Wícihitowin

Wícihitowin
Aboriginal Social Work in Canada

Edited by
Raven Sinclair (Ótiskewápíwskew)
Michael Anthony Hart (Kastitémahikan)
Gord Bruyere (Amawaajibitang)

Fernwood Publishing • Halifax & Winnipeg

Editing: Brenda Conroy
Cover Art: John van der Woude
Printed and bound in Canada by Hignell Book Printing

Mixed Sources
Product group from well-managed
forests and other controlled sources
www.fsc.org Cert no. SW-COC-003438
© 1996 Forest Stewardship Council

Published in Canada by Fernwood Publishing
32 Oceanvista Lane
Black Point, Nova Scotia, B0J 1B0
and #8 - 222 Osborne Street, Winnipeg, Manitoba, R3L 1Z3
www.fernwoodpublishing.ca

Fernwood Publishing Company Limited gratefully acknowledges the financial support of the Government of Canada through the Book Publishing Industry Development Program (BPIDP), the Canada Council for the Arts and the Nova Scotia Department of Tourism and Culture for our publishing program.

Library and Archives Canada Cataloguing in Publication

Wícihitowin: Aboriginal social work in Canada / edited by Raven Sinclair (Ótiskewápíwskew), Michael Anthony Hart (Kaskitémahikan) & Gord Bruyere (Amawaajibitang).

Includes bibliographical references.
ISBN 978-1-55266-317-2

1. Social work with native peoples—Canada. 2. Social service—Canada. 3. Native peoples—Services for--Canada. I. Sinclair, Raven II. Hart, Michael, 1965- III. Bruyere, Gord, 1962- IV. Title: Aboriginal social work in Canada.

E78.C2W575 2009   362.84'97071   C2009-904178-2

Contents

Section I — History and Theory / 17

Section III — Traditional Knowledge / 171

Dedication

To the Elders, who asked us to do this work.
To our teachers, who gave of their knowledge and understanding.
To our colleagues, who are working so hard in the front lines
so that we can be teaching and writing.
To our children, families and communities, who love and support us.
To future Indigenous social work practitioners and educators,
who will build upon and finesse the art of Aboriginal social work.

Contributors

Kathy Absolon (Minogiizhigokwe) is Anishinaabe *kwe* from Flying Post First Nation and teaches in the Aboriginal field of study. She has a background in Indigenous studies and Aboriginal social work practice. Kathy teaches holistic healing practices and Indigenous holistic thought. Her practice experience has been in working with individuals, families, groups and communities within Indigenous contexts. Kathy's research interests are in the many facets of Indigenous methodologies and worldview in Indigenous research.

Gail Baikie is a descendent of the Labrador Inuit. She has extensive social work practice, policy and teaching experience in the realm of Aboriginal community healing and development. Gail is currently an assistant professor in the School of Social Work at Dalhousie University and PhD candidate at Memorial University. Her scholarship is currently focused on Indigenous social work education and decolonizing the professional consciousness of Indigenous social workers.

Cyndy Baskin (On-koo-khag-kno kwe) is of Mi'kmaw and Irish descent. She is an associate professor in the School of Social Work at Ryerson University. Her research and teaching interests are bringing Aboriginal worldviews into education, Aboriginal research methodologies, structural determinants of health, Indigenous peoples and food security and youth and identity. Cyndy lives in Toronto with her family.

Gord Bruyere (Amawaajibitang) is Anishinaabe from Couchiching First Nation in northwestern Ontario. Most recently he was coordinator of Social Work at the Nicola Valley Institute of Technology, an Aboriginal public post-secondary institution. He has taught, developed curriculum and coordinated programs at eight mainstream and Aboriginal post-secondary institutions in social work, Aboriginal law and advocacy, political science, Indigenous learning and early childhood education. He has made national and international presentations on Aboriginal education and social work issues. He has published journal articles, book chapters and reviews that focus on Aboriginal issues in education, child welfare, traditional Anishinaabe family beliefs and anti-racism. He lives in Coquitlam with his partner Michelle.

Jacquie Green (Kundoque) belongs to the Killer Whale clan. She is from the Haisla territory and has been a visitor in Lekwungen territory for the last ten years. She presently teaches social work at the University of Victoria in areas of anti-oppressive practice and First Nations social work.

Michael Anthony Hart (Kaskitémahikan) is a citizen of Fisher River Cree Nation residing in Winnipeg, Manitoba. As a single father of two boys, Keesyk and Nostyn, Michael's interests focus on reaffirming Indigenous ways-of-being and helping while countering colonial oppression. He completed his PhD at the University of Manitoba while working at the faculty as a lecturer.

Michelle Reid (Juba) is from the Heiltsuk Nation at Wagisla on the B.C. central coast. Most recently she was an assistant professor at Thompson Rivers University School of Social Work and Human Service. She recently completed training as a registered art therapist in order to work in a meaningful way with Aboriginal people.

Cathy Richardson (Kinewesquao) is a Métis family therapist, researcher, child welfare advocate and activist. She is a faculty member at the University of Victoria in the School of Social Work. She is has developed the "Islands of Safety" child and family safety planning model for Métis Community Services in Victoria, B.C. She has written about Métis identity and responses to violence and mistreatment. Cathy is the co-founder of the Centre for Response-Based Practice and is interested in violence, resistance, language and restoration in contexts of social justice. She works with Aboriginal survivors of residential internment and community violence prevention in the north. She lives in Cowichan Bay with her husband and three children.

Dana Lynn Seaborn is a direct descendant of Métis Nation founder, Cuthbert Grant. She is the former executive director of Métis Community Services in Victoria and currently serves as president. She is dedicated to promoting Métis culture and has written and performed songs celebrating Métis history and identity. She is a recipient of a British Columbia Lieutenant Governor's Award for community service.

Raven Sinclair (Ótiskewápíwskew) is Cree/Assinniboine and Saulteaux from Gordon's and Kawacatoose First Nations. Her interests are Indigenous ways-of-knowing, doing and being. She completed her PhD at the University of Calgary and is an associate professor in the Faculty of Social Work at the University of Regina, Saskatoon Campus. She is a research affiliate of the Indigenous Peoples' Health Research Centre. Raven has a four-year-old daughter, Seth (Nípin).

Rona Sterling-Collins (Quistaletko) is from the Nlha'kapmx Nation, Interior of British Columbia. She is the owner of Sterling Consulting and works primarily with First Nations communities. She has a master's degree in social work from the University of Victoria. She is married and has a fifteen-year-old daughter and an eight-year-old son.

Commentary on Terms

Through the decades we, the peoples of this land we call Turtle Island, have been referred to by many terms. Terms such as Indian, Native, First Nations, Aboriginal and Indigenous have been used for and/or by us. We have been called more specific terms such as Cree, Ojibway, Iroquois, Huron and Chipewyan. Many of these terms, often English translations of Indigenous words, are held as unacceptable for many people, while being acceptable for others. We also hold our own ways of self-identifying, including Muskéko-Ininiw, Mi'kmaw, Gwich'in, Métis, Inuit, Anishinaabe, Nehiyaw, Gitksan, and Onkwehonwe. Some of these terms are used to refer to specific Indigenous nations, some refer to all Indigenous peoples, while alternative terms are used for other peoples.

All terms of identification have at least political, cultural and social ramifications. The debates about these ramifications are wide and varying. For example, some argue that the term "Aboriginal" is an appropriate term as it is connected to our rights as identified in the 1982 Constitution of Canada. Others argue that using the term Aboriginal is part of the colonial process of lumping Indigenous peoples together and treating us all the same despite our different cultures, languages, understandings, histories, ways of being and connections to the lands. Some might argue that by using the term Aboriginal we are acquiescing to political control over us and our lands. These political, cultural and social ramifications are highly significant and require much more discussion by us, the peoples of Turtle Island.

In the meantime, there is no consensus on what terms are to be used. As a result, Indigenous peoples on Turtle Island self-identify in many ways, including any of these terms. In following the traditions of many Indigenous peoples on Turtle Island, we have chosen to not predetermine which term an author should use and have supported the authors in using the terms they wish to use. Hence, the reader will observe that the most commonly used terms are Aboriginal and Indigenous, and these two terms are often used interchangeably. In some instances, the use of a term may reflect a particular time period. For example, in the 1950s and 1960s, the term Indian was commonly used, and hence, in discussions about that time period the term is appropriate. Later, in the 1970s and 1980s, the term Native was common, and so literature and discussions arising from that time may involve that term. Since the 1982 Constitutional amendment, Aboriginal was often deemed appropriate, although recently we see that Indigenous is being used more frequently. The use of terms in this book is an author's personal and/ or political choice.

Raven Sinclair (Ótiskewápíwskew)
Michael Anthony Hart (Kaskitémahikan)

Foreword

At the outset it is appropriate to commend the editors for assembling such an eminent group of Indigenous scholars to collaborate in the production of this publication. From the four corners of Turtle Island they bring a rich combination of traditional knowledge, clinical practice experience and academic expertise to the work.

Social workers and individuals in social work roles have been a significant presence in the lives of First Nations individuals, families and communities for the past fifty to sixty years. Based upon a Judeo-Christian worldview and tradition, social work theories and practices were developed to address the issues arising from the European industrial revolution and urbanization. The consequent policies and practices derived from a modern western liberal philosophy have for many generations been of major consequence for the social policies imposed upon First Nations.

The post-World War II period was a time of enhanced social awareness and a time of enhanced government-operated and funded social services. Within this context attention was focused upon the lack of child welfare services available to Native communities. As Fournier and Crey (1997) point out, submissions from the Canadian Welfare Council and Canadian Association of Social Workers to the 1947 Special Joint Committee of the Senate and House of Commons demanded social legislation and programming changes to protect Native children. In the subsequent *Indian Act* amendments of 1951, section 88 stipulated that all laws of general application in force in a province should apply on reserves, unless they conflicted with treaties or federal laws. Patrick Johnston (1983), in *Native Children and the Child Welfare System*, wrote that no consideration was given to the cultural differences or to the unique needs of First Nations individuals and communities. Consequently, nationwide, there is not a single First Nations family or community that has not been affected by the child welfare practices that resulted in what became known as the "Sixties Scoop," with an exponential increase in the number of children brought into the care of the state.

The authors in this collection comment on the progress made over the past half century in a few areas by both informed and sympathetic non-Aboriginal social workers and academics as well as their Indigenous colleagues. The current reality is, however, that the socio-economic circumstances and overall quality of life for the Indigenous peoples of Canada differ significantly from that of mainstream Canadians. Indigenous people remain disproportionately over-represented as users of health and human services and disproportionately under-represented as providers of those services.

Sharing stories that are at times deeply personal, the authors relate their experiences as students, clinicians and academics in dealing with the legacy of historical colonialism as well as the ongoing incidents of contemporary colonialism. The reader is informed and challenged by the authors' rich descriptions and multifaceted analyses. Maintaining fidelity to the journey of Indigenization of policy, programs, agencies, institutions and curricula is marked by the need for a personal and professional vigilance that does not supersede the holistic purpose of the journey itself.

Across Canada a handful of schools of social work have an Indigenous curriculum. Indigenous students continue to enrol in mainstream schools in a growing but limited number. With few exceptions, schools seldom have more than one Indigenous faculty member, and seldom is there more than minimal course content focused on Indigenous peoples. In 1974 the first Native students graduated with social work diplomas from the Saskatchewan Indian Federated College. That same year I had the privilege of meeting Dr. Marlene Castellano Brant for the first time at the Canadian Council on Social Development meeting in Calgary. To my knowledge it was the first time that either of us had had the opportunity to meet another Native person with a graduate degree in social work. Thirty-five years later it is an honour to have a small role in commenting on this publication, which reflects the work of eleven accomplished and skilled Indigenous social work scholars. Their teachings are recommended not as "recipes or formulae" for work with Indigenous individuals, families and communities but as a reference upon which each individual can develop an understanding and appreciation of what their role can and should be.

We often talk in terms of being on learning journeys, healing journeys, spiritual journeys and on physical journeys from place to place. With teaching from Elders, I have learned that when embarking on a journey of any nature it is important to have some notion of a destination or goal; otherwise we are adrift. It is also necessary to have a clear understanding of your point of departure. Take the time to situate yourself with regard in the four directions and your unique cultural and social traditions as you read *Wícihitowin* to ensure that the journey will be your own and that you will see through authentic and grounded eyes. *Kuk'chem* (thank you).

Dr. Richard Vedan
Secwepemc First Nation
Associate Professor, UBC School of Social Work

Section I — History and Theory

Thoughts Make Dreaming
Historical and Theoretical
Aspects for Indigenous Social Work

Gord Bruyere (Amawaajibitang)

> A dream is a scripture, and many scriptures are nothing but dreams.
> —Umberto Eco

It is a danger to remain unaware of what thoughts make dreaming. As Raven Sinclair points out, our Elders encourage us to know where we come from in order to know where we are going. It is important that social workers initiate and act upon an understanding of the world, of their particular society, and of the historical, cultural, social and political contexts in which they work. It is also crucial for social workers to situate themselves in terms of the implications of their personal and professional values, beliefs and practices. Too often we may unwittingly misstep or lose our way and hurt rather than help Indigenous families, communities and peoples.

What Raven Sinclair, Michael Anthony Hart and Gail Baikie offer us is the opportunity to situate ourselves with an eye to the horizon (remembering that there is a horizon behind us too). At the same time they allow us to stand and gaze into the depths and fathom what to expect when we immerse ourselves. What is compelling or even confounding is to apprehend that there are diverse ways of thought regarding Indigenous social work. There are many thoughts, many dreams. The thoughts that found their dreams are as different as the varied considerations they explore in their chapters.

There is another danger as you negotiate your way. To consider the chapters as all-encompassing, definitive or authoritative is to make the modernist mistake of assuming there is only one answer, that there is only one way to look and to walk. However, as this section of the book begins to show, and which subsequent chapters will illustrate, the questions of who Indigenous peoples are and what the solutions are to the problems or issues germane to Indigenous social work are not monolithic and are surely not that easy in any way. Yet this kind of understanding, this conscious dreaming if you will, or in other words a sound theoretical framework, will strengthen the relationships and actions that comprise good social work. Each of these authors offers a unique, particular dream. But each is founded on the same archetype. You are dreaming that you are embarking on a journey. Take this first step with an eye to the depths at your feet and an eye to the horizon.

Chapter 1

Bridging the Past and the Future
An Introduction to Indigenous Social Work Issues

Raven Sinclair (Ótiskewápíwskew)

Our Elders remind us that in order to know where we are going, we have to know where we have been. In the Canadian social work context that implies that as Indigenous social work educators and practitioners, we need to understand our personal histories and cultures and how the colonization of our lands has affected us as individuals, families and communities. It also requires us to have an understanding of the historical impact of colonialism in the contemporary social, political and economic contexts and to assess how these dynamics have influenced and are currently manifesting in the social work milieu. Further, given the mandate supplied by our Elders over fifty years ago when they articulated the need for Indigenous social workers to work with our people in culturally appropriate ways, it is our task to root ourselves in our traditional knowledges and cultures while simultaneously meeting the standards and rigour of mainstream social work education and practice. In terms of the social work profession more specifically, knowing where we have been includes understanding how the profession has interfaced with Indigenous people in Canada, how those encounters have been experienced by Indigenous people and how Indigenous people have responded to those interactions.

This book is a collection of writings by Indigenous social work academics across the country. It speaks to our collective past and illuminates, through the eyes of individuals from diverse nations, our understandings of our historical experiences as individuals and communities, how those experiences have shaped our individual paths, influence our current social work pedagogy and practice and inform our collective visions for a future in social work in ways that will meet the needs of the people we teach and for whom we engage in the helping field.

We are not alone in our endeavours and this collection does not emerge out of a vacuum. We draw upon the words of many Indigenous and allied academics who have gone before us and left beacons along the trail in the form of writings that have served to guide our thoughts and our work. We draw upon the support of all our relations who do the tough, emotionally challenging work on the social work front lines. We intend this book to be a resource for Indigenous and allied colleagues and perhaps as something upon which to build for the future generation of Indigenous educators and social workers. This work is a bridge between the past and the future.

The Past

> People become impatient with the repeated references by Aboriginal peoples to history and past injustices. "You cannot change the past," the argument goes. The point that is obviously missed is that the past is still with us in many ways and must be acknowledged in order to be accountable and responsible for the present and future. (Bruyere 1999: 177)

The encounter between Indigenous people and the social work profession in Canada has been controversial and tenuous at best. The early days of social work in Canada, framed by western philosophical influences and Judeo-Christian perspectives (Kreitzer 2006) within a postcolonial socio-political context, was an urban reform movement initiated by individuals intent on addressing poverty and child neglect. J.S. Woodsworth's push for a comprehensive social welfare program initiated formal social work train-ing in 1915 (Wharf 1990). Indigenous people in Canada first encountered the social work profession as wards of the federal government through the Department of Indian Affairs. Social workers were tasked to accompany Indian agents onto reserves to remove children to residential schools and later, in the 1960s and 1970s, to apprehend children deemed to be in need of protection (Miller 1996; Fournier and Crey 1997). Until the mid-1960s, Indigenous people were under federal responsibility in social welfare matters. The Hawthorne Report (1966), which condemned the terrible conditions on reserves and encouraged the extension of provincial welfare services to reserves, led to tripartite agreements for social and child welfare services to First Nations communities. Perhaps because the federal government agreed to pay all costs associated with child welfare of Indigenous children, the de-cade of the 1960s saw exponential increases in all provinces of Indigenous children in care (McDonald and McDonald 2007). Many critics argue that the Indigenous child welfare era of the 1960s and 1970s, which saw so many children removed from families and communities, was another colonial project, following on the heels of the residential school project (Johnston 1983). Many Indigenous peoples' perceptions of the social work profession are skewed as a result of the assimilative policy projects of governments, which were furthered in practice by social workers. "Social Work has negative connotations to many Indigenous people and is often synonymous with the theft of children, the destruction of families, and the deliberate oppression of Aboriginal communities" (Sinclair 2004: 49).

A shift in consciousness took place in the 1960s with a social movement spearheaded by developments in human rights in Canada and spurred on by a number of key documents. Harold Cardinal's (1969) book, *The Unjust Society*, left little room for doubt that Indigenous people were acutely aware of how unfair their treatment was at the hands of federal and provincial governments. Shortly thereafter, in 1972, the national representative body for status Indigenous people in Canada, the Assembly of First Nations, published a report entitled *Indian Control of Indian Education*, which immediately influenced all fields of education and gave rise to Indigenous social work programs in Saskatchewan and Alberta in 1974 (Sinclair 2004). The first class of social work diploma graduates from the Saskatchewan Indian Federation College in 1974 symbolized the manifestation of the call by the Elders, made many years before, to teach Indigenous social workers in an educational context that would respect Indigenous traditions and culture and incorporate these into the social work curriculum. This pedagogical approach to the western social work "helping" system, which had not been very helpful to Indigenous people, would, they hoped, enable Indigenous people to address the terrible social ramifications of Indian policies in Canada.

The Present

Until relatively recently, those of us who have worked in the field have had to satisfy our need for Indigenous writings about social work by scouring the limited collection of journal articles and hoarding assorted unpublished reports and documents that had emerged over the decades out of Aboriginal social organizations. To a large extent, we have had to rely on mainstream articles and texts and make our individual adaptations to the material. The paucity of Indigenous authored publications to date is not the result of lack of skill to write papers, chapters or books. Rather, the reality of our collective experience as Aboriginal people in a colonial and racialized country has left us little time for the luxury of, first, graduate and post-graduate education and, second, teaching, research and writing. Teaching, research and writing are luxuries that have been superseded by personal, family and community trauma. None of the scholars who contributed to this collection, or their families, have escaped the effects of the *Indian Act* in its various oppressive manifestations, the residential school project and its intergenerational fall-out or the "Sixties Scoop" and the Aboriginal child welfare era. These assimilative colonial projects have left our families and social systems in disarray and contributed many obstacles and challenges for Indigenous social workers and aspiring Indigenous academics. The high demand and need for skilled Indigenous social workers in all areas of social work practice in Indigenous communities has led to tremendous pressure on individuals with a social work degree, while colonial fall-out and funding restrictions create almost impossible working contexts in some communities. Indigenous social workers with university credentials often find themselves having to be all things to all people.

At the time of compiling these works into a collection, there was just one book about Indigenous social work in Canada, Michael Hart's (2002) *Seeking Mino-Pimatisiwin*, although there is a small collection of writings from the 1980s and early 1990s that have served and guided the growing cadre of Indigenous social work academics well. Several of these bear mentioning: Castellano, Stalwick and Wien's (1986) article "Native Social Work in Canada" was the first to assert that social work education for Indigenous people be grounded in Indigenous culture and that the community contexts of students be considered in program delivery. Morrissette, McKenzie and Morrisette's (1993) article "Towards an Aboriginal Model of Social Work Practice" also discussed the concept of infusing Indigenous worldviews into social work practice and introduced the importance of understanding colonization for both Indigenous and non-Indigenous people. This article is particularly interesting for their introduction of a continuum for individual identification with Aboriginal culture — a valuable concept in light of increasing urbanization of Aboriginal people as well as the de-culturing impacts of the residential school and child welfare systems for generations of Aboriginal people. Bruyere's riveting (1999) article "The Decolonization Wheel" articulates the insidiousness of colonialism as it plays out in contemporary society. Bruyere draws upon and critiques Fanon's decolonization framework and his key message resonates today: decolonization is not just an activity for Aboriginal people; it must be embraced by all social workers in order to tackle prevailing inequities and "isms" (1999: 178). Lastly, key writings from allied non-Aboriginal social workers have also been profoundly influential. Borg, Brownlee and Delaney's (1995) chapter "Postmodern Social Work Practice with Aboriginal People" calls upon social workers to adopt a postmodern perspective that criticizes systems of power and inequality as an avenue for genuine empowerment where allies support, but do not lead, Aboriginal people. They assert: "The ideal outcome of a postmodern social work model would be Aboriginal people as a unified people advocating for themselves... co-constructing their presents and/or futures with the assistance of the social work profession" (130).

This brief list is by no means complete and we are in the fortunate position of seeing the literature expanding in the last decade, giving us a foundation upon which to draw and grow our ideas. Many Indigenous authors and allies have contributed to our understanding in deep and meaningful ways (see, for example, Baskin 2002a, 2002b, 2005, 2006; Cross 2000; Coleman,

Unrau and Manyfingers 2001; Weaver 1997, 1998, 1999; Williams and Ellison 1996). A beneficial outcome of having an increasing supply of writing is that currently there are a good number of publications by Indigenous scholars articulating their experiences in social work pedagogy and practice, and the literature is more specific to social work specializations.

All of this writing and thinking has led us to formulations of an Indigenous-centred social work. I previously attempted a definition of Aboriginal social work that adequately summarizes the present direction of our collective efforts:

> Aboriginal social work can be described as a practice that combines culturally relevant social work education and training, theoretical and practice knowledge derived from Aboriginal epistemology (ways of knowing) that draws liberally on western social work theory and practice methods, within a decolonizing context. A decolonizing context is one which addresses the intergenerational and current impacts of colonization as manifested through colonial cultural and social suppression, intrusive and controlling legislation, industrial and residential school systems, the child welfare system, and institutional/systemic/individual racism and discrimination. Cultural relevance is manifested when practice and pedagogy mirror and support Indigenous and other ways of knowing, being, and doing. (Sinclair 2004: 76)

This definition will certainly evolve, but it still holds true, and the contributions in this collection elaborate on all the elements in this definition: social work education and training, decolonization and Aboriginal epistemology.

The Future

Recently, a colleague from Kanawake asked me, "Raven, what do you think about all this theory stuff?" My response was cautious. I said, "Makwa (not his real name), I think that in order to critique theory and its influences upon us as Indigenous educators, we need to know all about it." In our conversation I mentioned to him Sandy Grande's (2004) call for our collective engagement with mainstream theory in order to move Indigenous educators away from the "Native theory of anti-theory," which serves to limit our abilities towards political solidarity (2). Makwa and I agreed with Grande's conceptualization that engagement in abstract theory, given our collective urgency to attend to the practicalities of colonial turmoil, might have, until recently, seemed like a luxury for the academic elite. Our discussion revolved around the possibilities for learning that would come with developing deep understandings of the great non-Indigenous historical and contemporary philosophers, despite the fact that those writings are Eurocentric and, as Grande points out, often antithetical to the aims of Indigenous education.

The call to theory is an important one that Grande defines as "critique-al" work where engagement with critical and revolutionary theories might provide pathways to "spiritually vibrant, intellectually challenging, and politically operative schools for both Indian and non-Indian students" (3). St. Denis's (2007) discussion of anti-racism education in post-secondary institutions is one such example; she critiques identity and race theories to formulate a visionary approach to anti-racist education in the racialized Canadian context. Similarly, recent publications in Indigenous social work are indicating that Indigenous scholars are beginning to engage with the "dead White guys" (see, for example, Dumbrill and Green 2008; Hart Chapter 2) to provide new perspectives and foundations from which to approach social work theory, pedagogy and practice. There are many gems of wisdom to be found in dusty tomes that may resonate well with our perspectives:

> Constantly regard the universe as one living being, having one substance and one soul; and observe how all things have reference to one perception, the perception of this one living being; and how all things act with one movement; and how all things are the cooperating causes of all things which exist; observe too the continuous spinning of the thread and the structure of the web. (Marcus Aurelius, *Meditations*)

The contributions in this book provide a good overview of where we, as Indigenous educators, practitioners and students, have been and where we are going in Indigenous social work. In the spirit of our ancestors, we offer these perspectives and suggest that readers take what works, perhaps adding useful insights to your social work toolkits to be applied in your work in a good way. Build upon these ideas, offer suggestions and leave the rest.

Káhkíyáw Niwáhkómákánák — All My Relations

Chapter 2

Anti-Colonial Indigenous Social Work
Reflections on an Aboriginal Approach

Michael Anthony Hart (Kaskitémahikan)

One recent afternoon I attended a meeting of primarily non-Indigenous academics. Part of the discussion centred on the inclusion of anti-colonialism within the social work curriculum. I found it familiar and tiresome, that of all the topics within the meeting, this discussion drew the most critical attention. As most Indigenous academics will guess, the biggest question raised was whether anti-colonialism should be included within the curriculum. To be fair, most social workers do not write directly about anti-colonialism, although there are many indirect contributions to this critical stance; thus few social workers clearly understand what is meant by the term within an Indigenous context. Perhaps I should not have been tired of explaining the term and related concepts. Yet, I was frustrated that the same people would have no problem allowing similar concepts, such as anti-oppression, to pass with minimal discussion.

Despite the significance of this annoyance, an experience after the meeting created my greatest frustration that day. As I was leaving the building I ran into another meeting participant, who was, assumedly, knowledgeable enough of Indigenous views, concerns and experiences that she had taught others about these topics and participated in research on these matters. She asked for further clarification of the term anti-colonial as well as references to support my explanation, which I provided. While I appreciated her inquiry and effort to learn more, I was dumbfounded at one of her comments. I had just given her a brief explanation of anti-colonialism and identified an author on the topic, when she flippantly blurted out, "Of course, colonialism is over."

While we must speak out about the colonialism our peoples are facing, there are times when we just have to shake our heads in amazement, laugh and walk away so as not to be overwhelmed by the futility of the moment. This was one of those moments. As I walked away, I wondered how this person could teach others that Indigenous people continue to confront, and in many cases struggle against, colonial oppression if colonialism is over? If this was her perspective, how were the many times that our people had confronted the state and its institutions seen by her students? What kind of views were her students being taught about our sisters and brothers who continue struggling with the internalized oppression that manifests itself in addictions, violence and neglect? I realized that while I had to walk away from that moment, I have an obligation to write and talk about anti-colonialism.

We, the Indigenous peoples of Ininewi-Ministik,[1] have been confronting Amer-European colonialism for centuries. Although colonial processes have significantly influenced our ways of life, we continue to preserve and live our identities, beliefs, teachings and practices, and we have started to carry our collective wisdom into academia and professional practices. Social workers and social work educators must open up and articulate that wisdom in order to move this forward. One means for moving forward is recognizing, understanding and developing the relationship between anti-colonialism, Indigenism and social work. I have attempted, albeit indirectly, to address these topics through my writing on an Aboriginal approach to social work (Hart 1999, 2002, 2006). When I originally wrote about this approach, I was hoping to influence social work by Indigenizing it, at least to the extent an article could. I later stated that my intent was to "develop and present an approach to helping that will… stimulate our people to discuss and critique this and other Aboriginal approaches to helping" (Hart 2002: 12). While I more recently considered this approach to be anti-colonial, I have begun to question whether this is so. Accordingly, in this chapter I address whether this Aboriginal approach is a step towards anti-colonial, Indigenist social work. So that we may start to articulate anti-colonialism and Indigenism, we need to have, at least, a brief understanding of colonialism and the marginalization of Indigenous knowledge and ways of helping. With this basis we can ask whether or not an Aboriginal approach to helping anti-colonialism and Indigenism and in what directions we need to develop our perspectives and practices of helping.

What is Colonialism?

Colonialism has been addressed by many people; however, it has been defined only on occasion (Smith 1999). Further, colonial discourses are not homogenous or unitary (McLeod 2000). Indeed, understandings of colonialism continue to develop in sophistication and complexity (Slemon 1995). Elleke Boehmer[2] (1995: 2) explains that colonialism involves the settlement of territory, the exploitation or development of its resources and the attempt to govern the Indigenous peoples of the occupied lands. Leela Gandhi (1998: 16) defines colonialism as "the historical process whereby the 'West' attempts systematically to cancel or negate the cultural difference and value of the 'non-West.'" I (Hart 2002) have explained that colonialism is driven by a worldview and processes that embrace dominion, self-righteousness and greed, and affects all levels of Indigenous peoples' lives — the national, communal, familial and individual — and insidiously interferes with all aspects of Indigenous peoples' lives, including their spiritual practices, emotional wellbeing, physical health and knowledge.

Colonization connects directly to Indigenous knowledge through at least three means. One means is exclusion, or the absence of Indigenous knowledge, methodologies and practices, with Eurocentric scholars identifying their knowledge as superior (Battiste and Henderson 2000; Blaut 1993; Smith 1999) and excluding knowledge different from their own. Indeed, the colonizer's account of history as described by Albert Memmi (1965) and Fyre Jean Graveline (1998) exemplifies this exclusion. A second means is marginalization, or the process of putting peoples, individuals, ideas or additional matters on the periphery. In this process, it is important to note who holds significant power in systems such as academia and how such power is used. Ashcroft, Griffiths and Tiffin address this point:

> Education, whether state or missionary, primary or secondary (and later tertiary) was a massive cannon in the artillery of the empire. The military metaphor can however seem inappropriate, since unlike outright territorial aggression, education effects, in Gramsci's terms, a "domination by consent." This domination by consent is achieved through what is taught to the colonised, how it is taught, and the subsequent emplacement of the educated subject as a part of the continuing imperial apparatus… Education is thus a conquest of another kind of territory — it is the foundation of colonialist power and consolidates this power through legal and administrative apparatuses. (1995: 425)

Appropriation, a third means that connects colonialism to Indigenous knowledge, is explained by Graveline (1998) as the misrepresentation or partial representation of an idea or artefact without recognition of the sources of knowledge or inspiration while gaining prosperity, success and/or benefit from others' ideas. In experiences where Indigenous knowledge is appropriated, Indigenous persons, if not objectified, become virtual non-entities.

To thrive in this colonial environment, we, Indigenous peoples, have little choice but to participate in academic endeavours that either devalue or do not recognize our cultural identities. More specifically, Indigenous peoples' knowledge is given little, if any, legitimate academic role in higher education, and foundational aspects to Indigenous knowledge, such as spirituality intertwined with the land, are ignored. As a result we find ourselves learning and perpetuating predominantly Amer-European knowledge in Amer-European environments within the dominant Amer-European paradigms (Morgan 2003; Sinclair 2004).

As explained by Rains (1999), these actions compound the social ramifications in that the education we receive or transmit, or do not receive or do not transmit, is, in part, what sensitizes or desensitizes Indigenous peoples to the current political climate and the nature of the struggles being waged by Indigenous peoples. These actions, such as the marginalization of our traditions and cultures to the point where they are seen as obstacles to "progress," demonstrate that the colonial exploitation continues.

Marginalization of Indigenous Ways of Helping

While it has been suggested that Indigenous concepts and practices are beginning to be accepted within social work, social work education and practice are not free from colonial influence (Sinclair 2004). Too often our concepts and practices are "marginalized or viewed as secondary to the strategies and techniques emerging from the dominant paradigm" (McKenzie and Morrissette 2003: 262). This concern of marginalizing is heightened whenever we acknowledge the extent to which our instructing and learning in mainstream social work education programs are based on dominantly held, middle-class, patriarchal and White values (Mawhiney 1995: 226). For example, Raven Sinclair presented this ludicrous situation of an Indigenous social work student learning about cross-cultural practice:

> The cross cultural or minority "client" is automatically labelled as the "other." This forces the Aboriginal student to take a dominant subjective stance with respect to issues of diversity because they are never requested to examine their work with "White" individuals as cross-cultural. They are required to perceive of themselves and their people as the "other" who is in need of assistance. (2004: 52)

In other words, Indigenous social work students and social workers are most often required to take the dominating Amer-European perspective, with its associated values of individualism and self-efficacy. As explained by Kirmayer, Brass and Tait (2000), the approaches stemming from this perspective may not fit well either with Indigenous cultural values or the realities of Indigenous life. Further, discussions about integrating Amer-European and traditional Indigenous approaches, in order to address the problem of marginalization of Indigenous ways of helping, are for the most part concentrated in the realm of academia (Duran and Duran 1995). Sadly, this marginalization will continue to provide minimal, if any, support of Indigenous knowledge development (Nimmagadda and Cowger 1999: 274). Duran and Duran suggest that the problem does not lie so much with traditional helping practitioners in Indigenous communities as it does with Amer-European practitioners. "Western practitioners approach traditional healing methods with skepticism while expecting absolute faith from the traditionals in orthodox Western-orientated therapeutic strategies" (Duran and Duran 1995: 9). In light of such oppression, Kirmayer et al. (2000) and I (Hart 2003) suggest that there is a need to rethink the applicability of such difference in modes of intervention.

Anti-colonialism

Anti-colonialism is a social, cultural and political stance. As explained by George Sefa Dei (2000), it is anchored in the Indigenous sense of collective and common consciousness of colonialism as imposed and dominating. It sees colonialism as a persistent process. Graham Smith explains:

> I do not believe for an instant that we are in a postcolonial period. I do not think we have seen the last of colonization; on the contrary, it is very much alive and well. What has happened in recent years is the creation of an illusion that colonization is no longer practiced — that somehow the "white" world now understands this phenomenon and is able to desist from it. This, of course, is a myth.... What has happened is that the processes of colonization have been reformed in different and more subtle ways. Many of these new formations are insidious, and many of them have yet to be fully exposed. (2000: 215)

Similarly, Makere Stewart-Harawira (2005) observes that colonialism continues in territories such as Australia, New Zealand and Canada. In these places the relationships between Indigenous peoples and the states were reassessed and structures for more participatory forms of governance were negotiated to varying degrees. However, these actions brought new and increasingly influential forms of liberalism that shaped the relationships between Indigenous peoples and the settler societies in problematic ways. Of particular concern is the undermining of the Indigenous sense of the collectivity. Stewart-Harawira presented one example of such undermining where Indigenous identities have been reshaped and corporate institutions constructed as pseudo-traditional social and cultural institutions. "Within this neocolonial framework, Indigenous knowledge forms are subjected to commodification, on one hand, and, on the other, devaluation and margin-alization through reductionist reconstructions" (Stewart-Harawira 2005: 179).

Thus, anti-colonialism is understood to be the political struggle of colonized peoples against the specific and existing ideology and practice of colonialism (Ashcroft et al. 1995). According to Linda Tuhiwai Smith (1999), it is the proactive position of resistance that Indigenous people have adopted or should adopt to challenge these colonial frameworks. The challenge includes resistance to the operations of colonialism in political, economic and cultural institutions as well in as social systems (Ashcroft et al. 2001: 14). Anti-colonialism questions institutional power and privilege and the rationale for dominance, and acknowledges the intertwining role state, societal and institutional structures play in producing and reproducing inequalities. This line of questioning interrogates "the power configuration embedded in ideas, cultures and histories of knowledge production and use" (Dei 2000: 117).

In relation to ideas and knowledge production, Leanne Simpson (2004) outlines that anti-colonialism includes the development of strategies that have a focus on the recovery of traditional Indigenous knowledge. George Sefa Dei (2000) suggests that Indigenous knowledge is the entry point. He recognizes the importance of developing social understanding from Indigenous language, cognitive categories and cultural logic. Strategies based on such an understanding require deconstruction of colonial thinking in relation to traditional Indigenous knowledge. Hence, anti-colonialism also includes a critical analysis of colonialism and how it influences the construction of traditional Indigenous knowledge.

Significant, if not primary, to an analysis of the present state of Indigenous knowledge is an understanding of the concept of diffusionism. Anti-colonial thought works to denaturalize the discourse of diffusionism and spell out this narrative. In the context of African colonialism, Mary Louise Pratt (2004) noted this point in greater detail:

> Diffusion is often represented as a process of substitution and replication whereby, say... Western education replaces native education; the modern and universal replaces the traditional and local.... Imperial ideology naturalized or normalized this process (the substitution of an inferior paradigm with a superior one) as Peter Amato puts it, "the economic and political realities of the modernization of Europe had to create this modern Africa only insofar as it is their byproducts." Anticolonial accounts recover it differently, as structured intervention combining physical and epistemological violence. (452)

In place of diffusionism, anti-colonial writers present an alternate set of questions, techniques and strategies in order to create an anti-oppressive discourse, such as rereading the histories of colonized peoples in clearly separated stages: precolonial, colonial and postcolonial. Through the development and presentation of this discourse, anti-colonial knowledge producers remain aware of the historical and institutional structures and contexts that sustain intellectualism and intellectual projects (Dei 2000).

The concern over intellectualism plays strongest between proponents of postcolonialism and those of anti-colonialism. "For example, whereas postcolonial theorists depend on Western models, anti-colonial theorists work with alternative/oppositional paradigms, based on the use of Indigenous concepts and analytical systems and cultural frames of reference" (Dei 2000: 118). Further, anti-colonialists tend to see postcolonial perspectives as mystifying and co-opted (Pratt 2004: 451), whereas those representing postcolonial approaches tend to reject critiques of eurocentricism as too simple. In response, anti-colonialists point out that across the ideological spectrum the diffusion narrative continues to be reaffirmed in contemporary thought. In addition, the role of Europe's interactions with the rest of the world is marginalized or obliterated. Finally, anti-colonialists identify openly with a process of decolonization that is understood to be incomplete, while in postcolonial discourse, which assumes that colonialism has ended, that identification generally remains unstated (Pratt 2004: 451–52; Taoua 2003).

Academics, Indigenous knowledge holders and the political leaders of Indigenous nations and settler governments engaged in the protection, recovery and maintenance of Indigenous knowledge systems must work to dismantle the colonial project in all of its current manifestations (Simpson 2004; Smith 2005). Academics and new learners who are true allies to Indigenous peoples in the protection of our knowledge must "step outside of their privileged position and challenge research that conforms to the guidelines outlined by the colonial power structure and root their work in the politics of decolonization and anti-colonialism" (Simpson 2004: 381).

Another key trait of anti-colonial resistance is cultural revitalization for social transformation. Despite the physical and epistemological violence of colonialism, proponents of anti-colonialism are quick to point out that Indigenous knowledge and ways have not been substituted and replaced by diffusion (Pratt 2004: 453). Instead of the offsetting disregard of "tradition" and "culture" that is characterized in postcolonial discourses, and indeed by some colonial theorists such as Franz Fanon (1963) and Howard Adams (1999), anti-colonialism stands from a place of tradition, orality, visual representation, material and non-material cultures and Indigeneity, and validates Indigenous voice, words and languages.

On an international level, anti-colonialism moves away from a concentration on victimization to celebrate the political and material resistance of colonized groups. It also moves beyond the displacement that occurred through European expansion to address the inequalities and imbalances arising from the decolonization efforts of the recent past manifested in "Third World" nation-states. The Indigenous peoples' movement is, in this sense, pursuing a process of decolonization once removed (Niezen 2003: 196). It emphasizes the need to reject colonial power and restore local control (Ashcroft et al. 2001: 14). For the Maori, as an example, this restoration is one of the key elements to social transformation. It is what Maori name *tino rangatiratanga*, meaning "absolute self-determination, full authority, and complete control" (Smith 2000: 222).

Taiaiake Alfred (2005) notes a caution in following an anti-colonial agenda. He outlines how anti-colonial movements in the past, when paired with the rhetoric and politics of anti-imperialism, have led to nationalism — "an ideology of anti-colonialism geared towards regaining control of resources and imposing socially and culturally conservative cultures as counters to colonial corruptions" (62). This is quite clearly a situation of revolt as outlined by Albert Memmi (1965), who views revolt as being confined within the colonial apparatus since it is reactionary and dependent on the colonial situation. Thus, anti-colonialism needs to be able to move beyond such a limited outlook.

In summary, anti-colonialism includes actions such as social and political mobilization to de-legitimize and stop the colonial attack on Indigenous knowledge and peoples. It seeks to reaffirm Indigenous knowledge and culture, establish Indigenous control over Indigenous national territories, protect Indigenous lands from environmental destruction and develop education opportunities that are anti-colonial in their political orientation and firmly rooted in traditions of Indigenous nations. Anti-colonialism works to create the spaces needed for the recovery of Indigenous knowledge systems using the processes, values and traditions inherent in those knowledge systems (Foley 2003; Simpson 2004: 381).

Indigenism

Indigenism takes a particular anti-colonial stance. It is a progressive Indigenous viewpoint that opposes imperialism and colonialism, acknowledges the "fourth world" position identified by Manual and Posluns (1974), advocates for our empowerment (Churchill 2003, Niezen 2003; Walters and Simoni 2002) and seeks the ultimate goal of peace (Alfred 2005). Indigenism is also a process that acts as a counterweight to the hegemonic strategies of oppressive states (Niezen 2003). It is a global phenomenon where Indigenous organizations work both independently and together to form a transnational solidarity and invade institutional space from two directions, specifically the international and the local (Niezen 2003). For certain, it does not supplant the localized culture of any particular community as it is from these communities that it derives force (Alfred 1999: 88). Thus, it is also a local phenomenon, where our spiritual and cultural roots are protected and entrenched in the people (Alfred 2005). From another perspective, it is also the collection of theoretical, political and cultural discussions, analyses and critiques (Alfred1999; Guzmán 2005). In light of the dual emphasis on the local and global, the existence and expression of Indigenism is quite varied (Guzmán 2005).

The variability in Indigenous discourse raises an important point, identified by Devine Guzman. She explains that "any discussion of Indigenist discourse that fails to examine the regional and historical contexts to which that discourse pertains empties Indigenism of any possible value as an analytical tool or even a descriptive concept" (Guzmán 2005: 93–94). Thus, while recognizing the global scope of Indigenism, discussions have to be grounded in a place and time. Indeed, as explained by Jamies Guerrero (2003: 66), Indigenism can literally mean "to be born of a place." However, for Indigenous peoples, it also means that we live in relationship with the territory where we were born. Viola Cordova elaborates:

> It is not only Native Americans that have a sense of place that is very specific; most Indigenous peoples have a similar concept of bounded space. Their "place" is the foundation of cultural mooring and values; it is not simply "the environment" that they accidentally "occupy" — they are the children of that place. There is no artificial distinction between themselves and some alien "other" that is termed "nature." (Moore et al. 2007: 197)

Within this understanding of Indigenism, an Indigenous person has the responsibility to practise kinship roles in reciprocal relationship with his or her bioregional habitat, manifested through cultural beliefs, rituals and ceremonies that cherish biodiversity: this is the context of a Native land ethic and Native spirituality (Jamies Guerrero 2003: 66). This perspective is reflected by Ward Churchill (2003) in his focused discussion of Indigenism on Ininewi-Ministik. He saw Indigenous peoples as working together to establish our own frame of reference and our own future, one that is likely different from the Amer-European perspective, since colonialism and imperialism are equated with the Amer-European perspective. An Indigenist framework is essentially socialist, but from an Indigenous perspective. An example of a difference in the Indigenist and western conceptualizations of socialism is their view of the natural world. While a western perspective tends to hold nature as a thing to be subdued, controlled and exploited, an Indigenist perspective sees people as indivisible from and in relation with nature. Thus, an Indigenist cannot try to dominant nature.

According to Churchill (2003), an Indigenist considers the rights of Indigenous peoples as the highest priority and draws upon the traditions of Indigenous peoples to uphold these rights. An Indigenist outlook not only frames a person's critiques but acts as the lens for developing and espousing alternatives to the present social, political, economic and philosophical order. A significant matter for an Indigenist stance is the need to know history from an Indigenist perspective, including knowing past Indigenous leaders.

Similarly, D'Arcy Rheault, citing Paul Bourgeois and Don Longboat's commentary, explains that an Indigenist is usually, but not exclusively, an Indigenous person "who combines the abstract and theoretical thinking involved in the creation and transmission of Indigenous knowledge" (1999: 38). These thoughts are acted upon as the basis for daily living. As such, "the Indigenist is clearly a thinker and practitioner of Indigenous knowledge" (38). From this perspective, Indigenism is not only a stance, process and discourse; it is a way of life.

There are at least three requirements for collective Indigenous action: self-sufficiency, where the people have access to the resources needed to defy the colonial state and its institutions; reorganization, where the peoples' energy is channelled into contentious actions against the state and its colonial power; and reculturation, where the people come to understand that cooperation with the state is wrong and must be acted against (Tarrow 1998, cited in Alfred 2005: 63). Alfred (2005) also suggests that Indigenists (Onkwehonwe) resist colonial states on our own terms through creative confrontations that de-legitimize the state and its institutions. He identifies two ways of attacking the legitimacy of governing colonial institutions: active confrontation and withdrawal of consent and cooperation. Both of these means require non-violence and creativity. They also require enhancing our effective presence in the media. He explains that in today's reality, four approaches need to be followed:

1. unify the concerns and approaches of the different parts of the Indigenous peoples movement;
2. appeal to uncommitted people for their active support;
3. aggressively attack the hypocrisies and inconsistencies in Settler society to de-legitimize it or even win over various segments of the Settler society and the people who administer state authority; and
4. maintain consistency with the teachings and vision of peaceful coexistence that is the heritage of all Onkwehonwe. (232)

Further, Alfred articulates that the following five conditions are required for an Indigenist movement to succeed in a situation such as the oppression of Indigenous peoples in Canada:

1. the movement must have access to institutional power, such as government organizations and media;
2. there must be political and social divisions among the settler elite, in terms of either political parties, economic classes or ideologies;
3. the movement must have support and cooperation of allies in the settler society;
4. the state's ability or capacity for repression must be in decline, in either

physical terms, legal constraints or the political or social context; and

5. the movement must be capable of advancing its claims and de-legiti-mizing the state in the mass media (Alfred 2005: 64).

These conditions support one of the long term objectives of Indigenism; namely the transformation of the settler society's fundamental beliefs and attitudes.

In summary, Indigenism is grounded in place and time. It is locally based, but supports global connections between Indigenous peoples. It focuses on establishing our own frame of reference and knowing history from Indigenous perspectives. It recognizes and supports kinship roles between the earth, people and other life and emphasizes that humankind cannot dominate nature. It holds Indigenous rights as the highest priority for Indigenous peoples and relies on Indigenous knowledge for the basis of daily life. As such, it is a way of life.

A Brief Overview of an Aboriginal Approach

To consider whether an Aboriginal approach, as I have previously outlined (Hart 1997, 1999, 2002, 2006, 2007), reflects anti-colonial and Indigenist stances, I briefly present the approach here. This approach is based upon Indigenous relational worldviews and philosophies, particularly the Medicine Wheel and the understandings of respectful individualism and communitism. It holds spirituality as a central pillar and has several key concepts: wholeness, balance, relationships, harmony, growth, healing and *mino-pimátisiwin* [the good-life]. It also highlights the values of respect and sharing. The approach has particular views of people and of the helping relationship.

To begin explaining the approach, I must begin with spirituality, which is the recognition that there is another existence that is not of the physical world. Spirituality is so encompassing of traditional Indigenous life that it is respected in all interactions and is demonstrated through such activities as meditations, prayers and ceremonies. As such, I have recently recognized the need to emphasize spirituality as a central pillar of this Aboriginal approach (Hart 2007).

This understanding of spirituality is well demonstrated within Indigenous peoples' worldviews and philosophies. A significant and common component is respectful individualism, where individuals are provided with much room and freedom for growth, self expression and inner exploration. Individuals also come to know that they have a great responsibility to use this freedom for the collective wellbeing of the people and the life around them. Another significant and common component to these worldviews and philosophies is communitism, or the sense of community, tied together by familial relations and the families' commitment to it (Hart 2007). Each community member is oriented towards sharing our insights and supporting one another. Communitism also recognizes that we are communities of communities and that we must act respectfully towards other communities and their individuals as we are all connected. Indeed, many Indigenous peoples spend their first encounters with each other trying to find these connections.

Indigenous worldviews and philosophies, of the central part of Ininewi-Ministik particularly, have been modelled in fairly a common symbol, the Medicine Wheel. I understand the Medicine Wheel to be an ancient symbol of the universe that reflects the cosmic order and unity of all things. There is no absolute version of the wheel since Indigenous peoples have given it their own interpretations. Yet, the Medicine Wheel reflects and addresses several key and interrelated concepts common to many Indigenous methods of helping and healing, including the key concepts of the approach I outlined. The concept of wholeness is about incorporating all aspects of life and giving attention and energy to each aspect within ourselves and the universe around us. Balance as a concept is the dynamic where we give attention to each aspect of the whole, not focusing upon one to the detriment of other parts. Another key concept considers all aspects of the whole, including other than human beings, to be in relation to one another. These relationships require attention and nurturing, and when we give energy to these relationships, we nurture the connections. Nurturing the connections leads to health while disconnections lead to dis-ease. Harmony, the next concept of the approach, is ultimately a process involving all entities fulfilling their obligations to each other and to themselves. The concept of growth is a life long process that involves developing all aspects of ourself, the body, mind, heart and spirit, in a harmonious manner. Somewhat similar to growth, the concept of healing is a daily practice that is orientated to the restoration of wholeness, balance, relationships and harmony. Thus, we focus not only on "illness," but on disconnections, imbalances and disharmony. The final concept of the approach is *mino-pimátisiwin*, the good-life, or life in the fullest, healthiest sense. *Mino-pimátisiwin* is the goal of growth and healing and includes efforts by individuals, families, communities, people in general and all life entities.

The key values of this approach are respect and sharing. Respect is the showing of honour, esteem, deference and courtesy to all, including refraining from imposing our views onto others. Sharing includes the sharing of all we can, including knowledge and life experiences, and emphasizes that everyone is important. Sharing helps develop relationships.

This approach has a particular perception of people. Human nature is seen as good, although negative attributes can develop. It views people in the state of being and a state of being-in-becoming, as having a purpose and being active in striving to grow towards *mino-pimátisiwin*. People are understood as one aspect of life, dependent upon those who have lived before us and upon other life. Thus, people are social beings guided by good-conduct taught through such means as ceremonies.

Helping processes are focused on the relationships of the people being helped, including the relationship between the people seeking help and those offering help. The people offering help are not the experts. Instead, there is a focus on speaking from the heart, which suggests speaking with personal emotional experience, intuition and honesty. Finally, the helping process is a shared experience, thus the experience of the helping process is relevant to both the life of the person seeking help as well as the person offering help.

Anti-Colonialism, Indigenism and an Aboriginal Approach to Helping

I initially developed the outline of an Aboriginal approach through research in which I interviewed Indigenous people who utilized a particular Indigenous helping practice, namely the sharing circle (Hart 1997). At that time I considered Indigenous research methodologies and discussed colonialism in very limited ways. Later, I began to pay greater attention to colonialism as the context of an Aboriginal helping approach (Hart 2002). My thoughts at the time were that the approach was a step in the decolonization process. I thought I would be supporting Indigenous people by providing an explanation of how to approach helping them in a manner that was consistent with their worldviews, understandings and practices. By working in such a manner, I believed, and still believe, that we would be working at decolonization. But this is not necessarily anti-colonial or Indigenist.

Regarding anti-colonialism, my original approach does reflect some key attributes of decolonization. The approach attempts to denaturalize the colonial discourse in that it supports and is based upon Indigenous worldviews and practices. In this manner, it rejects colonial control to a degree. It definitely provides an alternative set of questions, techniques and strategies for helping Indigenous peoples. It utilizes Indigenous knowledge as its entry point, focuses on the locality of Ininewi-Ministik generally and central Ininewi-Ministik specifically, and is based upon the thoughts of Indigenous helping practitioners. Finally, to some degree it is an attempt at cultural revitalization as I relied on an Indigenous helping method as the basis for its development.

Still, this approach is limited in its anti-colonial outlook. Specifically, while it acknowledges colonialism, it does not speak directly to the point that colonialism continues as an imposing and dominating force. While the approach may be utilized to a degree as a means of critically analyzing colonialism, it is not based upon such an analysis. Nor does the approach provide for a political action to clearly reject colonialism. It could be used to explain the need for particular actions to recreate harmony and balance, but it does not call for the establishment of Indigenous control over Indigenous national territories, the protection of Indigenous lands from environmental destruction and education opportunities that are anti-colonial in their political orientation and firmly rooted in traditions of their nations. Finally, while the model is an attempt at cultural revitalization, in that I relied on an Indigenous helping method as the basis for its development, I used non-Indigenous means of research, namely ethnography, to support its development within a non-Indigenous institution, replete with its regulations and expectations.

A similar picture emerges when looking at this early articulation of an Aboriginal approach in the light of Indigenism. The approach is fairly grounded in a place — again that being Ininewi-Ministik generally and the central part of it specifically. It has established its own frame of reference that is based upon Indigenous thought. It encourages knowing history from an Indigenous frame of reference and directly emphasizes the practice of kinship roles, including the relationships between people, the land and other life. As such, the approach does speak, indirectly, against the domination of nature. It emphasizes Indigenous rights, particularly the right of Indigenous people to be supportive in a manner that is reflective of Indigenous worldviews and practices. It encourages the use of abstract and theoretical Indigenous knowledge as the basis for daily life and practice, ideally to be followed by the people being helped and the helpers themselves. As such, it is meant to be a way of life.

However, there are some limitations to seeing an Aboriginal approach as Indigenist. It does not clearly identify the connections to Indigenous peoples globally. I relied on non-Indigenous research methodologies to develop the approach, which raises some questions about how much the approach is based on Indigenous worldviews and practices. In addition, the approach is based in the English language. Concepts like the Medicine Wheel are not easily translatable in at least one Indigenous language, namely Cree, despite being around conceptually for generations. To be truly based in Indigenous worldviews, I suggest that at least the key concepts, values and practices need to be based in an Indigenous language or languages.

Perhaps the most obvious limitation of how the approach is not reflective of Indigenism lies in the name, "an Aboriginal approach." Alfred and Corntassel (2005) argue that the term "Aboriginal" works to continue the legitimacy of the colonial state. As a construction of the Canadian state, the term is part of a political, cultural and legal discourse that serves an agenda of silent surrender to an inherently unjust relation, where the Canadian state and its institutions attempt to gradually subsume and re-conceptualize Indigenous existence for their own political and economic gain. As such, we are being slowly destroyed as peoples. Alfred and Corntassel explain:

The acceptance of being "Aboriginal" (or its equivalent term in other countries, such as ethnic group) is a powerful assault on Indigenous identities. It must be understood that the Aboriginalist assault takes place in a politico-economic context of historic and on-going dispossession and of contemporary deprivation and poverty; this is a context in which Indigenous people are forced by the compelling needs of physical survival to cooperate individually and collectively with the state authorities to ensure their physical survival. Consequently, there are many "Aboriginals" (in Canada) or "Native Americans" (in the United States) who identify themselves solely by their political-legal relationship to the state rather than by any cultural or social ties to their Indigenous community or culture or homeland. This continuing colonial process pulls Indigenous peoples away from cultural practices and community aspects of "being Indigenous" towards a political-legal construction as "Aboriginal" or "Native American," both of which are representative of what we refer to as being "incidentally Indigenous." (599)

Without knowing, I have subsumed "Aboriginal." While I could argue that this approach is not Aboriginalist as described by Alfred and Corntassel, I cannot say with equal conviction that it is not contributing to the assault on our identities. When I wrote about this approach I was, and am, concerned that I am indirectly leading fellow Indigenous persons down the path of "pan-Indianism." I attempted to address the concern by emphasizing where this approach stems from, namely the central part of Ininewi-Ministik. I also acknowledged that this approach may not be fitting for all Indigenous peoples. Despite my efforts of speaking against colonial oppression and "pan-Indianism" in my writings about this approach, I never recognized the insidious effects of concentrating on the term "Aboriginal" as a means to identifying the approach. As such, one of the greatest weaknesses of this approach has been how I have referred to it. I will be referring to this approach here and in all future writings as the *mino-pimátisiwin* approach.[3]

Reflections

Overall, the *mino-pimátisiwin* approach to helping can be considered as generally reflecting an anti-colonial stance, while more closely reflecting an Indigenist one. The Indigenist reflection could be strengthened by clearly identifying the political intent of the approach. In particular, explanations of the approach should outline its context, where calling for the establishment of Indigenous control over Indigenous national territories and institutions is central. Most importantly, it should support the questioning and critical analysis of social work as an institution of colonialism. It should strengthen its base in Indigenous worldviews and practices by outlining its relationship to and reflection of Indigenous helping concepts, such as the Cree concepts of *wícihitowin*,[4] *kakéskihkémowin*[5] and *onasowéwina*.[6]

On the other hand, the dangers of not outlining the approach within such a context and not strengthening its base remind me of a story of our eldest brother, Wísahkécáhk. As told by Catherine Merasty and translated by Albert Umferville (cited in Brightman 1989), the story goes like this:

> Wísahkécáhk was walking around and he saw water birds by the river. He began to think how he could kill a lot of them. He went into the muskeg carrying a bag and filled the bag with moss. Then carrying the bag, he walked right by the river where many ducks, geese, and loons were swimming. Those birds were curious.
>
> "Hey older brother, what are you carrying in that bag?"
>
> "I'm carrying my songs." said Wísahkécáhk.
>
> "Songs?" those birds asked. Wísahkécáhk built a *míkíwáp* (three pole lodge) for the dance. All kinds of birds came there that night. Ducks, loons, and geese were there. Wísahkécáhk told the birds that there was a special dance that they should dance with their eyes shut. Wísahkécáhk began to sing. All the birds closed their eyes and began to dance. Wísahkécáhk kept singing. While the birds danced, he would grab them, one after the other, twist their necks, and throw them outside the lodge. He killed lots of ducks. Finally one loon got tired of dancing with his eyes closed and opened his eyes.
>
> "Oh, our older brother is killing us! Our older brother is killing us!" he yelled. It was almost too late. Wísahkécáhk had almost killed all of those ducks. That loon made a dive for the lake. Wísahkécáhk went after that loon and kicked it in the legs. That's why the loon have short legs today. (51–52)

Without identifying the context and firmly establishing the *mino-pimátisiwin* approach within Indigenous worldviews and practices, the approach would be like the songs in the story, attracting Indigenous helpers to social work only to have their necks wrung by the profession through the colonial foundations of its theory and praxis.

Further, I have come to realize that decolonization does not necessarily acknowledge the reality of colonialism on Ininewi-Ministik. My conversation after the meeting with an academic colleague demonstrated to me that individuals can partake in the idea of decolonization while maintaining the idea that colonization is over. It is like dancing to the songs of the *mino-pimátisiwin* approach with our eyes shut. We need our songs, but we have to keep our eyes open.

Moving Forward

Colonialism continues to exist, occasionally transforming shape like the tricksters in our traditional stories. We need to continually reflect on our practice to see how it represents the characteristics and goals of Indigenism and anti-colonialism. To me, this means as Indigenous helpers who happen to be social workers, we need to walk forward with at least two commitments in mind. First, we must acknowledge the existence of, and work against, colonial oppression. Second, we need to work from our hearts while reaching for our peoples' dreams and visions, where our hearts are firmly rooted in our peoples, traditions and cultures, and our dreams include peace for our peoples. These two commitments require us to be exceedingly clear about what perspectives, theories, approaches and practices we are following and how we use them. This includes the *mino-pimátisiwin* approach.

Notes

1. Ininewi-Ministik literately means the Indigenous Peoples Island and refers to the colonially named North America. It connects to a story of our oldest brother who recreated the Island from a handful of earth.
2. I referenced authors using their full names whenever I can so I may present a more personable sense of them and their work.
3. Even this title faces some challenges. Worldviews are significantly influenced by language. While I am not fluent in Cree, I know enough to explain that the language is rooted in verbs, unlike the English language, which is rooted in nouns. The title, the *mino-pimátisiwin* approach, reflects a noun base. To truly reflect my intent of the approach, the name of the approach should be rooted in a verb base, such as "approaching *mino-pimátisiwin*." This would reflect the teachings shared with me by several Elders regarding living *mino-pimátisiwin* as a process, not as some "thing" to arrive at. However, in using the title, "approaching *mino-pimátisiwin*," I am faced with the influence of the standards of the English language to objectify the title by putting the word "approach" after it, resulting in the "approaching *mino-pimátisiwin* approach." Clearly, this whole matter needs further attention.
4. Defined in an overly simplistic manner as the process of helping/sharing with one another
5. Defined in an overly simplistic manner as counselling.
6. Defined in an overly simplistic manner as laws.

Chapter 3

Indigenous-Centred Social Work
Theorizing a Social Work Way-of-Being

Gail Baikie

Indigenous Social Work within Recent History

In the 1980s, during my undergraduate degree, I was taught that there was only one social work — a discipline that had emerged from Euro-western history and social welfare contexts and was centred in Euro-western derived theories and methods. The unexamined assumption was that this knowledge and set of practices could and should be uncritically and universally applied to all peoples regardless of culture or political and historical circumstances. Locally derived Indigenous knowledge and skills were assumed to be personal, not professional characteristics, and therefore had no place within professional educational or practice settings. Over the course of fifteen years of professional practice with primarily Indigenous peoples and issues, I came to critique, resist and challenge these premises. I have not acted alone, and in recent years social work educational and professional institutions have, although still to a limited degree, accepted Indigenous perspectives and approaches as legitimate social work theories and practices. This is evidenced by the fact that Indigenous methods like the talking circle, family group conferencing and restorative justice now have some profile in the literature and are gaining popularity in social service settings. In addition, more mainstream agencies are working collaboratively with Indigenous peoples and communities and making an obvious effort to be more culturally sensitive. In the realm of social work scholarship and education, it is increasingly common to come across a chapter in a textbook, a scholarly article, content within the social work curriculum and, since the 1970s, social work programs for "Native" students.[1]

Since the 1980s in Canada, there have also been a few research inquires into social work education and practice that specifically include Indigenous social work education. For instance, in 1984 and 1985, the University of Regina was involved in a national initiative, "Indian and Native Social Work Education in Canada: A Study and Demonstration of Strategies for Change, which eventually became known as the Taking Control project.

Health and Welfare Canada provided funding in recognition that "social work education in Canada is out of touch with the social service areas relating to the social development and social circumstances of persons of Indian ancestry" (Stalwick 1986: xiv). This project clarified what was meant at the time by "authentic" Aboriginal social helping, specified the type of social work education required and documented the need for Aboriginal peoples to have autonomy over their social work education and social welfare services. Suffice it to say that the Taking Control project emphasized the distinct nature of Indigenous social work. Despite the position clearly articulated by these Indigenous social work leaders, subsequent investigations by the Canadian Association of Schools of Social Workers (CASSW) in May 1991 and March 2000 continued to position Indigenous social work within a multicultural or cultural diversity milieu (CASSW 1991). The CASSW standpoint in these reports is inconsistent with the Canadian Association of Social Workers' (CASW) 1994 submission to the Royal Commission on Aboriginal Peoples (1996), in which the organization apologized for the social work profession's problematic relationships with Aboriginal peoples and its dismissal of the Aboriginal worldview, and furthermore endorsed the right of Aboriginal nations to be self-determining.

Indigenous social workers and social work educators continue to resist attempts by mainstream social work institutions to either assimilate Indigenous social work within a Euro-western paradigm or categorize and marginalize it as "cultural." Rather, these leaders assert the distinct nature of the Indigenous social worker identity, knowledge-base, practices and political and social realities. For instance, an Indigenous social work educator's network, originally named Wunska, was formed in 1992 and later reborn in 2005 as the Thunderbird Nesting Circle. The organization's goals include supporting the scholarly development of Indigenous social work and self-government for Indigenous nations (Vedan 2005). Further evidence of a distinct Indigenous social work presence is an increasing number of Indigenous-focused health and social journals, including *Native Social Work*. There are regular local, regional and international Indigenous social work professional gatherings and conferences. For instance, in June 2007, an international conference called Indigenous Voices in Social Work: Not lost in Translation was held in Hawaii. We are also seeing the emergence of provincial and national professional associations, such as the Aboriginal Professional Helpers Society in Manitoba (Hart and Pompana 2003), in response to the fact that many Indigenous social workers believe that mainstream provincial bodies cannot (and should not) represent the interests of Indigenous social workers nor regulate their practices (Fiddler 2000). An exciting development on the international scene is the formation of the National Coalition of Aboriginal and Torres Strait Islander Social Workers Association in Australia.

While the profession espouses recognition of other ways of social help-ing, the evolution of Indigenous social work continues to be restrained, often implicitly, by dominant Euro-western assumptions that categorize and thereby limit Indigenous social helping to what is "cultural," "local" and "traditional." Many textbooks construct and practitioners perceive Indigenous social work to be simply a specialized field of Euro-western social work that specifically targets the social problems experienced by Indigenous peoples — such as the high rates of child neglect, violence, addictions and suicides — rather than as a distinct paradigm of social helping. Further confusion is created by social work literature, in which the term "Indigenous" is often used as a generic adjective denoting that a person, practice or knowledge originates from a specific location, as distinguished from generalizable or "universal" knowledge, theory or practices (Gray and Fook 2004), and may not neces-sarily refer to the First Peoples of a territory. This more general use of the term is insufficient for a discussion about Indigenous social work. A stream of thought called postmodernism challenges the modernist notions of a unified and universally applied set of theories and practices that underpins much social work education. Postmodernism claims that there are multiple ways-of-knowing, doing and being in the world and that no one way is privileged over another. This opens the door for context specific, hence "Indigenous" knowledge, identities and practices. Internationally, social work scholars have criticized universal approaches and advocated for more locally derived and therefore "authentic" forms of Indigenous social work education and profes-sional practices (Walton and Abo El Nasr 1988; Ragab 1990). Arguably, this amounts to a false "either/or" dichotomy (Berlin 1990) as effective social work practice requires both universalized *and* contextualized knowledge. Regardless of how it is packaged in textbooks or interpreted, many practitioners still assume that Indigenous social helping is subordinate or inferior to "real" social work, a point once argued to me by a national social work leader.

Contemporary Positioning of Indigenous Social Work

Despite the current challenge to modernism, the equitable inclusion of Indigenous social work remains an "illusion" (Roberts and Smith 2002: 189) as the discipline overall has not been critically reflective of its Euro-western assumptions, beliefs and values and has therefore failed to deconstruct and decolonize its own modernist professional culture. For instance, the univer-sally applied code of ethics and standards of practice do not account for the contextual, cultural and political realities for Indigenous social workers. Students and practitioners should not misconstrue the presence of Indigenous perspectives within social work as an indication of either the profession's commitment to respect the inherent right of Indigenous peoples to be self-determining within the realm of professional social helping or recognition that

Indigenous knowledges and practices have equitable status with Euro-western social work theories and methods. Indigenous social workers may argue that we do not need our knowledge and practices validated by the mainstream profession as to do so perpetuates the colonial relationship. This is a valid point but begs the question: How do we ensure the "professional existence" (Baikie 2008) of Indigenous social work in the absence of external recognition and sanctioning given that mainstream social work institutions maintain the legislative, structural and discursive power over what social work is, who practices, how they practice and where they practice?

To further complicate matters, the relationship between Indigenous peoples and the social work profession is strained largely due to the false assumptions that social work is an inherently "noble" profession, culturally neutral and without power. In Canada in the 1950s, changes to the *Indian Act* meant that that provincial laws of general application, including child welfare legislation, applied to federal Indian reserves (Shewell 2004). Euro-western social workers carry the legacy of having removed large numbers of Indigenous children from their families, communities and cultures (MacDonald et al. 2005; Johnson 1983). Most provinces currently regulate the profession and require all social workers to register with their provincial associations even though these organizations rarely recognize the ethical standards and practice competencies required to work effectively in Indigenous environments or with Indigenous peoples. These professional institutions, while having legislated authority, are often oblivious to the complex web of interjurisdictional (federal, provincial, Indigenous) social welfare policies and services and the cross-cultural nature of the work. Keep in mind that most cross-cultural social work theories and practices make the assumption that there is a culturally "neutral" (Euro-western) social worker who on occasion practices with an ethno-cultural client. One of the fundamental points in this chapter is that in our complex contemporary society, an Indigenous social worker is always working within, between and across culturally different contexts — Indigenous to Euro-western, Indigenous to Indigenous and even Indigenous to another ethno-racial culture. The power of the profession to regulate practices within Indigenous social welfare environments is further entrenched in recently negotiated self-government arrangements that specifically include the requirement for social workers, particularly in the field of child welfare, to be registered with and therefore regulated by their provincial professional associations.

As a result of these factors, many Indigenous peoples now find themselves in the paradoxical position of having to become professional social workers — as defined by dominant Euro-western discourses and institutions — in order fulfill their social helping roles and responsibilities within Indigenous communities. Indigenous social workers are at risk for identity and role dissonance due to the conflicting demands of their cultural, professional, social and political environments (Briskman 2003). This is exacerbated by dominant modernist ideals that separate a worker's personal life and their professional role. This means that the Indigenous social worker's Indigenous identity and characteristics are considered "personal" and "ethno-cultural" as opposed to a legitimate social helping way-of-being. Attempts by Indigenous social workers to integrate these identities place them at risk of being judged as biased and unprofessional (Weaver 2000; Bennett and Zubrzycki 2003). However, research is beginning to challenge such assumptions. For instance, Chung (2003: 271) found that non-Euro-western social workers "use their non-professional cultures and experiences as a means for helping." Furthermore, an emerging notion is that a social worker's ability to shift perspectives and approaches according to the cultural demands of their clients and practice contexts is a strength and indication of resiliency as opposed to a threat to the provision of professional service (Weaver and Yellow Horse Brave Heart 1999; Goulet 1998; Walley 1994, as cited in Taylor 1997; Lee 2001; Ford and Dillard 1996). It is important that beginning social workers do not misunderstand this argument. It is always unethical for any social worker to allow their individual personal interests and perspectives to interfere with their practice. Instead I am suggesting that Indigenous social workers bring other legitimate collective ways-of-knowing and social helping to their practice environments based on their worldview, which includes their cultural knowledge base and their individual and collective practice knowledge as social helpers. Clark (1995) explains that a worldview provides the "conscious mental platform on which we act", the "normative map of social behaviour" and is subconsciously supported by "unexamined beliefs and assumptions about reality" (65). As social workers we are practising in an era when we no longer have to be limited to perspectives, knowledge and skills derived either from the traditions of our respective Indigenous nations or submit to dominant Euro-western ideals. In fact, we potentially have access to tools and understandings derived from multiple Indigenous nations and other culturally diverse societies. The ongoing challenge is to be mindful of the potential risk of appropriation and exploitation of knowledge belonging to another society.

I argue in this chapter that Indigenous social workers can creatively engage with multiple social work ways-of-knowing, doing and being while maintaining an Indigenous-centred practice. In fact, my central thesis is that we need to reconceptualize our unique local Indigenous social work perspectives and practices within a global collective Indigenous-centred social work paradigm. In addition, we must recognize that Indigenous-centred social work is both distinct from and often compatible with dominant Eurocentric social work along as well as other culturally diverse ways of social helping.

By resisting the either/or categorizations or binaries characteristic of western modernist thinking (Berlin 1990), we open the possibility for conceptualizing an Indigenous–centred social work paradigm that is both localized and globalized, has both cultural and rights-based integrity, incorporates both traditional and contemporary knowledge and practices, focuses on both problems and possibilities and is both a specialized field and a generalized practice. I make these claims through theorizing Indigenous-centred social work using anti-colonial and postcolonial thought.

Theoretical Underpinnings for
Indigenous-Centred Social Work

The theoretical paradigm underlying Indigenous-centred social work foregrounds local and global Indigenous philosophies, values, experiences and ideas without precluding relevant and appropriate contributions from other cultures and societies, including Euro-western, which are primarily positioned as supplementary background. As Roberts (1990: 27) explains, a paradigm "consists of the fundamental worldview... [or] system of ideas, beliefs, and attitudes which provide both the background and the framework for theory development." However, Euro-western perspectives prevail and remain firmly entrenched in the social work curriculum and within social work practice. Anti-oppressive and other critical theoretical perspectives provide an intellectual means for continuing an internal challenge to Euro-western perspectives and neoliberal approaches within practice, but they too are problematic in that they assume that social relations are conflicted and adversarial, which is in direct contrast to the fundamental principle of social coherence inherent in most Indigenous perspectives. This is perhaps another unnecessary binary (Baikie 2008).

Fundamentally, an Indigenous-centred social work theoretical framework is enabled by an anti-colonial perspective. In this chapter, I also argue that there are relevant ideas from within postcolonial thought that augment and enhance a contemporary Indigenous-centred social work paradigm. Anti-colonialism critiques the historical and contemporary colonial suppression of Indigenous peoples by Euro-western forces, recognizes and supports efforts to resist, decolonize and reclaim what is cultural, and brings to the fore the unique nature- and rights-based nationalism of Indigenous peoples. Notwithstanding the limitations, postcolonialism does enable us to theorize the continued colonization of Indigenous societies within existing states, despite the decolonization of many African and Asian nations, to challenge the notion that Indigenous societies are homogeneous, to maintain both a local and an international perspective, to acknowledge both achievements in decolonization and the continuing challenges, and to consider the effects of dispersed populations, including the possibility of constructing new and sometimes hybrid collectives and identities, while ensuring the continued analysis of "conflictual cultural interaction" (Young 2001: 69).

As Young (2001: 12) asserts, a "postcolonial cultural critique involves the reconsideration of this [colonial] history, particularly from the perspectives of those who suffered its effects, together with the defining of its contemporary social and cultural impact." However, contemporary scholars argue that although many once-colonized nations (for instance India, and several African states) are now politically independent, Indigenous peoples remain under colonial rule in a state of "neocolonialism" (Smith 1999; Sinclair 2004). In this condition, Indigenous peoples remain "in a situation of dependence on... former masters... [where] physical force [is] no longer required because hegemony of the ruling class [is] sufficiently established at a cultural, ideological, economic and political level for it to operate by means of prestige and active consent" (Young 2001: 46). What this metatheoretical perspective suggests is that despite some political gains, many if not most Indigenous communities continue to be not just physically but also structurally, ideologically and discursively "colonized." The profession itself is implicated in this colonization agenda. Midgley (1981) accuses social work in the international arena of "professional imperialism," and Battiste (1998) asserts that education has been used as a tool for "cognitive imperialism" (20). Indigenous social workers, through professional training and multiple other influences, are conditioned by Euro-western thought, which frames and thereby restricts what they understand to be "reality" and the "truth." This means that Indigenous professionals are at risk for practising in a manner that continues to perpetuate the colonization of Indigenous peoples. I make the argument elsewhere that Indigenous social workers must decolonize their minds in order to liberate their practices (Baikie 2005).

Indigenous-centred social work does not preclude Euro-western ideas (Smith 1999) but instead foregrounds local and global Indigenous knowledge, identities, ways-of-knowing, values, attitudes, practices, protocols and concerns (Kovach 2005; Smith 1999). It enables us to recognize and respond to the postcolonial condition of "borders," which Giroux (2005: 2) explains as useful "for understanding the co-mingling — sometimes clash — of multiple cultures, languages, literacies, histories, sexualities, and identities.... [These are] contact zones where power operates to either expand or to shrink the distance and connectedness among individuals, groups, and places despite strong arguments for multiplicity."

In the end I have intellectual ground to further conceptualize Indigenous-centred social work and build on the pioneering work of past and present Indigenous scholars who have successfully articulated and asserted Indigenous social work knowledge as a distinct theoretical perspective and set of practice skills (see, for instance, Morrissette, McKenzie and Morrissette 1993;

Hart 2001). My intent is not to lay out a complete theoretical paradigm; the creation of contemporary Indigenous-centred social work will never be the product of one "expert" or the exclusive domain of researchers and scholars. Indigenous-centred social work will continue to evolve from the collective creative efforts of Indigenous social work students, practitioners, educators, scholars and researchers. This book itself is a contribution to this process. My goals are relatively modest. I argue that Indigenous-centred social work is distinct from Euro-western social work and I distinguish the more specific construct, "Indigenous-centred social work," from the more generic concept, "Indigenous social work." Finally, I identify Indigenous social workers, their ways-of-knowing and their practices.

What Is Indigenous Social Work?

Euro-western professional social helping emerged at the turn of the twentieth century in response to the needs of western societies to address the complex social problems created by industrialization and urbanization (Hick 2006). Its knowledge base is clearly grounded in western philosophies, which incorporate individualism and liberalism, and it has been strongly influenced by Christian morality. Indigenous social helping is historically rooted in collectivist and holistic philosophies and acquires a value base from Indigenous spiritualities (Hart 2001; Graveline 1998). Contemporary, professionalized Indigenous social work has developed in response to the devastating social conditions in Indigenous communities, which are primarily attributed to the colonization experience.

Most students, if not practitioners, have great difficulty answering the question: what is social work? Perhaps the best way to answer is to use a person-in-environment framework, a model widely understood to be the defining concept distinguishing social work from other professions (Kondrat 2002). As the term suggests, social work is concerned with the individual (physical, psychological, including affective and cognitive, and increasingly spiritual) and their environments (social, economic, political and some limited recognition of cultural) along with the complex dynamic interactions within and between these elements. An Indigenous social work perspective requires a reconceptualized person-in-environment perspective. First and foremost, Indigenous perspectives understand the person in their totality — physical, spiritual, mental and emotional (Hart 2001) — and do not separate the "inner space" from the "outer space" (Ermine 1999). Highwater (1981: 67, cited in Heshusius 1994) explains that "cultures, such as ancient Eastern or Native Indian, which in their organization of reality do not objectify nature, do not subjectify nature either. Theirs is not an alienated mode of consciousness that creates psychic distance between the knower and the known. For Indians, the oneness of consciousness... is a 'capacity for an integration of the self and the world that is learned'" (17). Mainstream social work is criticized for reducing the environment to the social environment, while Indigenous social work perspectives consider the natural environment as paramount (Zapf 2002). In addition, mainstream perspectives fail to account for colonial history and the contemporary complexity of practice contexts due to the intertwined Indigenous and mainstream neocolonial environments.

What Is Indigenous-Centred Social Work?

Indigenous-centred social work moves Indigenous practices out of the localized and disconnected while still accounting for both the global diversity of Indigenous peoples and their distinct ways of social helping. It considers collectively shared experiences among Indigenous populations, along with knowledges and practices that are either similar and or at least transferable across and between Indigenous populations (Baikie 2005). Yet, an Indigenous-centred social work perspective must not to be confused with a pan-Indigenous perspective, which fails to account for the diversity within and between Indigenous peoples and nations. A pan-Indigenous perspective essentializes an Indigenous way-of-being into very specific and unchanging stereotypical characteristics, such as the notion that all Indigenous peoples have a close spiritual connection to the natural environment. It fails to recognize that different Indigenous populations, such as the Inuit, Mi'kmaq, Innu and Haudenosaunee, are distinct cultural, political and social societies although they may share the common experiences of being Indigenous to a territory and having been colonized.

An Indigenous centred perspective accounts for both the similarities and differences among and between Indigenous peoples and nations and thereby enables a shared collective identity and shared practices without discounting variability. By way of illustration, many Indigenous and non-Indigenous people argue that the medicine wheel concept is not traditional to a specific Indigenous nation and therefore should not be claimed by or used within their community's programs and services. From an Indigenous-centred perspective, whether or not a knowledge or skill is authentic is largely irrelevant. What is more important is that a nation is open to the exchange of ideas and experiences and makes critical and conscious choices about what is locally relevant, culturally consistent and politically empowering. The use of non-traditional and even Euro-western knowledge or practices is not problematic as long as the community is exercising free will and operating in the best interests of their people. What is useful or pragmatic is more important than what is traditional or authentic. Furthermore, an Indigenous-centred perspective challenges the notion that culture is static and restricted to what was known or practised prior to European colonization. Instead, this orientation incorporates all historical and contemporary experiences, including current innovations emerging from Indigenous social workers practising in the complexity of their environments. The practice reality is comprised of a complex array of devastating social problems and tangled networks of inter-jurisdictional social welfare environments that have emerged as a direct result of colonization (Shewell 2004). The specific and unique nature of practice within these environments is a core characteristic of Indigenous-centred social work. However, it is also an environment of potential and possibility due to the inherent resiliency of Indigenous peoples and nations as evidenced by their increasing political autonomy and their success in reclaiming and revitalizing their cultures. It is also an unprecedented practice environment. Indigenous social workers cannot expect to be effective by simply applying either Euro-western or traditional Indigenous social helping knowledge derived from a different time and different realities. While often rooted in a "traditional" paradigm, new knowledge must and is being created by both scholars and practitioners to address current practice realities.

Indigenous societies are striving to reestablish their national boundaries, but the legacy of colonization and an increasingly postmodern world means these borders are porous and populations are mobile. The notion of "Indigenous" implies a people who are rooted to and within a particular geographical location. Colonization has meant that many have experienced dislocation from both their traditional territories and their legislated reserve lands. The notion of "diaspora" is useful for considering the implications of this phenomenon for an Indigenous-centred social work practice (Harvey and Thompson Jr. 2005: 1). The term diaspora is typically used to describe the forced migration and dispersion of a people from their homeland as is the case for Jewish and many African peoples. Indigenous peoples throughout the world are increasingly mobile and are forming new collectives ("urban Aboriginal," "residential school survivor" and "Indigenous social worker"), operating in new and divergent contexts (urban, international, mainstream) and creating new identities as Indigenous people within the diaspora (traditional, modern, First Nation, urban). As Rosaldo (1989) points out, "Neither 'we' nor 'they' are as neatly bounded and homogeneous as once seemed to be the case" (217).

Regardless of professional education and standards of practice, Indigenous social workers will often integrate their own cultural knowledge (for instance, see Mafile'o 2004; Lynn 2001) and the knowledge originating from other Indigenous nations into their professional practice, blurring the distinction between what is "cultural" and what is "professional." Thus, there has emerged a generic base of Indigenous social work knowledge and practices. For instance, in Canada, while use of the medicine wheel concept and the talking circle are not traditional to every Indigenous nation, they are widely understood in many Indigenous social work education courses to be foundational practice concepts and methods. In addition, restorative justice and family group conferencing models, originating with the Maori of New Zealand, are now achieving widespread appeal and use within both Indigenous and non-Indigenous social service settings.

An Indigenous-centred perspective recognizes that Indigenous nations have Indigenous rights. This is consistent with the fact that some nations, like Canada and New Zealand, have recognized Indigenous rights in their constitutional documents, i.e., the *Constitution Act* 1982 (Canada) and the *Treaty of Waitangi* 1840 (New Zealand). The specifics of these rights are currently being defined through negotiation and litigation. While most Indigenous nations have placed a priority on land and resource rights, the notion of rights can extend to social practices (for instance, customary adoptions, whereby children in need are cared for by relatives, community and kinship networks). While I have argued for the need for sharing among Indigenous nations, the assertion of a right to Indigenous social work practices incorporates a responsibility on the part of Indigenous social workers to also protect the knowledge from appropriation and exploitation. This is consistent with current dialogues and emerging protocols involving ethical research involving Indigenous peoples, which focus on the rights of Indigenous collectives to retain ownership and control of their knowledge. It could be argued, for instance, that Indigenous social work practices such as the medicine wheel, family group conferencing and restorative justice, while expanding the possibilities of healing for many Indigenous peoples, are also ripe for appropriation by the dominant mainstream.

Postcolonialism, along with critical theoretical perspectives, help bring to the forefront the right of Indigenous peoples to self-determination. The social work profession, mandated by codes of ethics to attend to social justice and human rights, has played a limited role in supporting the autonomous nature of Indigenous nations generally and of Indigenous social work practice and social welfare systems specifically. As previously pointed out, the Canadian Association of Social Workers (CASW 1994), in its brief to the Royal Commission on Aboriginal Peoples (RCAP 1996), proclaimed support for Aboriginal self-government. In addition, the International Federation of Social Workers (IFSW 2004) released a policy paper in support of the collective right of Indigenous peoples throughout the world to be self-determining. Unfortunately, neither the CASW nor the IFSW has adequately considered the implications of self-determining Indigenous nations on either social work education or the regulation of the profession. This is evident in the latest iteration of the CASW Code of Ethics (2005), which is completely mute on the issue of Indigenous autonomy.

Who Are Indigenous Social Workers?

In any society, social responsibility manifests itself into various forms of social helping —informal, natural (O'Gorman and Delaney 1996), mutual aid, self-help and formalized paraprofessional and professional helping (Farquharson 1999). Volunteerism and other less structured forms of social helping within contemporary modern society have been displaced by more "expert" professionalized services. However, there appears to be renewed recognition of the intrinsic value of informal social helping as a characteristic of resilient and healthy individuals and communities (Waller and Patterson 2002).

Indigenous peoples and societies are distinct and diverse, but tend to share some experiences and characteristics. Traditionally, knowledge and practices with respect to social obligations, helping and healing evolved over time, were accumulated collectively and transmitted intergenerationally (Ermine 1999). Elders have a tremendous responsibility as the conduits of this store of traditional knowledge and skills. The transmission (teaching) and acquisition (learning) occurred within the mediums of stories, ceremonies and the traditional practices inherent in daily living. Spiritual leaders and Elders often had specific responsibilities for health and healing practices. A general principle of reciprocity ensured that the community responded to those affected by health and social issues pertaining to disease, hunger, child welfare and matters of social deviance and social control. Often women played many of these social helping roles (Anderson 2000). Waller and Patterson (2002), by way of illustration, studied the traditional helping structure in the Dine tradition and concluded that "helping one another is a way of life. Human beings are inextricably connected to one another and to nature through a complex web of relationships including blood relations, clan relations, tribal relations, and relationships to all human beings and other aspects of the natural world. Mutual dependence and cooperation are givens and individual standing in the community is largely related to the extent to which a person is helpful to others" (73). The study identified important distinctions between Dine and more mainstream informal helping models. The Dine view problems and solutions as spiritual in nature, understand and respond to problems in a holistic way and view need as non-stigmatizing and relationship categories as not mutually exclusive. The provision of services is typically active and pragmatic as opposed to Euro-western approaches, which tend to be more passive, often using talk as the primary means to provide emotional support or assist clients in solving problems.

These traditional and carefully balanced systems of knowing and helping were disrupted by European political, economic and social welfare forces. Out of this chaos and into the "Indian social welfare system" (Shewell 2004) emerged the Indigenous paraprofessional social helper. While not completely displacing traditional helpers, the Indigenous social service worker became a legitimized holder, applier and generator of social helping. After many years of dedication and commitment, many would also acquire the more traditional status of Elder in their communities. However, the Indigenous paraprofessional, a manifestation of colonial authority, was typically subordinate to "real" social workers — the products of Euro-western professional socialization. Colonial structures throughout the social welfare system determined that the knowledge and practices of these often young and inexperienced university graduates was superior to the cultural knowledge and practice wisdom of their Indigenous colleagues (see, for instance, Mastronardi 1990, who describes the experience of subordination by Inuit community workers in the field of youth protection in Northern Quebec). In recent years a distinct Aboriginal professional social work sector has emerged (Fiddler 2000). Figure 3.1 is an adaptation of Farquharson's (1999) continuum of social helping into a non-hierarchical circle of Indigenous social helping.

In conclusion, the responsibility for social helping traditionally rested with Indigenous social helpers. However, due to colonization, these social helpers were displaced by Euro-western social welfare services, professional social helpers and, by the later part of the twentieth century, professional social workers. Today, this responsibility is being reclaimed by Indigenous social helpers including the more formalized Indigenous social work professional.

Figure 3.1 Circle of Inidgenous-Centred Social Work

The challenges are huge. Indigenous social workers must contend with the destructive legacy of decades of colonization on both the psychological and spiritual "inner space" and the social, physical and structural "outer space" (Ermine 1999). The reality is that the profession of social work is supported by Euro-western ideological hegemony or "the unquestioned dominance of all conformist ideas that support the interests of the group promoting them" (Mullaly 2002: 79). Indigenous social workers are continuously influenced by this hegemony through their personal and professional socialization and are not immune to developing a false consciousness through internalized oppression. In other words, Indigenous social workers experience cognitive and practice dissonance due to conflicting Indigenous and Euro-western social work ways-of-being messages about what is "real" or the "truth." For instance, Euro-western social welfare legislation and policies may specify that only the biological parents or "legal" guardians can make decisions for a child. However, within the Indigenous community the grandparents and other members of the extended family have obligations and expectations to be meaningfully involved in the decision-making. Thus, an Indigenous social worker may have great difficulty remaining Indigenous-centred while incorporating other ways-of-knowing. Some critical theories, such as Gidden's structuration theory, suggest that our inner and outer worlds exist in a recursive relationship, and this notion is consistent with Ermine's (1999) conceptualization of the unity of the inner and outer space within Indigenous thought. What this means is that Indigenous social workers, while influenced and impacted by the powerful ideologies and social structures of colonial society, are also active participants in the creation and maintenance of colonized relationships. To borrow a metaphor from Kondrat (1999), we are all dancers in the neocolonial dance. Colonizing influences tend to operate below conscious awareness. The logical analysis is that if Indigenous social workers have a colonized consciousness they are seriously at risk for perpetuating colonizing practices. On the upside, because Indigenous social workers are active agents in colonization, they can be and are active agents in decolonization. To maximize opportunities and minimize risks, individual and collective efforts to develop critical consciousness are required (Sakamoto and Pitner 2005) and can be achieved through critically reflecting on the influences of Indigenous and Euro-western worldviews and using other consciousness raising techniques (Baikie 2008).

Where and How Do Indigenous Social Workers Practise?

Indigenous social workers are required to work in practice settings that are complex and uncertain. These environments are complex because of the political and philosophical tensions inherent in Indigenous and Euro-western colonial relations, which translate into a vast array of both locally derived and state-imposed social policies, institutions and service agencies. The uncertainty arises because anti-colonial and postcolonial ideas challenge the Euro-western scientific knowledge base as a means for solving problems for all populations. Indigenous social workers must critically analyze when, where and with whom they will use either Euro-western or Indigenous de-rived knowledge and practices. Postcolonial thought also raises the possibility of creatively drawing upon knowledge from diverse cultures (including the diversity of Indigenous cultures) or creating new Indigenous knowledge ap-plicable to contemporary social challenges. Suffice it to say that Indigenous social workers require a diverse knowledge base and tool kit, creativity and the fortitude to get into the messiness of their practices.

Many Indigenous leaders argue that political autonomy, hence libera-tion from colonial domination, is necessary for their communities, nations and citizens to regain health and wellbeing. This is consistent with an anti-colonial nationalism perspective, which emphasizes strategies to decolonize lands, resources and socio-economic and political systems. The intent is to reestablish boundaries that distinguish an Indigenous society from the non-Indigenous society. It means establishing places and spaces where Indigenous ways-of-knowing, doing and being are reclaimed, redefined and represented. While this argument has merit and is therefore supported if not facilitated by Indigenous social workers, there remain limitations and risks. In this contemporary era of global interdependency, most if not all Indigenous societies can never be completely autonomous. Smith (1999), for instance, quite rightly points out that in several states, like Canada, Australia, New Zealand and the United States, the colonizers are unlikely to leave. Furthermore, it is generally understood that due to the economi-cally globalized nature of our world, all nations and states are implicated in and must conform to the power of Euro-american economic, political and ideological interests.

If the experience of many decolonized states in Africa and Asia are any indication, then any level of enhanced political autonomy may place Indigenous societies at increased risk for social strife and social stratification. Historically, in Indigenous societies, collectivist notions of social obligation, like sharing and caring (Vedan 2005), minimized the gaps between those that "have" and those that "have not." Colonization produced whole communi-ties of "have nots." It is becoming apparent in Canada that as Indigenous nations achieve gains in political and economic autonomy, some are reaping benefits will many others are not, and the gap between them is widening. Neither whole communities nor subgroups of disadvantaged populations is an acceptable scenario from any social work perspective and one that our discipline professes to challenge and change. My main point is that even if Indigenous communities regain a measure of independence and social and economic wellbeing, there will continue to be social implications. Indigenous social workers will need to continue to work with those on the margins of both non-Indigenous and Indigenous societies and to challenge social conditions both within and outside Indigenous nations that advantage some and disadvantage others. Furthermore, Indigenous nations remain imbedded globally if not locally within the Euro-american dominant systems, and discourses and efforts to mitigate the impacts of individual and collective subordination will need to continue.

Within the diaspora, Indigenous peoples are dispersed throughout the state and subjected to structural oppressions, including racism, that place them at continued risk for social and economic disadvantage. Indigenous individuals, communities and nations must also contend with the intergenerational trauma created from the legacy of colonization (Wesley-Esquimaux and Smolewski 2004). Arguably, this new and complex practice realm requires a more formalized and professional Indigenous social work. Given its colonial legacy, mainstream social work education and practice is not well positioned to prepare Indigenous practitioners for these realities. Traditional methods are also likely insufficient.

Indigenous-centred social work is distinct in terms of how knowledge is derived and used. Knowing about a phenomenon and having the technical skills to apply knowledge are privileged within a social work dominated by a Euro-western scientific perspective (Sheppard et al. 2000). On the other hand, an Indigenous-centred social work values pragmatic, tacit (Osmond 2006), or culturally implicit, knowing, coming-to-know and knowledge generated from practice experiences (Fook and Gardner 2007). Thus, how we understand Indigenous social work, at least during this historical moment, requires us at times to shift our professional gaze from knowing about and applying social work skills on the client-in-environment to learning from the dynamics of the practitioner-in-context (Baikie 2008). This means that Indigenous-centred social work is only partially about working with clients and equally if not sometimes more about working with and within the dynamics and cultures of the various Euro-western and Indigenous policy and practice settings, which likely impede and sometimes enable our work with clients and broader social problems. Researcher-generated knowledge can be relevant knowledge for Indigenous social work practice, and this is currently emanating from more structured research processes, including those that use Indigenous and decolonizing research methodologies (Smith 1999). At this point in time, our deductive knowledge base is limited, but what does exist is a wealth of inductively generated theory-from-practice (Fook 2002), otherwise known as "experiential knowledge" or "practice wisdom" (Dybicz 2004). This shouldn't come as a complete surprise to the Indigenous student or scholar as Indigenous people have typically valued the practice wisdom of

Indigenous social helpers over the university-acquired expertise of "professional" social workers.

A highly skilled and structured Indigenous social work profession is required to address the social and psychological devastation resulting from decades of colonization. The practice arena for most Indigenous social workers often extends into multiple and complex practice contexts that may or may not be inherently Indigenous and may be on the border between what is Euro-western and what is Indigenous. For instance, an Indigenous social worker is just as likely to practise in a hospital for the general public with clients from multiple ethno-racial backgrounds as she is to work in an urban Native friendship centre with Indigenous peoples from across the country and around the world. Even localized practice settings have become increasingly complicated. Indigenous social workers find themselves working within quasi-autonomous social welfare institutions such as a child welfare service operated by an Indigenous community but legislated by a provincial government. Many local cultural healing and helping practices are being revitalized and an Indigenous social worker may just as easily work within a community or wilderness-based healing program that relies almost exclusively on traditional Indigenous knowledge. This means that an Indigenous social worker must be extremely flexible, creative and innovative and able to draw on multiple sources of knowledge — the knowledge base associated with their own culture, knowledge shared by other Indigenous societies and a more generic Euro-western social work knowledge — and they must create their own knowledge through experimenting within and reflecting on their own practice (Schon 1987). In many ways, Indigenous social workers are pioneers in these contemporary practice contexts and need to and are finding ways to work not only with the impact of colonization on Indigenous peoples and communities but also strategically with, within and across cultural and contextual boundaries.

Indigenous social workers share a collective need to address the neo-colonial social and political uncertainties and complexities inherent in their contemporary practice environments, including the expectation that they be competent to practise in both Indigenous and non-Indigenous contexts, to work across contextual and cultural boundaries and increasingly to find ways to develop and operate within the unprecedented nature of services and programs being created within quasi-autonomous, including some self-government, arrangements. Unfortunately, social work education often fails to adequately prepare practitioners for their daunting tasks. Thus, an Indigenous-centred social work education must continue to evolve and to prepare and position Indigenous social workers to decolonize their practices, their identities and their minds in order to recreate Indigenous-centred social work in meaningful and effective ways.

Cross-cultural and cross-contextual challenges facing Indigenous-centred social workers include the following:

- incorporating and valuing Indigenous knowledge (including philosophies, cultural "tacit" knowledge, traditions and languages) in the face of widespread dismissal and resistance;
- recognizing and responding to different sociological trends for Indigenous and mainstream populations such as a higher population growth, younger population, more poverty and high rates of substance abuse, violence, suicide and racism;
- responding to the dynamic and shifting priorities, accountabilities and structures within Indigenous communities and nations resulting from either the devolution of programs and services from the federal government or negotiated self-government arrangements, all of which have as yet unknown implications for the health and social wellbeing of Indigenous populations;
- challenging mainstream stereotypes of the sameness of Indigenous people, and acknowledging and accommodating the differences between and within Indigenous groups (including the variability to which an Indigenous person identifies with traditional or contemporary Indigenous culture);
- dealing with conflicting cultural and professional identities and expectations of the social work profession, the social welfare service system, Indigenous communities and of themselves as Indigenous peoples;
- overcoming past educational experiences that result from, and perpetuate, limited access and opportunities for Indigenous social workers;
- overcoming limited access to relevant social work resources including funding, Indigenous social work educators, Indigenous social work materials and texts, resource people, relevant mentoring and field practice environments and professional development opportunities;
- recognizing and responding to negative perceptions of social work by many Indigenous peoples and communities and the ambivalence many social workers feel in identifying with the social work profession; and
- addressing the lack of legitimate space for Indigenous-centred social work within the profession (social work education, professional associations, practice environments) and lack of acknowledgement of its current and historical contributions to the profession and to social welfare services (adapted from Baikie and Bella 2003).

I end this discussion by emphasizing that Indigenous social workers are restrained by social structures and colonizing ideologies that cloud their awareness, but practitioners also resist these constraints through their day-to-day practices (Weaver and Yellow Horse Brave Heart 1999). Thus, Indigenous social workers are creating knowledge that ensures that their practice is "culturally safe"[2] and therefore does not unwittingly "diminish, demean and/or disempower" Indigenous people and communities but instead "recognizes, respects and acknowledges" Indigenous cultures and rights (Wood and Schwass 1993). This means that Indigenous social workers must practise in ways that are accountable to Indigenous peoples and communities, that adhere to their integrity as Indigenous people and Indigenous social workers, that adhere to Indigenous ethical standards and that create new knowledge that enables effective practices in their diverse neocolonial contexts.

Indigenous-Centred Social Work Is Real Social Work

The theoretical assumptions underpinning this chapter are primarily anti-colonial. I write from a stance that recognizes that social work theories and practices are not immune to the relations of colonial domination and oppression. As Indigenous social workers we must re-centre our Indigenous knowledges, skills and practice realities. This requires us to continuously resist antagonists who challenge the status of Indigenous-centred social work as not "real social work," who try to subjugate our knowledge and skills to the margins as a cultural or specialized approach, or attempt to appropriate segments into the mainstream knowledge base without recognition and acknowledgement. The notion of Indigenous-centred social work provides an opportunity for Indigenous social workers to collectively resist domination by centring Indigenous philosophies, values, histories and theories in all their multiplicity — similarities and differences, points of congruence and divergence. The fundamental point emphasized in this chapter is that Indigenous-centred social work denotes a social work way-of-being that is distinct from, but potentially compatible with, perspectives and approaches associated with Euro-western centred social work. The implications of this thinking for Indigenous social workers are profound. First and foremost, the Indigenous social worker no longer has to transform into a generic Euro-western social worker in order to be considered a professional social worker. Unfortunately, this remains the intent of many social work education programs, which are based exclusively in a universalized knowledge base and whose explicit or implicit goal is to indoctrinate all social workers into a Euro-western worldview. This is also the intent of most social work regulatory bodies and national associations, whose premises regarding ethics and practice standards are still very Eurocentric. Even though there have been a number of discussions and attempts at professional organizing, much stills needs to be done, and it will require the concerted efforts of Indigenous social work students, practitioners, educators and researchers, along with their supporters.

At this stage it is imperative that the Indigenous social workers have ways of understanding and articulating the meaning of Indigenous-centred social work practice. This chapter and textbook are contributions to this reconceptualization, which affirms and centres the knowledges, practices and identities of Indigenous social workers; situates their knowledge base within the broader national and international collectivity of Indigenous social work knowing, and positions Euro-western social work as a choice not an absolute requirement. It is my intention that the term Indigenous social worker acquires a new and more comprehensive meaning. No longer would the word "Indigenous" be just an adjective denoting a worker's cultural/racial identity. Rather the term "Indigenous social worker" would be understood in its totality, including as a noun, denoting a distinct social work, and as a verb, denoting ways of relating and practising. Theorizing Indigenous-centred social work moves the term Indigenous social worker from a personal to a collective way-of-being.

Notes

1. Castellano, Stalwick and Wien (1986) categorized Indigenous social work education programs as autonomous models of social work education emerging as in-service staff training but without official accreditation; affiliated autonomous programs controlled by Native organizations but connected to and sanctioned by an existing university; and special Native programs offered by mainstream institutions with short-term contract funding.

2. The concept "cultural safety" is attributed to Maori nursing educator, Irihaprti Ramsden. In New Zealand, cultural safety is now considered a necessary outcome of competent nursing services. How this concept applies to competent social work practice is a matter to be discussed within the profession. From my perspective, the primary notion needing to be considered is not as much "safety" as it is "cultural accountability" and the maintenance of "cultural integrity" for the Indigenous social worker, the Indigenous client and the Indigenous practice context.

Section II — Practice

Dreaming Makes Action
The Practice of Indigenous Social Work

Gord Bruyere (Amawaajibitang)

Hold fast to dreams for if dreams die, life is a broken-winged bird that cannot fly. —Langston Hughes (1959: 97)

During my social work education, I had a tough time balancing school, faced a shortage of resources, was involved in a cross-cultural love relationship and had ongoing issues with drugs and alcohol. At the same time, I was really struggling with my identity as a man, as Anishinaabe and as whatever professional role I was going to take on as a social worker. It was not too different from what many social work students are forced to deal with now that I think about it. I was fortunate that I was able to go see an Elder. He had a way of putting things into perspective and of seeing through my fallacious thinking and justifications. Anyway, I sat with him and recounted my litany of complaints and whined about how difficult my life was. I finished by saying, "I just wish my life was easier!" He sat there for awhile, silently smoking his pipe at the kitchen table. I could hear children playing outside and the wall clock ticking. He leaned forward a bit. So did I because I was so eager to hear him tell me how to solve my problems. He just looked at me and absolutely stopped me in my tracks when he said, "What makes you think it's supposed to be easy?"

As a social work educator, I have often encountered students who want me to tell them what Indigenous peoples want to be called — Aboriginal? Indian? First Nations? Native Americans? What? Many times they have asked me what Indigenous peoples want. Do you mean like a new pony or the newest brand of body wash? How about clean running water? However, the question that most often causes me to take a deep breath and wait before I speak is when students want a list of approaches and practices that are effective with Indigenous peoples. They want a tool box, or even better, they want an all-in-one tool that they can apply to any people or any situation.

I cannot say I blame them. We all want something that will keep us afloat. We all want to know that storms will pass or that our dreams will make sense. What Rona Sterling-Collins, Raven Sinclair, Michael Anthony Hart, Cathy Richardson and Cindy Baskin offer you may provide some of that. Their narratives and analyses are replete with practice examples and opportunities to enhance a social worker's ability to work respectfully with Indigenous peoples. But be careful. These are particular dreams and the actions they forebode are unique to those dreams. There are many practice contexts and issues that they do not explore, and what they offer may or may not be effective in any given situation. Much of it may. Much of what they have to say has not been presented in contemporary social work literature. In any case, you will find your own way to understand the action of your dreams and find that Elder within yourself to help guide you to what is true.

Chapter 4

A Holistic Approach to Supporting Children with Special Needs

Rona Sterling-Collins (Quistaletko)

The Beginning of our Journey

I begin this story with tears in my eyes. Sharing my story about my son Wyatt is emotional because he is incredibly "special" in every way possible and it is an honour to share this journey with him. I have decided to share this story as my own, although my husband and my eighteen-year-old daughter are very much a part of this journey. They might, one day, want to share the story from their own place of heart. I have chosen to write this chapter as a sacred narrative. Following the tradition of my ancestors, I share this story with a reminder that our stories and our experiences are as important as academic research. We learn from many approaches to teaching. In my story, I will share our joys and struggles with Wyatt and autism. I highlight the signs of changes, growth and regression of his disorder. I contextualize our journey utilizing the medicine wheel framework, which reflects Wyatt's development in the four quadrants of physical, emotional, intellectual and spiritual. In honouring Wyatt, a holistic perspective to his life is the only method that can provide a snapshot of who this incredible person is.

Helping those with autism first requires contextualizing the dynamics of autism in terms of the physical and social aspects of autism spectrum disorder. To support Aboriginal families and communities, service planning and delivery needs to incorporate an Aboriginal worldview. There is great benefit to ensuring social workers serving Aboriginal children and families have a strengthened awareness of special needs, and I include a section specific to ways social workers can support children and families with special needs that bridges cultural relevancy into contemporary services. The essence of my story is to provide hope to other Aboriginal children and families with special needs. I am on an amazing journey with Wyatt and it is my hope that this story will touch others in order that they can serve as advocates for children with special needs.

A Special Son

"Your son has a special spiritual gift." — words of a spiritual Elder
soon after my son was diagnosed with autism

Wyatt was born on November 21, 1997, arriving three weeks early but healthy
and strong. I was told by the Elders before he was born that he had waited
a long time to come back to this world, and that he had an old spirit. While
in my womb, he visited my sister in her dreams to introduce himself.

Wyatt was a happy and delightful baby, meeting all expected milestones as
an infant and toddler. At eighteen months, he was chattering. Then, over the
next year, I began to notice a regression in his speech and in his interactions
with others. It was though as he was retreating into a world of his own. He
was losing interest in interacting with us, his speech and language regressed,
and he was not responding to us. We could walk into a room where he would
be playing on his own, and if we spoke to him, it seemed he did not hear us
and he carried on without looking up. We took him to our family doctor who
thought it was too early for a formalized assessment of any kind and said that
boys sometimes develop speech later than girls. We asked for a hearing assessment, thinking it possible that Wyatt had a hearing impairment, as he often
did not respond to our verbal communication and acted as though he could
not hear us. The hearing assessment conducted by an audiologist indicated
that his hearing was fine; in fact, it was highly sensitive. We then requested
a referral to a pediatrician, which involved a wait time and a commute to
an urban centre for the appointment. The first pediatric appointment we
attended was not helpful and I did not feel any further ahead from the visit.
We went back to our family doctor and requested to see another pediatrician.
Again, this involved a wait time.

As time passed, Wyatt's behaviours became increasingly difficult and
hard to manage. Our greatest challenge was his propensity to bolt with no
fear and little understanding of danger. He would leave the house, unan-
nounced, often without a jacket or shoes and wander off, day or night.

While we waited months for and between appointments, I began researching child development delays and special needs on the internet as I
suspected something was "wrong." At the time, we said "wrong" because we
didn't have a clear understanding of what was going on in Wyatt's world,
we just knew his development was uneven. Although he was exceptional in
some areas, in others he was not meeting the developmental criteria for his
age range, particularly in the areas of speech and language development.

A cousin from my paternal side (Allyson Sterling) has a son about the
same age as Wyatt. She too was struggling with her son's behaviours and
development. They, however, lived in Calgary, where access to special needs
services is far superior to access in other provinces. When her son demon-

strated unusual behaviours, she was able to get a diagnosis for him when he was two years old. He was diagnosed with autism spectrum disorder, specifically pervasive development disorder, not otherwise specified (PDD-NOS). She shared information with me about her son's behaviours and they sounded remarkably similar to Wyatt's behaviours. When I told her about Wyatt's symptoms, she recommended that I research autism.

I first read about autism on the internet; however, the first website I reviewed did not have a broad enough description of the disorder. At first glance, it did not seem to fit Wyatt. He was not rocking back and forth, nor was he flapping his arms. I remember searching websites until late at night, reading about many different types of special needs and thinking that none of the descriptions seemed to fit. They created more questions and confusion for me. In frustration, I resumed my search through materials on autism. This time I found better websites, and the information started to ring true for us.

By this time, Wyatt was over four years old, and my husband and I were both exhausted and deeply stressed. We needed supports and services. We had enrolled him in preschool, but he didn't function well and we had to stay with him, which didn't allow for any kind of break or respite for us. We were assigned a Supported Child Development Worker to accompany him to preschool. This particular provincial program is one of the few universal programs available for special needs children, if the child is able to meet eligibility criteria of the program. The program requires that the child have an assessed delay and be enrolled in a licensed childcare setting. Unfortunately, in rural communities, it is difficult to secure workers who have specialized training in the field of autism. Although the intent of the Supported Child Development Program is provide support of a one-to-one worker in a licensed childcare facility, we were faced a couple of challenges. The worker had generalist early childhood education training and not specialized training. The second challenge was that Wyatt was over-stimulated in the childcare centre, and the noise, fluorescent lights and many children caused him to act out with aggressive or unpredictable behaviour, including bolting from the building. Unfortunately, the Supported Child Development Program does not have the flexibility to provide service in the home or in a smaller group environment that is not licensed according to provincial standards. Further, the program is not culturally relevant or family focused, which posed a challenge to us and other Aboriginal families. Over the years of receiving some minimal service from this program that has not fully met Wyatt's unique needs, I have lobbied for more Aboriginal services for children and families with special needs.

After Wyatt turned four years old, we were called to our second appointment with a pediatrician and he gave us the first diagnosis. He agreed that Wyatt displayed signs of autism. That set the ball in motion. He wrote up his assessment to support our application for special autism funding from the provincial government. The application was denied because the diagnosis was not considered comprehensive enough. We were referred to Vancouver Children's Hospital for a comprehensive assessment but had to wait six months for the appointment. In the meantime, I continued educating myself about autism. I went to a national conference on autism in Toronto, I joined two autism support societies, and I read books and researched sources on the internet constantly. It was comforting and enlightening to read stories written by other parents who were experiencing the same struggle as us. There were times when I felt completely alone and isolated. Learning that other parents shared the same struggles helped me to keep moving forward. Koegel and Lazebnik (2004: 9) said in their book, *Overcoming Autism*:

> Keep trying different teaching methods until you find the one that works for your child. Above all, don't lower your expectations: expect your child to overcome the symptoms of autism and lead a rich and fulfilling life. Your continued perseverance is your child's biggest asset. If you give up, your child will never make it.

In October 2002, Wyatt was almost five years old and we finally had our appointment in Vancouver. Wyatt was assessed by a child psychiatrist who specialized in autism. While my instincts told me it was autism, I still had a small window of hope that it would be something of a lesser magnitude. At the end of the session, the psychiatrist confirmed that Wyatt had autism. This is a diagnosis that continues to have its challenges and mysteries, because many children are on the autism spectrum without having the absolute diagnosis of autism. Within a couple of months after the diagnosis, we returned to Vancouver for a speech and language assessment and a psychology assessment.

I felt a certain relief to finally have a diagnosis, but at the same time, I was also devastated. I had no idea of the level of grief that a parent could feel when their child is confirmed to have special needs by a medical specialist. It took me months to process my grief in private, and I do not feel as though the grief has completely passed. Maybe it never will. I cried a lot. I tried to negotiate with the Creator. I blamed myself. I blamed others. I was angry. I was hurt. At times I felt depressed. Despite my grief, I made an agreement with myself that I would not let my grief consume me and that I would continue to fight for services for Wyatt. I established contact with two autism societies, and I am grateful to the Creator for putting me in touch with two workers who also have sons with autism. They were a lifeline at that time. Their sons were older and they shared information and personal stories that gave me hope. I was reminded that I have a special son and I needed to do my best for him, despite all the challenges we would face.

About Autism

Autism is a complex developmental disability that is the result of a neuro-logical disorder that affects the functioning of the brain and that has an impact on development of social understanding, communication, behaviour, interests and activities (Autism Society Canada 2007, Autism Society of America 2007, Ohio Developmental Disabilities Council 2007). According to the Diagnostic and Statistical Manual of Mental Disorders (DSM-IV) of the American Psychiatric Association, there are five autism spectrum disorders (ASD), of which the first three occur most commonly:

1. autistic disorder (also called autism, classic autism and AD);
2. Asperger's disorder (also called AS, Asperger syndrome);
3. pervasive developmental disorder, not otherwise specified (PDD-NOS);
4. childhood disintegrative disorder (CDD); and
5. Rett's disorder (Ohio Developmental Disabilities Council 2007).

Autism is referred to as a "spectrum disorder" because there is a con-tinuum of severity or developmental impairment. Typically, children and adults with ASD have communication and social characteristics in common, but the conditions present over a wide spectrum, with individual differences in the number and particular kinds of symptoms; severity – mild to severe; age of onset; levels of functioning; and challenges with social interactions (Autism Society Canada 2007).

It is estimated that one in every 165 children is challenged with ASD in Canada. In the United States, one of every 150 births is affected by autism. Alarmingly, ASD is on the rise. Prior to the mid-1980s, the rate of autism was estimated to be one in 2,000 children; recent rates represent a 1200 percent increase! (Edelson 2006).

Autistic disorder or autism occurs most commonly and PDD-NOS is the second most common form of the disorder. It is also referred to as atypical autism. PDD-NOS children have impairments in social interaction or restricted activities and interests, but the strict criteria for autistic disorder are not met (Autism Society Canada 2007; Autism Society of America 2007).

Autism is four times more prevalent in boys than in girls. It knows no racial, ethnic or social boundaries, nor does it reflect family income, lifestyle or educational levels. It can affect any family, and any child. Unfortunately, I could not find any specific statistics in Aboriginal communities although through my informal networks, I have learned that Aboriginal communities are dramatically affected. In my own community, I am aware of five boys who are diagnosed on the autism spectrum.

The unanswered question is: What causes autism or ASD? There are many theories and, given its growing prevalence, there is ongoing research, but at this time there have been no conclusive determinations. Speculation on the part of researchers and parents point to a number of possible causes, which include genetics, vaccines containing low level traces of mercury (called thimerosal and used as a preservative), the mumps-rubella (MMR) vaccine, environmental pollutants, diet, disrupted immune systems, mineral imbalances, food allergies and stress in pregnancy (Edelson 2006; Hamilton 2000; Siegel 1998; Autism Society Canada 2007; National Institute of Mental Health 2004). There may be more speculations, but at this point in time, there is no final determination of the cause of ASD.

There are three common characteristics of ASD in children:

1. *Difficulty with social interaction*: Children with ASD tend to lack interest in other people, or they may be interested but not know how to talk, play with or relate to others appropriately. Initiating and maintaining conversations is a challenge.
2. *Difficulty with communication*: Children may begin to develop speech and language skills but these skills may be lost, or they may develop very slowly or never develop at all. Without appropriate early intensive intervention, about 40 percent of children with ASD do not talk. Children with ASD also have difficulty interpreting non-verbal communication cues and gestures.
3. *Repetitive behaviours and restricted interests*: Children with ASD may have repeated ritualistic actions such as spinning, repeated rocking, staring, finger flapping, hitting self or other subtle or apparent behaviours. They may also have restricted or persistent interests, intense preoccupation or obsession with one thing, idea or activity. Changes in the environment or routine may trigger acute distress for the children.

Children with ASD may also have additional problems and challenges, for example, sensory problems. Many ASD children are highly attuned or even painfully sensitive to certain sounds, textures, tastes and smells. Some children find the feel of clothing on their skin unbearable. Some find sounds, such as those made by vacuum cleaners, fluorescent lights and telephones to be painful. Often the children will scream and cover their ears. Children can be hypersensitive or hyposensitive to stimulation.

Children with ASD may have unique abilities, such as an accurate and detailed memory for information and facts, high visual recall and superb ability to manipulate data for useful purposes. They may be able to concentrate for longer periods of time on one activity or task.

Some children with ASD may be faced with additional challenges that can include mental retardation or scoring high or low in particular skill areas, having seizures (one in four children with ASD develops seizures), fragile X syndrome (affects 2 to 5 percent of people with ASD), which is a chromosome disorder causing mental retardation, and tuberous sclerosis, which is a rare genetic disorder that causes brain tumors (1 to 4 percent of ASD children will also have tuberous sclerosis) (National Institute of Mental Health 2004; Autism Society Canada 2007).

A Holistic Perspective

The medicine wheel framework — physical, emotional, intellectual and spiritual aspects — has been a valuable tool for describing Wyatt's development. In 2004, I was invited to present at a national Health Canada meeting on special needs in Aboriginal communities. My presentation was from a parent's perspective. As I began to prepare, I realized that a medical perspective was limiting as it described autism from only the physical and intellectual perspectives. It did not explore the emotional and spiritual aspects of the disorder. For Aboriginal people, this is a significant omission.

The medicine wheel is an ancient symbol used today by many Aboriginal people. It is a framework that helps us to see the interconnectedness of all beings and forces existing on physical and spiritual worlds (Long Claws 1994; Four Worlds Development Project 1984). It is a holistic approach, which assists people in understanding the connection between head and heart, physical and spiritual. Each individual travels within their own medicine wheel. The goal is to achieve harmony and balance within one's self and interdependence and interconnectedness with all living things in the universe (Long Claws 1994).

My intent in using the medicine wheel framework was to touch people's hearts. I believe that without the connection to our heart and emotions, it is far too easy for folks to intellectualize about special needs without fully grasping the impacts of the disorder on children and families. The philosophy of the medicine wheel has also helped me to connect to the spiritual component to Wyatt's development. The Elder told me that my son had a spiritual gift and I needed to honour that important message. According to Meadows in *The Medicine Way*,

> The Medicine Wheel was developed by some tribes more than others, but to many it was the principal method of explaining life and a means to personal empowerment and life enhancement. This circle of power — the Medicine Wheel — served many purposes. It was a map of the mind. It was a chart to lead its user to the discovery of the Inner Self, to the divinity within, and to acknowledge the true purpose of one's life. It was a working tool with which to fashion one's own self-development. It was a device for tuning in to the Earth's psychic energies and to the unseen forces of Nature. It was

a working laboratory in which metaphysical tasks could be safely carried out. It was both a teaching aid and a learning package that uncovered the meaning behind some of the deepest mysteries of life. (1990: xvii)

A holistic perspective supports Wyatt's overall development; his strengths can be utilized to assist in the areas that need support. Presenting a holistic perspective feels the most fitting and respectful to Wyatt.

The Physical Aspect

The physical manifestations of Wyatt's autism have been the most obvious ones. He is hypersensitive to sounds, sights, touch, taste and smells and his sensory system becomes acutely overactive. This causes sensory integration difficulties for him, meaning that he has difficulty processing loud sounds, bright lights, some textures and tastes. Loud noises cause him anxiety, and he usually will raise his voice to the noise-level in an attempt to drown them out. He will also cover his ears and he likes to wear hoodies to help muffle noise. Rough and scratchy materials bother him. Until Wyatt started school, we had a difficult time keeping clothes on him, and we have learned that he prefers soft cottons without confinement, and no shoes. If he could, he would go barefoot all the time. His most recent fixation is to take his socks off and flush them down the toilet, throw them on the top shelves of closets or hide them in the freezer. Generally, it is his way of letting us know that he does not like wearing socks!

He finds everyday lighting hard on his eyes and if he could, he would wear sunglasses all the time to filter out the light. We have learned that the hum of florescent lights can bother him. Wyatt is sensitive to smell and when he smells food, he gets over-stimulated, which causes him to impulsively jump up and down or twirl around. He likes orange coloured foods (oranges, cheese, carrots, goldfish crackers, etc). He will attempt to eat most foods and we are fortunate that he is not overly tactile-sensitive to food as other children with ASD can be.

Until Wyatt's seventh year, bath times were incredibly stressful for him. He liked playing in water, but absolutely despised having his hair washed. Because the whole experience was stressful for him, we would often resort to sponge baths in order to avoid the crying and screaming. When he entered grade one, the school included a swimming program twice a week. Over the course of that year, he learned to tolerate having water on his head and face with the help of Speedo goggles. Wyatt can now swim independently, will put his face into the water, and does not need the goggles in the bathtub. Haircuts are also a sensory issue for Wyatt. He hated haircuts and would cry, fight and scream. It was as though the haircuts "hurt" him. Haircuts are still somewhat of a challenge; he doesn't like them but with preparation ahead of time, he tolerates them. Wyatt is also sensitive to teething and nail cutting. He is currently losing his baby teeth and cutting adult teeth and this has been very painful for him.

According to research, sensory motor processing challenges limit the experiences and the environments in which an individual with ASD can function successfully. Sensory motor processing involves the ability to take in information from the environment, organize it, make sense of it and formulate a response. When the sensory system is not functioning well, we may have difficulty paying attention or formulating a response that makes sense. In addition, we may shut down or overreact to incoming stimuli and have difficulty moving safely and freely (Ohio Developmental Disabilities Council 2007). According to Kranowitz (1998),

> The brain of the hypersensitive child registers sensations too intensely… the child may misinterpret a casual touch as a life-threatening blow, may feel he will fall off the face of the earth if he is nudged, or may withdraw from unfamiliar people or situations. He may be distressed by changes in routine, loud noises and crowded settings. (57)

She also notes that children can have a combination of hypersensitivity and hyposensitivity. This essentially signifies that the child is oversensitive in some areas and under sensitive in others. This off and on processing can be bewildering to the adults who care for them (Kranowitz 1998).

Another challenge that we have faced from the time Wyatt was three years old is his propensity to bolt or run away. He gets fixated on something and wanders off to investigate. He does not have any fear, nor does he have the reasoning skills to fully understand danger. Between three and six years old, Wyatt would wander out of the house day or night, shoes or no shoes, in any kind of weather condition. He would usually wander to my parents' home to hang out and visit. Sometimes he would wander across the ranch, which is approximately 160 acres in size. There were several occasions when he ran toward the main highway, and each time we caught him just as he slowed enough to cross the cattle guard, only feet from the highway.

From time to time, Wyatt still wanders on the ranch, but has learned to put his shoes and coat on first. His most recent fixation is my father's cattle. He loves animals, including horses and cows. Last year he went through a phase when he would run to my father's barn and herd the cattle into the corrals, where he thought they needed to be. It was absolutely unnerving and stressful for us. Yet, he has never been harmed.

Dr. Temple Grandin, an internationally recognized author who has autism, loves animals and has a special affinity with cattle, believes that her autism has provided her with unique gifts that allow her special insights into animal behaviour. She is an expert on cattle psychology, an inventor of devices and facilities for handling them and a passionate advocate for their humane treatment. She also wrote two books to share her story about her journey with autism.

> Temple, now forty-seven, has never ceased to ponder and explore her own nature, which she feels is quintessentially concrete and visual (with the greatest strengths, and the weaknesses, which may go with this). She feels that thinking in pictures gives her a special rapport with cattle, and that her mode of thinking is, albeit at much higher level, akin to their own mode of thinking — that she sees the world, in a sense, with a cow's eye.... clearly, there is a continuum of experience extending from the animal to the spiritual, from the bovine to the transcendent. (Sacks 1995: 15–16)

Through Temple's writing and hearing her speak in person, I have learned a number of important facets about autism: 1) that my son is highly visual and may think in pictures and not in words; 2) that he loves animals and cattle and has a special rapport with them; and 3) that his level of thinking may be at another level than the average person but his functional skills such as communication and socialization may be impaired.

Communication involves both understanding language (receptive skills) and providing information (expressive skills). The abilities of children with ASD vary widely. Regardless, many children with autism experience difficulty with non-verbal communication (eye contact, smiling, facial expressions). Children with ASD often fail to understand words or phrases that are abstract, or have a double meaning, and tend to interpret things literally. Some children exhibit echolalia, which is the tendency to repeat words, signs, phrases or sentences spoken by other people. Some children use this as a communication method or a means to regulate their own behaviour (Autism Canada Foundation 2008).

Wyatt's speech and language is delayed. I would estimate his language level to be equivalent to that of a two to three year old. The most challenging part of his speech and language delay is that he does not like to talk. He uses very short sentences to express himself. With the help of visual aids called "picture exchange symbols" and more recently an electronic communication device, Wyatt is slowly progressing in his speech and language. I believe that Wyatt has good receptive communication (he takes information in and understands what is being said) but his expressive communication is delayed. In addition, he has echolalia.

Over a three-year period, Wyatt had speech and language therapy sessions on a regular basis. A therapist would come from Kamloops, approximately 90 kilometers one way, or we would take him there. However, because of the shortage of speech and language therapists in the province, we have not been able to secure a new therapist for him for a year and a half. In the meantime, he receives limited speech and language services at school. We are very concerned about his speech and language development as we are acutely aware of the impact delays will have on his ability to have relationships with other people. I notice that Wyatt is often left out of conversations because of his communication difficulties.

Occupational therapy (OT) is imperative for Wyatt because of his overactive sensory system and his sensory integration difficulties. We do not have access to therapists in our rural community and again, we commute him to Kamloops each week for occupational and music therapy sessions. The occupational therapy provides Wyatt with the opportunity to decompress and release the build up of sensory pressure. His favourite OT activity is vestibular movement, in which he swings and spins at the same time. He often spends thirty minutes in the swing at each session and suffers no dizziness or unsteadiness. We have learned important exercises and activities from the occupational therapist that I consider have been necessary for Wyatt's overall functioning. I believe occupational therapy activities are one of the necessities for children with ASD because of the sensory integration issues that often accompany this disorder. Every child is different, so the sequence and kinds of activities that an occupational therapist provides will be based on each child's particular needs and sensory issues (Kranowitz 1998). The following are some benefits that occupational therapy exercises may provide:

- development of better body awareness and improvement in postural security;
- improvement of tactile discrimination and reduction of tactile defensiveness;
- improvement in balance, bilateral coordination, motor planning, fine motor skills, extension against the pull of gravity, and flexion;
- reduction in gravitational insecurity; and
- improvement in ocular control and visual-spatial perception (Kranowitz 1998).

The biggest lesson we have learned in the physical realm is that most of Wyatt's behaviours are sensory-driven. If he is acting out, this is a cue that there is a sensory issue occurring. We might ask ourselves (and him): "Is he over stimulated? Is it too loud? Is he hungry? Is he tired? Does he need deep pressure release?" We are better able to understand his behaviours by being aware of his sensory system. It is believed that these sensory difficulties stem from neurological dysfunction in the brain. We are bombarded daily with thousands of sensations. Our ability to integrate these sensations by attending to the important ones and filtering out the non-essential inputs helps us to function efficiently. Without smooth functioning of this system, the person is unable to accurately interpret his environment, respond and adapt (Autism Canada Foundation 2008).

Hence, if Wyatt is having a sensory issue, we know that he will act out in some way — by screaming, by having erratic behaviour, by whining, by covering his ears and so forth. We are getting much better at offsetting issues before they occur, which has made life easier for all of us.

Educational-Intellectual Aspect

Individuals with ASD have their own strengths and unique abilities, often having accurate and detailed memories for information and facts, high visual recall and a superb ability to manipulate data for useful purposes. They have unusually good spatial perception and exceptional long-term memories, allowing them to excel in the areas of music, math, physics, mechanics, science and technologies and architecture (Autism Society Canada 2007). We know that Wyatt is smart, but he processes information in a way very different from people who do not have autism.

Once Wyatt was officially diagnosed with autism, we were able to access provincial funding under a special autism program. This program provides funding to families for early intensive therapies and supports, but only until the child reaches the age of six. We received the funding for one year and were able to contract with an autism program from Kamloops to provide twenty hours per week of one-to-one services in our home. The intensive program, based on the applied behavioural analysis (ABA) model developed by Dr. Ivar Lovaas in 1987 (Simmons 2006), has had remarkable success with many children with ASD. We found that a blend of ABA and hands-on activities was the most helpful for Wyatt. It is unfortunate that we had only one year of this important service, as early intensive interaction is the most effective for children with ASD (Koegel and Lazebnik 2004).

When Wyatt turned six years old, we enrolled him in kindergarten, and a full-time special education assistant was assigned to him. We were very nervous about him going to school because of his hyperactivity and bolting. To our surprise, he loved school and responded well to the structured environment. He is now in grade three and is integrated into the classroom environment with his education assistant available to help him. I have worked hard with the school to establish a team-based approach to his individual education plan and the goals set out for him. I feel fortunate to have these school services in place, as I know that many families do not have the same experience and find the school system is not meeting the needs of their children.

An important aspect to Wyatt's development is that he is socially nurtured in school. Because he is in the same school moving forward with the same group of children, he is very much adored and supported by most of the other children. Many of the little girls nurture and mother him along while the boys look out for him. Wyatt now stays at school for lunch every day with the help of an aide. He eats in the lunchroom with the other children and then has the opportunity to play and socialize on the playground. Staying at school for lunch is new routine that commenced in grade three. It is an important step toward developing his social skills and it also gives us a break during the day.

Autism has had an impact on Wyatt's ability to play and learn through typical teaching methods. He generally lacks spontaneous and imaginative play, but there are activities that he does enjoy, including play dough, art, drawing, colouring, painting, puzzles and hands-on type of activities. Because he is highly visual, he learns best by seeing and experiencing. He loves singing and music and has an incredible memory for remembering tunes and songs. He is slowly beginning to grasp the concept of money and time. Abstract ideas are more difficult for him. He takes things very literally. "They are literal in interpretation of others' comments and actions and have difficulties with insight into others' actions and perspectives" (Ohio Developmental Disabilities Council 2007). In the last year, he has finally taken to computer games and can navigate himself on the computer independently.

At school, he has a modified language arts and math program but is able to join the rest of the class in music, art, physical education, and on occasion, social studies and science. Wyatt's memory is exceptional so once he grasps a concept, he will not forget it.

Emotional Aspect

Children with ASD often have impaired social communication skills and little or no interest in people. Their interactions with people might be considered strange as they usually do not understand non-verbal communication and facial gestures. They may have difficulty expressing their own feelings and understanding the feelings of others (Autism Canada Foundation 2008; Autism Society Canada 2007; National Institute of Mental Health 2004). Wyatt does have some emotional challenges, because his social communication and interactions with others would not be considered typical, yet he loves people and is very interested in others around him. His eye contact is improving but he does not always understand non-verbal communication and facial gestures. If someone is crying, he will not understand it and may start laughing without the understanding that his behaviour is inappropriate in such a situation. He is very sensitive and his feelings can easily be hurt, but he cannot grasp the concept of "other" yet. Generally, he is a happy little guy and it is not often that he is sad or cries. He does make facial gestures in the mirror to himself and sometimes he can be overly dramatic. He sings and hums often and chats to himself.

The emotional impacts of Wyatt's special needs have been stressful for our family. His dad made the decision to give up his full-time employment, pension and benefits to be a full-time caregiver in the home when it became clear that our stress levels were unmanageable when we both worked. Wyatt's sister, who is seventeen years old, is very supportive of him and probably has not received her fair share of family attention because of Wyatt's high needs. The stress of having a special needs child in the family has also had a marked impact on Wyatt's grandparents, aunts, uncles and cousins. Last year, I arranged for a professional to provide a family workshop on autism. I believe it was helpful to the extended family to learn more about autism and about how best to support Wyatt. It has been a learning experience for everyone close to him.

As Wyatt's parents, we have been challenged to the extreme in our relationship. Fortunately, we have overcome the challenges thus far. We were able to get respite funding approximately two years ago, and we are finally taking short breaks as parents. We had our first ever one-week trip away when Wyatt was eight years old. I strongly promote the concept of respite. It is important that parents have the opportunity to maintain their relationship, just as we maintain everything around us if we want it to function well.

Keeping Wyatt safe from harm has been a big job, and at times, it was our sole focus. Another parent of a boy with autism told me that when Wyatt turned six he would start to calm down. I remember counting down the time until he turned six, because he was so hyperactive and I was exhausted. Although Wyatt is settling over time, he continues to be busy. At all times, both his dad and I are on alert, always checking to see where Wyatt is and what he is doing.

I cannot imagine the emotional challenges that Wyatt faces each day in struggling with autism. He wakes up each morning smiling and happy. He is excited to go to school, despite the many challenges he will endure throughout the day. He works hard every day. He models to us how we should always do our best. I am humbled by having such an incredible person in my life.

A father of an autistic son wrote in his book:

> Chris (my son) is the one who's worked hard. He's the hero. It's his strength that should be admired. He's the one who did not allow himself to be trapped in this disorder. He's the one who is strong. I hope a bit of his determination came from me, but I know that most of it comes from his amazing human spirit. He and all the others fighting to get out of this disorder's trap are my heroes. (Davis 2001: 368–69)

Spiritual Aspect

Just after Wyatt was officially diagnosed with autism, I had a Spiritual Elder come to the house to see him. I was in emotional turmoil and she calmly told me that Wyatt has a special spiritual gift. She said that children with spiritual gifts often come with a "dis-ability." She said that he was fine. The Spiritual Elder put everything into perspective for me. She did not discredit or underplay the challenges we would face, but she contextualized the situation in a spiritual and cultural manner. I learned that Wyatt has a special ability and he can see what most cannot see with the human eye. He is close to the spiritual world. More recently, I was reminded that my spiritual development and growth will support Wyatt's, that our paths are intertwined, not separate and distinct. These teachings are not new to us. Sometimes we just need to be reminded of our cultural and traditional teachings, which is why our Elders are so important.

I have noticed that Wyatt sees what many of us cannot see. For example, I believe he has invisible friends that he plays with. Sometimes I watch him giggling and running back and forth, as though he is playing tag with someone. When I ask him who's there, he says "right there." He also has a connection to family and extended family members. Whenever a death is about to occur in our family, Wyatt seems to be visited by spirits several days prior. Again, he acts as though there is someone in the room but I cannot see anyone. He will also wake up very early, at 4 or 5 am on these occasions, and chat and play in his room.

Coincidentally or not, I met a spiritual channeller when Wyatt was nine years old and we became friends. She visited us for a weekend and shared spiritual information with me about Wyatt that has assisted me to continue to support his spiritual development. She said that Wyatt communicates in another arena that is not of this earthly world. In other words, he can communicate on another plane but is often confused because many of us cannot communicate with him at that level.

I am aware that Wyatt has a strong connection to animals, to the point that I am convinced that he has a spiritual connection to them. Therefore, animals respond differently to him. He has walked up to a wild horse and was able to touch it where the owner could not. Wyatt loves animals. He enjoys his dog and cat, and the cattle and horses.

We do not often speak about the spiritual realm of our development because it can be complex and more difficult to explain. According to Meadows,

> True spirituality cannot exist without free will. That Will is the power to determine – to make choices and decisions. Free will is the liberty to choose. It is a primary and fundamental liberty that is essential

to your own wellbeing, to your own spiritual growth, development
and evolution, and that of others. (1990: 202)

We each need to connect to our spirituality in whatever way works. Some
may find it through organized religion, others may seek a connection to the
mother earth and all living things, some may meditate, and there are many
other forms of spiritual empowerment. For myself, I have found that as I ask
for spiritual teachers, they somehow come into my life. To support Wyatt, I
need to continue to develop my own spirituality.

Meg Blackburn Losey (2007) wrote a book entitled *The Children of Now*,
which is about children who are spiritually special. They are a new generation of children — undeniably evolved beyond previous generations — who
come to our world with very special gifts.

> Often, because of certain stimuli or changes within the relationships
> of energetic functioning, a child of the new evolution may look
> different or even overtly dysfunctional. In other words, some of the
> New Children do not appear to function "normally" on a mental,
> emotional, or physical level. Some of the children experience all
> manner of apparent disabilities, from minor to substantial. Many
> of them seem to be profoundly physically disabled while exhibiting
> a spiritual clarity that demonstrates a mastery and wisdom beyond
> that of most adults. Those who appear to be profoundly affected
> often do not or cannot speak and many communicate telepathically
> more easily than most of us do with words. Some children also do not
> behave normally as expected in certain situations. Others seem to be
> "spaced out or not with the program." That is because their program
> is far beyond our simple everyday one. (Losey 2007: 48–49)

While I feel vulnerable in sharing my perspectives on spirituality,
particularly as they relate to Wyatt, I also feel compelled to do so because
I believe that in order to achieve holistic balance, one requires harmony in
the quadrants of the physical, emotional, intellectual and spiritual. In other
words, we must talk about spirituality and the dimensions of it that are often more difficult to explain. Many of us could benefit from expanding our
own thinking and belief systems about holistic balance and harmony and
considering the relevance and importance of spirituality.

Service Challenges for Aboriginal Families

There are several key service challenges facing many Aboriginal families with
special needs children, whether they are diagnosed or undiagnosed. Through
my work, I have travelled to many Aboriginal communities across British
Columbia and have gained a stronger understanding of the issues faced by

communities, and the obstacles confronting families with special needs children. Communities that are remote, isolated and rural are faced with many challenges in securing services and therapists for children and families. In 2007, I had the privilege of working in Aboriginal communities in my nation and a neighbouring nation to conduct a needs assessment around special needs. I learned that the challenges that I endure as a parent of a special needs child are common among families in Aboriginal communities. In the community work that I do, there are service challenges that many Aboriginal families and communities are posed with, which include the following:

- little or no services available for special needs children and families;
- lack of information or awareness about mainstream programs and restricted eligibility criteria to access mainstream services, when they are available;
- wait lists for services and lack of transportation;
- family lifestyles and issues are some times are a barrier;
- lack of community capacity (trained workers and programs) to assist children and families with special needs;
- lack of specialized staff in early childhood education centers and schools;
- high costs to travel in and out of isolated and remote communities to access services and therapists;
- little or no access to specialists to diagnose special needs children or provide follow up supports;
- lack of supports to offset stress on families, extended families and childcare providers in communities who have or work with special needs children;
- lack of respite services available to families with special needs children;
- lack of adequate services and supports for school-age children within and out of school;
- lack of funding or community capacity for childcare centres, trained staff, equipment and resources, specialized services and transportation;
- parents are uncertain about accessing services, they may be intimidated by the paperwork, the assessment process and factors to accessing mainstream services that are not culturally sensitive;
- support for siblings and extended family members is a gap area;
- education and awareness about special needs with community service providers, family members and communities is a gap area; and
- services are often not culturally relevant, are not inclusive of culture and language and are not family-focused.

This research conducted was specific to Aboriginal communities and the findings are reflective of Aboriginal participants. (Sterling Consulting and Nzen'man 2007)

As we consider the many challenges facing Aboriginal families and communities, it becomes clear that Aboriginal children with special needs have multiple barriers in addition to the disability or disorder they live with on a daily basis. Many Aboriginal children are not assessed or diagnosed; many do not have access to services or therapies and are generally having to cope with what little resources are available in their communities. This puts stress on the child, the family, the overworked community service providers, the extended family and the community in general. It is not due to lack of interest or intent: it is due to lack of funding and services or access to services.

Aboriginal Services and Worldview

In British Columbia, many Aboriginal communities are developing a new program called Aboriginal Supported Child Development (ASCD), which is similar to the mainstream Supported Child Development Program but will be developed and delivered by Aboriginal communities. ASCD provides culturally appropriate support services to children with special needs. Services are provided in childcare centres or home and community environments. Developed and run by local Aboriginal communities, programs are culturally responsive to their community (Aboriginal Supported Child Development 2008).

I have the honour of working in my nation with Nzen'man Child and Family Development Centre Society on the development of this program for our communities. It is an exciting time as it is the first program that will be community-based for Aboriginal children and families with special needs. Although the levels of funding are minimal, we are committed to ensuring that services will be available to those children with the highest needs.

Cultural and spiritual connections are what make this program unique to Aboriginal communities. Aboriginal Supported Child Development provides services for children who require extra support in the following domains: physical, cognitive, communicative, social, emotional and behavioural. Services are provided for children from birth to twelve years of age who have a developmental delay or disability. Services for youth aged thirteen to nineteen may be provided on an individual basis (Aboriginal Supported Child Development 2008).

In a needs assessment (Sterling Consulting and Nzen'man 2007) conducted in the Nicola-Thompson-Lillooet Zone in the interior of B.C. regarding special needs, the Aboriginal parents, service providers and communities identified the following themes as priorities for development and delivery of the Aboriginal Supported Child Development Program in our zone:

- be flexible in eligibility for services — ensure there is flexibility so that children requiring extra supports (intellectually, physically, socially, emotionally) can receive those supports;
- provide outreach services — bring the services to the child and family (in the home, in the community, whatever works best for the family);
- include families and communities in programming — the program must be inclusive of the family, extended family and the community;
- include cultural activities into the program;
- develop a good recruiting and training program for Aboriginal workers;
- ensure policies are flexible;
- be inclusive of other service providers into the programming — develop networking and collaboration of services;
- ensure better coordination of services;
- get sustainable funding for the program;
- develop linkages with the schools;
- ensure the program is holistic;
- create more awareness and education of special needs to parents, service providers, communities, extended families;
- provide transportation for families; and
- provide parent services and supports.

Aboriginal communities are striving for self determination at all levels of community development. Aboriginal special needs are not a new concept. We have always revered our "gifted ones" through time. Today, we are incorporating the traditional and cultural ways with contemporary services.

Despite the challenges, I am amazed at the strength and resiliency of families and communities. Families, service providers and communities do their best to work with children with special needs, being inclusive and supportive to children and families as much as possible. This is often done with little funding and resources. The reality is that in many Aboriginal communities, the staff of community service programs provides the primary support system for families because of the lack of specialized resources. I have met parents of children with special needs who don't have access to specialized services or therapists, have no respite services and don't have a full understanding of their child's disability or disorder. However, what they do have is a sense of family and community responsibility, cultural and traditional values and unconditional love for their children. It is common in Aboriginal communities for folks to be accepting of children with differences. Among our people, Wyatt is accepted as part of the whole and for who he is. Fyre Jean Graveline articulates the commitment:

We are able to see ourselves and our immanent value as related to and interconnected with others — family, community, the world, those behind and those yet to come. Through embracing this worldview, each individual becomes intensely aware of personal accountability for the welfare of others. (1998: 58)

Supporting Children and Families with Special Needs

In my journey with Wyatt, I have learned to navigate the system to access services and supports although there have been many limitations and hurdles. I have found the process very frustrating and time-consuming. As a community practitioner and a sessional instructor in an Aboriginal social work program, I have also come to realize the important role that social workers have in Aboriginal communities. Social workers are often the touchstone for a range of services. It is imperative that social workers gain foundational knowledge and skills to support Aboriginal children and families with special needs. The social worker's key role is to serve as an advocate for the child and family. The following is a list of key supports that the social worker can provide to families:

1. Support and encourage parents to get a diagnosis in order to access services and resources. Getting a medical assessment and diagnosis may assist families in accessing funding, services and resources for their child that otherwise would not be available to them.
2. Act as a sounding board for parents. Allow them to vent, talk and share about how they are feeling, particularly if they have just learned of the special needs of their child. Assist the parent in linking with the appropriate resources for a qualified assessment of their child. Attend the appointments with the family to support them. Assist the family in taking notes and in record-keeping as the family will require a file of information for their child. Bring a backpack with activities and snacks to the appointments for the child. Assist the family in asking pertinent questions to the medical professional. Recognize that parents may be overwhelmed, stressed or grief-stricken and need a support system. Assist in setting up a professional support system for the parents. Refer them to the appropriate services if you think they require grief counselling or marital counselling.
3. Support the extended family. The grandparents and extended family members will also be impacted by the diagnosis of the child. Arrange for a family talking circle and other support systems that the family may require. Assist in setting up a special needs workshop with an external facilitator who can share important information and resources. You

might also bring in an Elder or cultural advisor who can support the family from a traditional perspective.

4. Assist the family in accessing services and resources. The parents may not know how to begin to access services and resources for their child. Assist them in this process by making telephone calls and appointments. Assist the family with the paperwork if they request. You might attend the first sessions with the family until they are underway. Assist the family in becoming informed about what is available and how to access it. Learn about the limitations of services as well; some interventions only work on a small number of symptoms. Be informed about the degree and the extent of the service (Koegel and Lazebnik 2004).

5. Assist the family in developing a holistic plan for the child and family. This should include services and supports in the quadrants of physical, emotional, intellectual, spiritual/cultural. Draw on the strengths of the child and the family. Areas of strength can be used to support areas that need improving. In addition to developing a holistic plan, it's important that a team approach (where possible) be set up for the child and family. Involve other service providers who can provide services and supports for a coordinated approach. Ensure that the service best meets the needs of the child and family. For example, consider a home visiting or outreach approach for services. Be inclusive of the family in the programming; services should be available for both the child and the family.

6. Support the family in celebrating the progress of the child. Koegel and Lazebnik recommend that "it's also important that you celebrate improvements, no matter how small. It's easy to keep thinking about how far behind your child is, but if you focus on the improvements he's made, you'll realize how far he's come. And be sure to share your joy in his progress with the people who love him and you" (2004: 21). As the social worker, you can support the family in these celebrations and you can help to point out the progress and the strengths of the child.

7. Assist the family in accessing financial resources for services. As a social worker, you will probably have more connections than the family about where to seek funding for services for their child. Recognize that the family may be financially stressed and may need support with funding. There are various programs that are available to special needs children that can be contacted for information and referrals. Families may need support such as transportation to get to appointments.

8. Assist the family in maintaining a record of reports and notes by using a binder or folder to hold all the documents together. This will help the family as they access services for their child. Service providers and specialists often like to review reports and information concerning the child. You might need to assist the family in understanding some of the

terminology of the reports and assessments, as they can be medically based.

9. Remember that there is incredible stress on the siblings of children with special needs. Support for the family should include helping the other children to understand what is happening. Siblings may be embarrassed, worried, frustrated or possessive of their special needs sibling. They may be concerned for their parents and concerned about the future.

10 Assist the parents to seek respite. It is imperative that parents take breaks from the children as a couple. They need time for themselves. The siblings also need breaks from time to time and consideration should be given to them as well. Support the family in securing respite funding or services. Support the family in securing appropriate caregivers who can care for the child and keep the child safe while they take their breaks.

11. Take time to do research and gather information on the special need of the child. Parents may be interested in more information but may not have the time to research for it. Research on the internet, bookstores and the library for information to share with the family. Look into foundations and organizations that specialize in a particular area. These organizations are usually non-profit and can be a great source of information and support to the family.

12. Arrange networking meetings. Assist the family in the planning of services for the child by setting up networking meetings with the parents and various service providers that will be involved with the child. Again, a team of service providers who can work together for the benefit of the family will be extremely helpful. It will also take the pressure off one service provider to do everything.

13. Link the family. Gather information on support groups and organizations which are available for parents to join. It is helpful for parents to get useful advice from other parents having similar challenges. There are on-line supports available if they cannot attend in person. They can also sign up and receive packages and information in the mail from many non-profit organizations.

14. Support the home environment. The home environment may need to be altered or structured for the child, depending on the special need. The child may need special equipment or materials. Network with the health professionals and other service providers. Ensure the family has the opportunity to learn how to support the child. For example, sensory integration activities and exercises may be taught by an occupational therapist and the family can incorporate these activities on a daily basis.

15. Assist the family in developing self-care plans. Utilize the medicine wheel framework, if the family approves, to assist the family in developing self-care plans. Families with special needs children have high stress

and experience burn out and exhaustion. Therefore self-care plans that consider emotional, intellectual, physical and spiritual wellbeing will probably be helpful for the family. Further, families may feel socially isolated as going out with the child or having people to their home can be stressful. Ask the family what social supports they might need.

16. Encourage parents to utilize cultural and traditional systems. If it is appropriate and the family wishes, you could assist the family by setting up cultural and traditional support systems for them. Cultural and traditional supports could include visits with Elders, spiritual leaders, cultural and traditional resource people and attending ceremonies or other cultural or traditional activities. Consider how cultural and traditional activities can be included directly into the child's program and ask the family what they might like to see.

17. Support the community to build capacity around special needs. This could include professional development, training and mentoring of staff who work with children. It could include family and community workshops on special needs topics. It could include proposal writing and seeking funding for more services for children and families with special needs. It could include creating more awareness about special needs in the community and with leaders.

A complementary approach that integrates the work of the medical professionals, the specialists, the therapists, the family, community and the cultural and traditional systems will support a holistic plan for families and children with special needs. Aboriginal social workers can be instrumental as advocates and liaison people who facilitate the holistic plan. The systems can work in tandem to balance and harmonize services in and for the best interests of the child. Aboriginal families and communities have inherent strength in their culture and traditions that are woven into the fabric of who we are. We need to utilize this inherent strength for the benefit of the special children of our communities.

A Holistic Approach to Autism

Although research to understand the causes of autism spectrum disorder continues, there is awareness about the challenges of children with ASD. When we first learned of autism, I had to seek out people who had training and understanding of the disorder. This was difficult in a rural community, and at that time, I had to look outside of the community for supports. Today, there are some early childhood educators, teachers, special education assistants and parents in my community who know about ASD and have knowledge and skills to support children on the spectrum. There have been great strides in a short time.

Writing my story has been a great conduit to renew my faith and hope at all levels. I continue to be inspired by Wyatt and his unique and beautiful personality. It is so important that those of us serving Aboriginal children with special needs, whether we are parents, extended family, service providers, social workers or community members, utilize a holistic perspective.

I have renewed hope and faith that services for Aboriginal children and families with special needs will be developed to reflect cultural relevancy and holistic programming. I am excited about the new Aboriginal program starting up in my community and I look forward to culturally understanding the children. If we take into account the quadrants of the medicine wheel framework — physical, emotional, intellectual and spiritual — we are better able to understand and plan for the child from a strengths perspective rather than a deficit perspective. Wyatt's intuition and spiritual dimensions are incredible strengths that offset the social and communicative challenges with which he struggles.

My journey with Wyatt has its joys, laughter, tears and frustrations. However, I know that Wyatt chose me to be his mother and I agreed, and so it is that we are on this journey together. It is my hope that my story will inspire and lend support to others, particularly those working in Aboriginal communities and to other parents who have children with special needs. I hope that social workers and service providers of Aboriginal communities will continue to serve as advocates and support systems to families with children with special needs and encourage and promote a holistic approach to planning and service delivery. In essence, it is our hope, faith and commitment that children need from us.

Chapter 5

Identity or Racism?
Aboriginal Transracial Adoption

Raven Sinclair (Ótiskewápíwskew)

My name is Ótiskewápíwskew and I am Cree-Assinniboine and Saulteaux from Gordon's and Kawacatoose' First Nations in the Treaty Four area of southern Saskatchewan. In 1965 I was apprehended by child welfare services in Saskatchewan and a year later, adopted into a White Anglo-Saxon Protestant family. I was five years old at that time. I was raised in a culture that is significantly different from my Nehiyaw and Anishinaabe heritages and, as a result, I was indoctrinated into a Euro-Canadian lifestyle and worldview. As a young adult, I became curious about my own adoption, and having met other adoptees in increasing numbers, I developed a curiosity about this thing called the "Sixties Scoop," especially after someone matter-of-factly informed me that I was a "Scoopee." As a young adult, university became an avenue of discovery for me and I eventually focused my studies on Aboriginal people in Canada. I switched disciplines from psychology to social work in the mid-1990s and began to concentrate on the Sixties Scoop and the transracial adoption (TRA) of Aboriginal children.

What I found is that the apprehension of Aboriginal children by the Canadian state between 1960 and the early 1980s, now referred to as the Sixties Scoop, has emerged as a problematic project of Canadian-Aboriginal relations. The evolution of Aboriginal child welfare is seen by critics as a post-residential school program enacted by Canadian governments to further an assimilationist agenda of replacing Aboriginal peoples' cultures with Euro-Canadian culture and values (Chrisjohn and Young 1997; Sinclair 2004). The adoption of Aboriginal children into non-Aboriginal homes, specifically, is perceived by some as fulfilling the criteria for genocide as outlined by the United Nations where children from one ethnic group are forcibly transferred to another to ensure that culture, language and traditions are irrevocably altered (Chrisjohn and Young 1997).

The literature informed me that the transracial adoption of these Aboriginal children has had negative outcomes in terms of high adoption breakdown rates and identity problems for adoptees. Meanwhile, the general transracial adoption (Black-White, Korean-White, for example) success and failure rates are similar to same-race adoption rates. The marked difference between the success of Aboriginal TRAs and other TRAs raised a number of questions and I decided to find answers by pursuing a masters degree and a doctorate dedicated to this specific topic. I pursued my PhD with the intention of discovering how Aboriginal children experienced their adoptions and how they grappled with identity issues. Mostly I wanted to give a voice to the adoptees, something that was clearly missing in the literature. In the course of my research, I interviewed sixteen adoptees from across the country, and I reviewed eighty Aboriginal TRA narratives from other sources.

After six years, three of which were spent mulling over the data — the narratives of my participants in addition to narratives from other sources — it emerged that Aboriginal transracial adoptions have been unsuccessful because of the interplay of a number of factors. Analysis of the research data indicated that the source of problematic Aboriginal TRA outcomes rests less with identity issues, which is the prevailing concern articulated in the literature, and more with racism (both intra-familial and social), which is articulated by the adoptees. The research gave primacy to the articulations of adoptees, and their narratives clearly linked the negative outcomes of Aboriginal TRA to the socio-cultural context of racism in Canadian society.

Much has been written about Aboriginal child welfare (Bennett, Blackstock and De la Ronde 2005; Levitt and Wharf 1985; McKenzie and Hudson 1985; Sinclair, Phillips and Bala 1991; Timpson 1995; Wharf 1993), and much has been written about the colonial experience of Aboriginal people in Canada (Chrisjohn and Young 1997; Duran, Duran and Yellow Horse Brave Heart 1998; Frideres 1988; Miller 1996; Milloy 1999; Neu and Therrian 2003). This chapter presents a slice of the Aboriginal experience in Canada with a focus on the child welfare era that began in the 1960s in order to provide the context for the transracial adoption of Aboriginal children. A more important purpose is to articulate the issues as they are understood from the stories of adoptees who have experienced transracial adoption. Their recommendations invite a paradigm shift in adoption practices and specifically, in Aboriginal TRA, in order to focus on issues that may better meet the needs of Aboriginal children in care now and in the future.

The Sixties Scoop

The large-scale apprehension of Aboriginal children in Canada between 1960 and the mid-1980s was first coined the "Sixties Scoop" in a report written by Patrick Johnston (1983), *Native Children and the Child Welfare System*. Johnston undertook extensive research, and his findings were validated through the many groups that provided him with statistical data, including governments, Aboriginal organizations and band councils (P. Johnston, personal communication, December 8, 2005). The term "Sixties Scoop" was applied because, first, Johnston observed in the statistics that adoption as the mechanism to address problematic child welfare issues had resulted in obvious increases in Aboriginal child apprehensions in the decade of the 1960s (National Archives of Canada Vol. 6937). Second, in many instances, Aboriginal children were apprehended from their homes and communities without the knowledge or consent of families and bands (Johnston 1983; Timpson 1995; RCAP 1996; Saskatchewan Indian 1977). Johnston was provided with the term "scoop" by a B.C. social worker who told him "with tears in her eyes — that it was common practice in B.C. in the mid-sixties to 'scoop' from their mothers on reserves almost all newly born children. She was crying because she realized, twenty years later, what a mistake that had been" (P. Johnston, personal communication, December 8, 2005).

During the Sixties Scoop era, Aboriginal children were apprehended in disproportionate numbers (to non-Aboriginal children) throughout Canada, and many were subsequently adopted into non-Aboriginal homes in Canada, the United States and overseas (Sinclair 2007a). Statistics from the Department of Indian and Northern Affairs Canada (INAC) indicate a total of 11,132 status Indian[1] children adopted between 1960 and 1990 (Hall, cited in RCAP 1996). Because of inaccurate recording of information, the actual numbers are believed to be much higher. Although INAC maintained a list of the adoptions of status Indian children called the "A List," many children were never recorded as such. For political or social reasons, Aboriginal children were sometimes recorded as Métis or French in child welfare documents, perhaps to increase their chances of adoption placement. From a social desirability perspective, the less Aboriginal a child appeared to be on paper, the more "adoptable" the child might be (Sinclair 2007a). Similarly, children who were members of sibling groups were often recorded as "singles" (Kimmelman 1985), likely to increase their adoptive appeal to prospective families. Through multiple placements and inaccurate records, tribal connections were sometimes completely lost (Fournier and Crey 1997; Sinclair 2007a). In terms of the numbers that are available, we see that approximately 70 percent of apprehended Aboriginal children were adopted into non-Aboriginal homes (Fanshel 1972; Fournier and Crey 1997; Timpson, 1995; York 1992), and in the 1970s, one in three Aboriginal children were separated from their families through adoption or fostering (Fournier and Crey 1997).

The adoption of Aboriginal children, in some provinces, did not follow the regular adoption processes. In Saskatchewan, for example, the Adopt Indian and Métis (AIM) program was developed specifically to facilitate the adoption of Aboriginal children. In some cases adoptions practices were coercive, covert and illegal (*Saskatchewan Indian* 1977: 11). The testimony of Patrick Rich, an Innu from Newfoundland, illuminates one such approach to apprehension and adoption. Rich and his wife Germaine had two children removed at birth, and when they attempted to have them returned they were initially told that their house was too crowded. Then they were told that their house was too cold. Finally, they had their day in court.

> And social workers told us Mary Jane [one of their daughters] been adopted and told us Germaine [the mother] signed the papers. And Germaine spoke to me in Innu and said, "I never sign any papers for adoption." So he [the social worker] came back two weeks later and show us the papers. First he showed us Roxanne's paper with Germaine's signature on it. Then he came back with Mary Jane's papers which had Germaine's name on it, but it wasn't her signature. Germaine spoke to her in English and said, "That's not my signature." (RCAP 1996, P. Rich, Sheshatshiu, Nfld 92-06-17 133, 124)

Occasionally when families made concerted efforts to locate their missing children, officials lied, misled and withheld information (Fournier and Crey 1997).

Eventually, the increasing public outcry on the part of Aboriginal politicians led to an inquiry in Manitoba in the mid-1980s. Justice E. Kimmelman's report on adoption practices in Manitoba during the 1960s and 1970s revealed that the child welfare adoption practices, as implicated by the case files of adopted Aboriginal children, were substandard and appalling. Kimmelman reviewed fifty-four case files representing the adoption of ninety-three children and "searched in vain to find in at least one file some details indicating why approval had been given to the adoptive family over other applicants. Were there other applicants? Did the Executive Director give final approval?" (Kimmelman 1985: 59). Indeed, files were so inadequate that the mere existence of a case summary resulted in a positive comment about the file.

To explore why Aboriginal children were apprehended at such alarming rates, Fournier and Crey (1997) point out that living conditions in most reserves in Canada were appalling after decades of government manipulation and financial mismanagement,[2] but rather than funnel resources into programs and infrastructures that might address the problems, governments supported social welfare departments to step in and remove the children. Joyce Timpson, a social worker from northwestern Ontario who completed a report on Aboriginal child welfare for the Royal Commission on Aboriginal People, noted that Aboriginal families were dealing with the fall-out of the residential school project and were experiencing severe upheaval as the result of social, economic and cultural changes. She observed that the federal government's "willingness to pay child-in-care costs, along with federal and provincial governments' resistance to supporting preventive services, family counseling or rehabilitation, were major factors in making apprehension and permanent removal of children the treatment applied most often in problem situations" (Timpson, cited in RCAP 1996: 21).

Thus, the Sixties Scoop evolved into a campaign that was supported in principle by governments and furthered in practice by agencies at the child welfare front lines. The Sixties Scoop was one of the products of a national government interested in reducing fiscal responsibility for Indians through their assimilation into the mainstream (Neu and Therrian 2003),[3] provincial governments eager to have jurisdiction over child welfare and a newly developing field of social work staffed by enthusiastic, yet naïve, social workers. As a case in point, once respective governments had clarified jurisdiction issues with respect to child welfare and per capita child welfare payments to provincial governments were promised, the number of Aboriginal children in care increased *400 percent* in the ten year period between 1955 and 1964 (RCAP 1996; Fournier and Crey 1997). The "economy" of child welfare had begun. The decade of the 1970s marked increasingly high rates of Aboriginal children in care in Canada: 44 percent in Alberta, 51 percent in Saskatchewan and 60 percent in Manitoba (McKenzie and Hudson 1985: 126). Hence, the Sixties Scoop was a by-product of the interaction between key economic policies, the residual influence of an assimilationist agenda, an untried child welfare bureaucracy and a very large socio-economic and political divide between Aboriginal and non-Aboriginal people, which left Aboriginal people vulnerable to bureaucratic decisions and interventions.

Resistance to Aboriginal Transracial Adoption

Resistance to Aboriginal child welfare involvement emerged during the Indian social movement of the 1960s, which came on the heels of the 1960 Bill of Rights in Canada. Perhaps because of the Bill and the subsequent acquisition of the federal franchise in 1961, Aboriginal people became more politicized in matters concerning them. Lobbying efforts of the social movement that began in the field of education with the dissemination of the position paper "Indian Control of Indian Education"[4] by the National Indian Brotherhood (1972), the precursor to the current national organization, the Assembly of First Nations, had a direct influence in the area of child welfare. Assuming "control" thus extended to other socio-political spheres (Sinclair 2007a). In 1981, the Chief of Splatsin (Spallumcheen Indian Band) in British Columbia, Wayne Christian, became concerned about the high numbers of apprehensions and subsequent TRAs of children from his own community. His efforts to resist these practices initiated a movement among Aboriginal leaders to voice discontent about child welfare approaches (McKenzie and Hudson 1985), contributed impetus for the Manitoba inquiry and ultimately led to Aboriginal-controlled child welfare.

Unfortunately, the involvement of the child welfare system is no less prolific in the current era. Dr. Lauri Gilchrist of Keyano College noted that given current child welfare statistics, the Sixties Scoop has merely evolved into the Millenium Scoop, where long-term institutionalization is the predominant outcome rather than adoption. Long-term institutionalization is an unfortunate outcome of the post-Manitoba Inquiry moratorium on Aboriginal TRAs. Given that there are more children in care now than during the Sixties Scoop era and there is a reluctance to make Aboriginal children available for adoption, there are few alternatives available. Although adoption practices are undoubtedly more stringent, formalized and accountable than they were in the 1960s, where Aboriginal children used to be taken into care by White social workers, now there are many Aboriginal social workers, recruited into the ranks of social services and operating under the umbrellas of First Nations child and family service agencies, who are the ones doing the scooping (Sinclair 2007a). Currently, Aboriginal children are still in care in disproportionate numbers, but for a multitude of reasons beyond just apprehensions by "overzealous social workers."[5] The economic system that rests upon the Aboriginal child welfare system has become firmly entrenched in the last half century.

Identity Conflict Paradigm

A primary concern with respect to Aboriginal children in care has been that these children suffer from a loss of cultural identity and therefore experience conflict with respect to their cultural identities. The identity conflict or "identity crisis" paradigm has deep roots in much of the writing and thinking about Aboriginal child welfare and Aboriginal TRAs in Canada. Brad McKenzie and Pete Hudson, in a 1985 article, articulated: "There is… evidence that native children raised in non-native homes are more likely to experience an identity crisis in adolescence, leading to acute social and psychological problems when they find they no longer fit in the society to which they have been socialized" (127). Sherri Swidrovich (2004: 110) astutely observed that McKenzie and Hudson's claim originated in reference to one 1979 study of ten psychiatric patients who had experienced psychiatric care. Swidrovich noted:

> Clearly, in terms of making a determination about relative outcomes in substitute care the mental health status of the study's subjects introduces a bias and makes it entirely inappropriate to simply extrapolate the findings from this small group to the general situation of Native children in care.

Of course, the authors are not to blame that almost every writer about Aboriginal transracial adoption has referenced them since the time their article was published. Unfortunately though, their comments have become central to the adoption discourse, and "truth" about adoption and identity conflict has been created, even in the absence of research in the area.

Exacerbating the limited literature on Aboriginal TRA specifically is the plethora of literature on transracial adoption generally (focusing primarily on Black/White adoption in the United States) that indicates favourable adoption outcomes. The conclusions of the collective body of studies indicate that the majority of studies on Black and other ethnic minority children who were transracially adopted found that adjustment outcomes were positive and comparable to outcomes for *same race* White adoptees (Bagley 1993; Feigelman and Silverman 1984; Grow and Shapiro 1974; Lindholm and Tavliatos 1980; Simon and Alstein 1992) and that transracial adoption generally results in positive outcomes for the adoptee and their adoptive family (Bagley 1991, 1993; Bagley and Young 1984; Bagley, Young and Scully 1993; McRoy at al. 1984; Shireman and Johnson 1986; Silverman and Feigelman 1990; Simon and Alstein 1981, 1992). For example, Bagley (1993: 285) reported in a longitudinal study of Afro-Caribbean adoptees that outcomes were excellent. Just 10 percent had poor adjustment. He described the children as "well prepared by transracial adoption to participate in a multi-cultural, multi-racial society," while Silverman and Feigelman (1981) concluded favourable to excellent adjustment outcomes for children of various ethnic groups (Korean, Chinese, Latin American) who were placed in White adoptive homes, and a slightly lesser degree of success, approximately 50 percent, for Black children who are adopted into White homes. In a later study, Feigelman and Silverman (1984) noted that approximately 75 percent of transracially adopted children adapt well, while Grow and Shapiro had concluded in 1977 that 77 percent of African-American adoptees in their study were well adjusted. Generally "adjustment" and "success" in the studies are determined through the results of several tests and interviews with parents and teachers as well as children's scores on identity tests (Grow and Shapiro 1974). In some studies, adjustment is based on parental ratings of children's adjustment (Zastrow 1977).

These rates are consistent across studies, with results showing that TRA success statistics are comparable to same race adoption adjustment. Interestingly, two groups in particular — Korean and Columbian children — fared even better than Caucasian-Caucasian adoption in terms of adjustment. Maladjustment, according to Silverman and Feigelman (1981), was correlated with two specific factors, including placement after age five and the negative attitude of friends and family to an interracial adoption. Transracial adoption, it appears, is highly successful. The majority of the studies contradict the negative hypotheses held by many of the researchers that transracial adoption was imminently doomed to failure and would result in poor adjustment and outcomes (Chestang 1972; McRoy et al. 1982). In the early 1970s, the vociferous outcry from the National Association of Black Social Workers (NABSW) in opposition to the adoption of Black children into White families, coined the "anti-transracial adoption movement" by Simon and Alstein (1992: 14), had likely fuelled the widespread belief that transracial adoption was ultimately harmful for children and families.

The research, instead, found that adjustment among adopted children was good and these consistent findings contributed to new perceptions in some cases. Ladner (1977: 254), a Black social worker, studied Black/White TRA adjustment with initial skepticism. She eventually concluded: "There are Whites who are capable of rearing emotionally healthy Black children."

Because the transracial adoption literature often concludes with percentage outcomes that are favourable, readers might be inclined to believe that the favourable findings are universal and applicable to all transracial adoptions and that the experience of success is life-long. However, the adoption research area is not entirely robust and, until recently, long-term outcomes were absent in the literature with few exceptions (Baden 2002; Simon and Alstein 1992). Because of the lack of research and outcome data, the risk is that the findings of TRA studies on children have been and will be inappropriately applied to adult outcomes and all transracial adoptions. For example, Resnick stated: "The wealth of follow-up studies done so far on Asian children adopted by American and European parents suggest that their early adjustment to their new environments have generally been a happy and positive experience" (1984: 282). Resnick was applying those findings to Latin American adoptees.

Sorosky, Baran and Pannor (1975: 18) aptly observed that the transracial adoption literature is an emotional topic that is prejudiced by groups that occasionally have a vested interest in the research outcomes. They argued that for every research study that emphasizes a favourable outcome, there is a contradictory study to be found. For example, one article stated that age of placement is not a factor in outcomes (Holtan and Tremitiere 1996), while another states that age is one of two key factors in adoption outcomes (Feigelman and Silverman 1984). In the course of reviewing the literature, it became evident that, while most reports conclude with favourable outcomes, issues of concern pertaining to adjustment and identity are discussed in every instance, although there is a general blurring of the two issues. Most reports emphasize one or two points that the authors see as particularly problematic despite the favourable outcomes. For example, several authors noted that adopted children of colour are uncomfortable with their appearance and do not feel "pride" in their cultural heritage (Feigelman and Silverman 1984; Grow and Shapiro 1974; Kim 1978). Similarly, several authors note that extended family acceptance and attitude towards the TRA is correlated with adjustment outcomes (Feigelman and Silverman 1984). Hence, it would not be appropriate to make an unequivocal statement that TRA has either positive or negative outcomes when the literature clearly indicates that TRA is a blend of both, depending upon many factors. Mostly, it does not make sense to apply blanket conclusions to TRA outcomes. Aboriginal transracial adoption is a case in point.

Studying Aboriginal Transracial Adoption

Few of the early seminal TRA studies cover the issue of Aboriginal transracial adoption other than to give it cursory mention. In a few studies, Aboriginal adoption was subsumed into the "other" ethnic category (Simon and Alstein 1977, 1992). According to the contemporary literature, Aboriginal transracial adoption presents an extremely problematic situation, the etiology of which has not been fully articulated. Reviewing the early literature might lead one to believe that adoption outcomes for "Indian" children were positive (Fanshel 1972; Simon and Alstein 1977, 1983), although Simon and Alstein (1992), in a follow-up study, concluded that Aboriginal adoptions seem to comprise a "special case." More recent research alludes to problematic outcomes in Aboriginal TRAs (Bagley 1991; Holtan and Tremitiere 1996).

Adjustment to adoption in Aboriginal children appears to deteriorate as the children get older, with reported adoption breakdown[6] rates of 50 percent by age 15 (Bagley 1991), with Marie Adams (2002) noting that rate is as high as 95 percent. Interestingly, Holtan and Tremitiere (1996), American researchers who reported on TRA in the 1970s, alluded to deleterious outcomes and limited social and economic success for "Canadian Indian" adoptees. Until 2004, no studies examined the experiences or long-term adjustment of Aboriginal adults who were transracially adopted as children, with the exception of Christopher Bagley (1991), in whose longitudinal study participants had reached early adolescence.

In recent years, much interest has been directed at the Sixties Scoop and a critical mass appears to have been reached with respect to research on the topic. Six theses have been completed on the Sixties Scoop in Canada within the last five years (Arsenault 2006; Carrière, 2005; Nuttgens 2004, Sinclair 2007b; Sindelar 2004; Swidrovich 2004), four articles have been published within the last two years (Kulusic 2005; Carrière 2005, 2007; Sinclair 2007a) and several book chapters are currently being published. Four of the studies were exploratory studies designed to shed light on the lived experiences of adoptees, with the fourth focusing on mental health issues. The earliest study, Simon Nuttgens (2004: 51), asked the question: "What are the life-stories of Aboriginal adults who were raised in nonAboriginal families?" in order to learn how Aboriginal adults raised in non-Aboriginal families made sense of this experience through their personal life stories and to create a portrait of "being raised in a family of different cultural and racial origin." Similarly, Sindelar's (2004) study asked multiple exploratory questions included how Native adoptees define themselves in terms of identity and culture, search and reunion strategies, and how adoptees experienced "claiming" identity vis-à-vis adoption and reunion. Arsenault's (2006: ii) exploratory study sought to "hear the voices of Aboriginal adoptees; to understand how adoption has influenced Aboriginal adoptees lives, and to gain knowledge that can make a difference in the practice of the adoption of Aboriginal children." Another researcher who examined the Scoop in order to deliver adoption recommendations was Jeannine Carrière (2005), who sought to analyze identity and especially "connectedness" to birth families and culture as determinants of mental health. For the most part, these studies illustrate the childhood and growing up experiences of adoptees, their experiences of reunion and repatriation, and their experiences of what can be categorized under the rubric of "reconciliation" on multiple levels. The study that stands out in the group is Cheryl Swidrovich's (2004) project, which sought to deconstruct the "polemical discourse" of the Sixties Scoop in order to reconcile positive adoption experiences of ten adoptees. Swidrovich's analysis and findings provide a unique critical perspective of the Sixties Scoop discourse and her main point about providing discursive space for positive adoption experiences is well taken.

The collective theses of the last several years delve into the life stories of adoptees and contribute a rich array of information about the lived experiences of Aboriginal TRAs where no information existed previously. As initial forays into a new area, they are generally exploratory in nature and, with the exception of Nuttgens (2004: 184), whose interest was to highlight key issues to "serve as a point of reference for further sensitive discussion as to this practice," the researchers provide some general recommendations to address the problematics of Aboriginal TRA (Sindelar 2004; Carrière 2005; Arsenault 2006).

My own research articulated the lived experience of adoptees and included a wealth of stories about birth family and culture, apprehension and relinquishment to child welfare authorities, adoption placement, childhood, adolescent and adult experiences, reuniting with birth families, and reacculturating to birth cultures and nations.

Identity or Racism?

Interestingly, there was little discussion about the issue of identity by adoptees in my research. It took several years, a deliberate search for "negative data" and a suspicion that something was missing in the findings to realize that sometimes the absence of information can be extremely informative. If, as a cultural identity perspective suggests, identity is the predominant problematic issue and the main reason for Aboriginal adoption breakdown, one could assume that this issue would emerge in adoptee narratives, especially as adoptees recount their teen years. This is what the literature has told us, so should we not hear about troubled identity stories from adoptees? On the contrary, cultural identity was rarely discussed by adoptees. The lack of information was validated by the findings of another researcher, C. Swidrovich (2004: 120), who noted: "It should be noted that when sharing their experiences, none of the thirteen participants in (my) study included any discussion about identity problems or difficulties they might have encountered growing up."

Most of the adoptees in my own research indicated that Aboriginal identity was actually neither part of their consciousness as a child nor did they want it to be. For one adoptee who is now an adult, it still is not an issue. Indeed, their Aboriginal identity only became a matter for consideration or concern as they began to learn about negative stereotypes and images about Aboriginal people.

> We certainly didn't consider ourselves Indian kids and I certainly didn't consider myself an Indian kid until probably mid-way through my elementary school life. (Lacey)[7]

Being identified by others as Aboriginal and being "lumped" in with Aboriginal people was mostly distasteful and traumatic. Many adoptees in their teen and early adult years began to recognize that their Aboriginality was related to their poor social treatment. Identity only emerged as an issue once adoptees became adults or became aware of a sense of loss in their lives. For others, identity became integrally tied in with searching for belonging through reunion and repatriation. One described his search for identity as grappling with the "good Indian/bad Indian" stereotypes that he had internalized growing up. Another participant, who sought help in a moment of crisis, was not seeking help for identity problems; she was seeking help from the abuse and turmoil of her home environment:

> I tried to get some help talking to different people and finally went to the Native Child and Family in Toronto and talked to a couple of people there and started getting some help, but they didn't know how to help me and they told me that you know. Like we have no idea what you've gone through, we have no idea. It's different than the residential school, we went through residential school. You didn't have anybody. We at least had each other. (Sally)

Paul made a clear link between being singled out and ostracized and his own acting out behaviours; for him the issue was not identity.

> That turned into me having behavioural problems in school and at home because I just didn't feel part of, you know, I was always kind

of centred out in class. And then from there I would have behavioural problems and when the teacher asked me something or if I didn't have my homework done or something like that it centred me out. And I kind of basically dealt with that with having temper tantrums.

Very few adoptees recount any suggestions or support for pursuing their cultural identity, and those who did get encouragement were generally not interested. Most would likely agree that their contexts were closely aligned with prevailing adoption mythology that the adopted child is subsumed into the adopted family as if "born to them" (Thompson 1999).

Stories about racism abounded in the narratives that I witnessed. As I re-examined the literature it became apparent that because most researchers have not given precedence to racial issues, they have interpreted racism/ostracism and the emotional consequences of those experiences as identity or adjustment issues. For example, discomfort with their physical appearance and lack of pride in their cultural heritage was interpreted as the child having substantial identity issues (Bausch and Serpe 1997; Feigelman and Silverman 1984; McRoy et al. 1984).

Even the most recent and accurate interpretations of the issues conclude with identity as the problem. For example, Simon Nuttgens (2004: 187) articulates racist social discourse as significant and observes that attachment is not the problem for participants in his study, but he concludes by discussing identity:

> It can also be said that if it were not for the presence of racist discourse towards Aboriginal people, the probability of a more positive outcome would have been greatly increased. It seems that the difficulties which arose did so not due to the inability of Aboriginal children to attach to nonAboriginal parents per se, but due to inability of such children to acquire a positive Aboriginal identity in the face of a society which devalues and denigrates this aspect of their being.

Here again is a researcher concluding, based on accepted discourse, that identity is the issue, when, given the stories, it is more likely that the difficulty is not about acquiring a positive Aboriginal identity but about acquiring positive self-esteem in the face of racism. Even if children have a healthy identity as Aboriginal children, they still suffer the effects of racism. The voices of adoptees assure us that the children were not invested in an Aboriginal identity; indeed, most opposed it. They were invested in love and nurturing, and the absence of that, combined with abuse, became the problem issues. It is adults and academics who concern themselves with fitting children's maladaptations into theories of identity.

Colour-Blindness

In contemporary society, there are very few redeeming characteristics attributed to "Aboriginality." Canada has been very proud of its international
reputation as a land of equality replete with a national mythology that this
is not a racist country (Boyko 1995; Frideres 1976; Hughes and Kallen
1974; Sinclair, 2007a; Schick and St. Denis 2001). This discourse of denial
has repercussions for adopted children and families. For example, adoptive
parents who believe in the mythology will obviously not be able to prepare a
child to deal with issues that "do not exist" in this country. Adoptees raised in
an atmosphere of racial denial will of course be confused when confronted
with ongoing racism. For adoptees whose families chose to take a "colour-
blind" approach, the results are equally problematic. To echo the words of
Howard McCurdy, a Black Canadian adoptee who presented at the First
International Transracial Adoption conference held in Montreal in 1969,
"Although the Caucasian parent adopting a part Black child may not see his
child as that different, society does" (Bernard 1969). The good intentions
behind a colour-blind approach are naïve and destructive.

> The goal of racial justice in adoption requires that we see and ac-
> knowledge the color of a person's skin and, more pointedly, what
> that skin color represents in contemporary U.S. [or Canadian]
> society…. Colorblindness marks a path of least resistance — not a
> good sign when dealing with entrenched social problems like racism,
> sexism, homophobia, and other mechanisms of social exclusion.
> (Fogg-Davis 2002: 34)

The denial/colour-blind approach places children at risk for psychological
harm. To use an analogy from childhood, colour-blindness as an approach
to dealing with racism is like covering one's eyes and believing others cannot
see you (Sinclair 2007b).

O'Brien Caughy, O'Campo and Muntaner found a strong correlation
between parental openness to talking about racism and its effects, and their
child's acting out behaviours.

> In fact, parents who denied experiencing racism had the highest
> behavioural problems among their children. On the other hand,
> parents who reported actively coping with racism experiences or
> taking some sort of action in response to racism also reported fewer
> behavioural problems in their children. (2004: 212)

Although the authors' conclusions pertain to non-adopted African-American
children, it is likely that their findings can be applied to the Aboriginal TRA
context. Aboriginal children in substitute care are exposed to "subtle forms

of discrimination [that] continue to interfere with the lives and life chance of various racial and ethnic minorities" (Elliot and Fleras 1992: 44), and Palmer and Cooke (1996: 717) noted that "Socially, [First Nation] children are often excluded; majority teenagers, in particular, gravitate toward others like themselves, ignoring those from visible minorities. Social exclusion creates a climate in which adolescents are likely to drop out of school."

Children Just Want to Belong

Adolescence is a vulnerable time and is, unfortunately, the time when most Aboriginal youth become exposed to racism in the extra-familial social contexts (Cournane 2007). The vulnerability of adoptees is enhanced when their adoptive contexts are abusive and their adoption "tenure" is tenuous. Occasionally adoptees have been returned to care even during their teen years (Palmer and Cooke 1996), like a puppy returned to the pound. In my study, one participant was informed that family heirlooms were going to her non-adopted sister to "keep it in the family." The implication is that the child does not really belong to the family.

Children and adolescents may innocently contribute to their own racial dilemmas through denial, because an adopted child who experiences racism and discrimination may not share such encounters with their family because it is not part of the family ethos. Kim (1978) explains that for a child who wants to fit in, bringing in information that highlights their difference might be emotionally challenging. Children who experience racism when their families do not, see this as proof that they are inherently "different" (Kim 1978). As a result, many TRA children deal with racism in isolation. Marilyn and Loyal Rue (1984: 249) astutely recognize the challenge of racism for the adoptee:

> Racism, even its non-violent forms, is still pernicious. The difficult thing about racism in our particular situation is that when it is directed at [our adopted son] Carl, he must deal with it alone. He does not have the comfort of knowing that the rest of the family shares in his experience. If we were an entire family of minorities, his situation would be much different in this respect. And since neither of us has ever been the victim of racial prejudice, we are ill-prepared to help him develop the skills useful in combating it.

Researchers who allude to racism but do not adequately follow it up or who digress to identity issues fail to make the connection to coping strategies and skills that children and youth need to deal with discrimination. For example, Bagley (1991) suggested that as the result of widespread discrimination and prejudice, adoptive parents cannot transmit an adequate sense of ethnic identity to their children. This concept was alluded to early in TRA history by Chestang (1972) and Kim (1978) and is supported in several studies that theorize that adoptive parents cannot adequately role model coping skills for the discrimination that adoptees face in society (Bensen 2001; Triseliotis 1989). Although ethnic identity is very important, it is likely the aspects of ethnic identity that pertains to a sense of belonging, security and social support that mitigate the harmful effects of discrimination and prejudice.

Hawley Fogg-Davis (2002: 32) refers to the set of skills learned within same-race families and cultural groups to deal with racism as "racial navigation." Racial navigation, according to Fogg-Davis, accounts for the external gaze — the application of racial stereotypes onto an individual — as well as their own self-conceptions. Learning how to navigate racial issues, she argues, must be an explicit and conscious activity that occurs through critical dialogue.

> Racial navigation aims to make explicit the interplay between race-conscious social structures and individual self-understanding... racial navigation is a dynamic process that actively cultivates a personalized racial self-concept through familial conversation as well as through critical dialogue with others.

Applied to Aboriginal TRA, the lack of racial navigation skills leaves youth particularly vulnerable to internalizing the harmful effects of racism. The turmoil that results from racism, which often manifests in the adolescent years, is very likely the reason that an adoptee engages in destructive and harmful behaviours to themselves, their adoptive family and their environment (see, for example, Adams 2002 and Gilchrist 1995).

Transracial Aboriginal adoptees are in unique contexts, which likely contribute to mental turmoil. Most are raised in an environment of privilege, power and high social status (Ryant 1984).[8] Although their economic status is higher than average, they are inevitably forced to confront an inferior social status consistently ascribed to ethnic minority group members (Kim 1978). Not only are Aboriginal adoptees' ethnic and cultural identity wrapped up in cultural stigmatization, their identities are most likely associated with poverty and other negative stereotypes as well. In Canada, economic status is personal status; however, in our stratified society, colour automatically equates with a lack of status (Boyko 1995). Upon becoming aware of these issues, adoptees describe internalizing racism or stereotypical perspectives and, consequently, distancing themselves from other Aboriginal people and from their Aboriginal identity. For an adolescent, being Aboriginal can have severe repercussions in terms of justice and politics. On the one hand, the child is raised to be a member of the dominant ethnicity and culture; they are raised to be members of the White majority. On the other hand, they are treated as a member of a stigmatized minority by their peers, society at large and possibly by relatives and friends. They may be racially profiled by police and others in positions of authority. They are associated with harmful negative stereotypes by virtue of their appearance, and they are associated with Aboriginal political and social events, regardless of whether they identify politically and sociologically as Aboriginal.

Development theory would refer to these pressures as role ambiguity, role confusion and role strain (Shriver 2004). Although it is beyond the scope of this chapter to delve too deeply, mainstream developmental theory helps clarify the challenges that adoptees face. Symbolic interaction, for example, holds that "people are seen first and foremost as beings who interact with one another based on shared meanings and symbols. Thus human interaction is symbolic interaction" (Robbins, Chatterjee and Canda 1998: 268). People assign social meanings to their experiences, and human behaviour is a function of social behaviour. Personality, therefore, stems from social constructs and interactions. "According to symbolic interactionism, it is through contact with others in the social group that children learn a sense of 'I,' 'my,' and 'mine,' as well as a concept of 'we'" (LaRossa, cited in Hollingsworth 1999: 443). If reflection then is the means by which we come to our self-concept and self-conceptions, the implications for Aboriginal adoptees are quite frightening. Indeed, the implications for the development of self-concept are of great concern for anyone who exists in a hostile, abusive or oppressive environment.

If we create meanings and symbols in our interactions with other people, what happens when those meanings and symbols are constantly changing? For Aboriginal people in Canada, social interaction is a continual guessing game. One individual may be extremely friendly and engaging, and the next individual may be blatantly hostile. For the Aboriginal adoptee in their formative years, it would be difficult to create and rely upon consistent interpretations of meanings and symbols in such a social environment.

The Locus of the Problem

From the stories, narratives and testimonials of adoptees, many Aboriginal adoptees have struggled greatly to "fit" into White society outside of their family context. Some were not allowed to fit even within their family context, with constant reminders of their racial difference through abuse and intra-familial racism. The problem with viewing identity as the issue is that the locus of the problem then rests with the child. The literature thus states that adolescents "no longer fit" rather than that "a racialized society does not allow them to fit." Sixkiller Clarke, in analyzing the impact of racism in the education system, notes: "For too long, we have explained the failure of Indian students as a 'within child' deficit... We have failed to look beyond these problems, because if failure is not the fault of the child, then it lies elsewhere... (1994: 121). Frideres (1988: 43) pointed out the problem two decades ago:

> For too long theorists have viewed the Indian Problem as "a problem Indians have." They have not viewed it as a "White problem." This has resulted in a failure to take into account the existence of external structural factors that have impinged upon Native people.

By defining racism as an adoptee identity issue, the burden for the problem is placed upon the already-burdened Aboriginal child, adolescent and adult. The adoptee is held responsible for deficits in their identity constructions, and structural issues are overlooked. It is interesting, yet appalling, that reports consistently locate the problem within the children. One article in the *Globe and Mail*, which examined a study tracking a hundred Aboriginal children placed for adoption in Pennsylvania, interpreted adoptee behaviour in this way:

> A lot of the kids placed in Pennsylvania had very little contact with any native culture, and we suspect they shaped their behaviours on the stereotypes of the "dangerous savage" that they were hearing about. (Philp 2002)

There is no mention in the article of racism, social ostracism, isolation or abuse, any of which might result in problematic behaviours.

Individualizing the problem does not just affect adopted children. Adoptive parents are occasionally targeted as failures despite their best efforts to provide their child with a sense of cultural identity (Adams 2002). If identity issues are further misdiagnosed as adoptive family failure, quests for solutions will also be misdirected.

The Lost Identity Paradigm

The identity conflict paradigm places the onus on adoptees for having "lost" their identity in the first place. Such deficit perspectives are perpetuated by the well-intentioned whose labels infer that the problem or the outcome rest within the adoptee. Examples include pathologizing adoptees as "Split Feathers"[9] (Locust 2000) and "Lost Birds" (origin unknown) replete with "syndromes" resulting from their experiences. In adoption circles, labelling Aboriginal children automatically as having special needs (Adams 2002: 179), ostensibly to augment advance supports for the transracial adoption, is another pathologizing strategy.

> I get really resentful when people start talking about, you know, all these people who don't have language and culture because I'm, like,

where the hell were you? Where the hell were you thirty-five years ago when I was born? Where the hell were you when I was adopted? Where the hell were you for my mother? (Sally)

A commonly accepted phrase regarding Aboriginal TRA is "lost identity," as if adopted children, even those adopted at birth, had their Aboriginal identity intact and dropped it by the wayside. "They also suffered a loss of Aboriginal identity, culture and heritage" is a common phrase in the literature (Arsenault 2006: 87). An article referred to the adoption of American Indian Children in this way: "America's 'lost birds' fly home: Adopted Indians find way back to their tribes" (Arrillaga 2001). It is interesting to make the assumption that a child, raised from birth in an adoptive home, would experience any loss pertaining to identity at all. It would make sense for a child adopted at an older age to articulate loss in that context, assuming that their birth family's Aboriginal identity was intact and that the identity was transmitted to the child before adoption placement. This line of reasoning assumes that identity is a static, unchanging variable within the human character and even Aboriginal children adopted at or shortly after birth have an Aboriginal identity intact. Given that sociological thought informs us that "ethnic identity is a variable and not a constant" (Frideres 1988: 149), one has to question why this leeway has not been afforded to Aboriginal children in non-Aboriginal homes. For example, when non-Aboriginal children have turmoil in adoptive and foster care, they are not portrayed as having identity conflicts. The majority of studies on African-American transracial adoptees examine "adjustment" as opposed to identity.

None of the adoptees who spoke to me discussed loss of identity, culture and heritage, other than in retrospect. One spoke of loss in relation to not knowing she could go back to her community, "I really felt um really empty and lost but I didn't know that, that was there that I could go back to." For the most part, discussions about loss pertained to loss of family and the absence of love, nurturing and belonging. The concept of loss is central to adoptee experiences but it encapsulates a great deal more than cultural identity. More often than not, loss referred to enduring emotional and attachment loss.

It's also the loss of even being able to connect and have close relationships with brothers and sisters from my adopted family. I don't spend Christmas with family, I don't go to family dinners, I don't participate in and I actually don't actually celebrate um any holidays. Valentine, birthdays, Easters, these are all nightmare days for me. Christmas is still a horrible time. I'd far rather be locked in a room and, and send my kids to their father's where they can go and have a Christmas where they can enjoy it. Cause I just don't see it, I don't feel it, I don't relate to it. (Sam)

Often the sense of loss, and the loneliness that it implies, was an impetus to searching for birth family and community. Other reasons included curiosity and maturity, that is, simply that the time had come to look for birth relatives and community connections. Hence, it seems to be more appropriate to consider that identity seeking and eventual acculturation is indeed an "adaptive response" (Frideres 1988) in adoptees rather than a deficit within the adopted child. In almost every instance, the decision to seek birth family and community coincided with learning about Aboriginal culture, and in almost every instance, it was a clear choice made by the adoptee. Some waited longer than others and some searches took much longer than others. However, none of the narratives that were reviewed indicate that the search and developing of cultural identity was something that was outside the agency of the individuals. Indeed, these participants were very clear about their decisions.

> It really wasn't until I was sort of nineteen when I left high school and went off to do university when I really started to open up and grow up. And sort of be more accepting and, and see more the diverse people and then that's when I really wanted to start leaning more about, about my culture and everything like that. (Tasha)

> I want to find out at this point of my life, like it's, I'm twenty-six now but I want to find out who I basically am and where I came from and what that part of me is cause I never got a chance to experience it. (Kendra)

Revising the Discourse

The etiology of the Aboriginal TRA problem takes on more clarity when racism is pulled from silence and denial through the narratives of Aboriginal adoptees (Adams 2002; Arsenault 2006; Carrière 2005; Fournier and Crey 1997; Nuttgens 2004; Sindelar 2004; Stolen Generations 2003; Swidrovich 2004). Adolescent behavioural problems, adoption breakdowns and adult psychological turmoil are linked, in adoptees' testimonials, to the intra- and extra-familial racism and abuse experienced by adoptees and the emotional fall-out from those experiences of racism. The issue of identity links with racism to contribute to the problem because adoptees are socialized to have a White identity and subsequently denied access to White society. Hence, it is their White identity socialization in the face of an unaccepting social context that is the problem, not the biological Aboriginal identity that adoptees are held accountable for "losing" in their adoptive experiences. The identity paradigm does not hold the system accountable for its own weaknesses relative to Aboriginal TRA, nor does it provide the space for additional considerations of abuse as well as multiple pre-adoptive factors such as neglect, abandonment and violence that might be playing out in the adoption scenario (Adams 2002). Considering that not all Aboriginal children have had negative pre-adoption experiences, the identity conflict paradigm also does not create the space for simple grief at the separation from birth mothers and families.

Ironically, racism is very likely one impetus to seek out cultural identity and community belonging. Many adoptees are emancipated early due to abuse, isolation and intra-familial racism. Even the best intentioned adoptee families can be guilty of subtle racism, which can have a negative impact on the adoptee. In my own experience, I grew up believing that Canada was not a racist country and that my family was not racist. However, several memories have never left my mind. In one memory I became aware one day that my brother and sister were getting ready to go somewhere. When I finally asked where they were going, they dashed out the door without an explanation. Later my sister informed me that they did not want me to come along to the movie because they were embarrassed to take me along. Ironically, the movie they went to see was *Billy Jack*, a 1971 film about a "half-breed" karate expert who fights for the rights of Aboriginal people. My family is a "typical" Canadian family and they are well-intentioned and kind. Their goodness, however, did not extend to understanding my experiences as an Aboriginal child in a non-Aboriginal context. To this day, they rationalize that I had problems growing up, not that my context was problematic.

In summary, Aboriginal children, adopted or not, are generally subject to racism. Aboriginal children who are socialized to have a White identity are still subject to racism. The common denominator is, of course, racism. This is important for two reasons. First, labelling someone as having an "identity" issue locates the responsibility for the problem on that individual. Hence, Aboriginal children in non-Aboriginal homes become somehow responsible for the confusion and turmoil they experience as Aboriginal children in non-Aboriginal homes; as if the child changing their identity will magically alter their intra- and extra-familial contexts. This burden is compounded in situations where abuse and other pathological conditions exist. It is time to observe that perhaps the problem is not located within the child.

Second, by attending to racism as the problem, the locus of responsibility is contextualized structurally and systemically. Children are relieved of the burden of responsibility for situations in which they had no power. Externalizing the problem is critical to the welfare of Aboriginal children because maintaining the illusion that TRA is problematic because of cultural identity issues will not lead to solutions that help children deal with the reality of racialization in Canada.

Suggested Practice Shifts

In response to the misdiagnosis of the problem, adoption agencies and adoptive families have sought to find solutions to identity problems, and large sums of money are being directed into "cultural identity" programming in child welfare across the country. Some of conventional adoption prescriptions emphasize the importance of instilling a cultural heritage in the child through books, movies and culturally relevant events such as powwows (Adams 2002). Unfortunately, these are idealized versions of Aboriginal culture and not realistic as a means for instilling identity. Indeed, chances are high that what children observe will more readily match the negative stereotypes learned in the course of their daily lives through media and education. Such shallow approaches to dealing with the issue will likely only exacerbate the problem and create more conflict for the adoptee. As one researcher noted, it was usually the transracially adopted teenagers who wanted to change the subject when "ethnic" discussions were initiated at the dinner table (Simon 1998). By paying more attention to racism and strategies for dealing with it, children and adoptive families will be addressing a core issue in transracial adoption. In the long-term, this will serve to enhance awareness for everyone working in the field of adoption and involved in the adoption triad.

The following practical recommendation are found in Palmer and Cooke's (1996) discussion of countering racism with First Nations children in substitute care:

- Discuss race with children and caregivers; acknowledge racial differences and the existence of racism in its various forms.
- Help children deal with racism through teaching and action plans; advise children that racism is illegal.
- Children need confidence that people in authority [social workers, teachers, foster parents, adoptive parents, police] will take action to support them in countering racism.
- Children need to be coached in how to respond to racism in effective ways.
- Aboriginal children need cultural connections and supports (721.)[10]

These recommendations should be implemented across the board in social service agencies dealing with Aboriginal children. It is absolutely critical that Aboriginal children be given the supports and strategies to deal with and counter racism. To not act given the abundance of adult testimonies indicating lifelong dealings with racism both within and outside the adoptive family is to be complicit in abuse of Aboriginal children.

The following recommendations come directly from the participants:

- Resources should be directed to family preservation.
- If children must be placed, extended birth family placements should take place.
- Education of potential adoptive parents is necessary.
- Stricter selection guidelines and screening process are needed.
- People need to know that adoption is a privilege and not a right.
- Legislation must protect the rights of children and First Nations.
- Adoption agencies should collaborate with First Nations on behalf of children.
- Siblings should be adopted together wherever possible.
- There must be willingness to support the child to acculturate and maintain cultural ties.
- Openness in adoption will help with maintaining birth and cultural knowledge.
- There should be ongoing ties between adoptive families and supportive resources.
- Elder Support for adoptees should be in place.
- Adoptees should automatically receive treaty and band information at age eighteen.
- A national adoption registry should be developed to facilitate reunification.

In addition to the participants' recommendations, the following recommendations are provided. As Sindelar (2004) noted as one of her theme headings, "Once you adopt a non-white child, your family's not white." The recommendation pertains to the concept of constructing a "bicultural family" identity once an Aboriginal child is placed into a non-Aboriginal home for adoption. Constructing a bicultural family identity requires a paradigm shift in the perspective of adoptive families and it may be essential to the wellbeing of Aboriginal transracial adoptees. For example, the third group in the three groups of families studied in the McRoy, Zurcher, Lauderdale and Anderson (1984) study described themselves as bicultural as the result of bringing an interracial child into their home. Rue and Rue (1984) said the same thing. When the Rue family decided to adopt a child from Thailand, they immediately conceived of themselves as a Thai-American family. This approach counteracts the prevailing adoption myth that children, regardless of their ethnicity, are subsumed into their adoptive family and culture "as if born to them" (Thompson 1999).

Adoption ideology has only recently begun to consider the notion that because the child is of another ethnicity and will be entering into a family of another culture, that the whole family is, therefore, reconstituted into a blend of all the cultures involved. The respectfulness of this approach might be significant in terms of the intrinsic inclusiveness of the child's birth heritage that is implied when the family as a whole assumes a bicultural identity, as opposed to the child's standing alone in their "transraciality." Families who subscribe to a biracial identity may ensure that their child has ongoing contact with Aboriginal people, culture and communities. Ideally, adoptive families would engage in "sustained and meaningful relationship with the Aboriginal community" (Nuttgens 2004: 171).

A corollary benefit of adopting a bicultural paradigm is that it may also serve as a gatekeeping mechanism. Acceptance or rejection of a bicultural family paradigm by prospective adoptive parents may well reveal their levels of racial tolerance or intolerance (Sinclair 2007b).

A second recommendation that may provide support for addressing problematic areas pertaining to identity issues is to utilize Baden's (2002) cultural-racial identity matrix as an assessment tool to help adoptive children and their families recognize that identity is indeed a fluid and multidimensional dynamic. Baden (2002) presents a racial-cultural identity matrix as a method of helping adoptees to determine their sense of identity. Baden states: "Neither the proponents or opponents can purport a 'best way' to identify as a transracial adoptee" (189). The model is an assessment tool that is inclusive of a multi-faceted cultural identity. The model includes adoptive family culture and birth family culture as ends on the continuum, and adoptive family identity and birth family identity on opposing axes. The model does is not dichotomous; adoptees do not have to choose either their birth identity or their adoptive identity. There are enough factors in a cultural-racial matrix from which to choose so that the individual will fit somewhere within the continuum without being pathologized and without altering how they actually culturally identify. This approach is person-focused rather than ideologically focused. In terms of intervention, the model could help the worker to start where the adoptee is in terms of their identity and the model supports what adoptees already know — that their identities are multi-faceted and intricately tied up on multiple factors in their lives. Weaver, citing Oetting and Beauvais (1991), explains:

> Attachment to one culture does not necessarily detract from attachment to another and multiple cultural identifications are not only possible but potentially healthy. (Weaver 2001b: 8)

The cultural identity matrix would be useful for post-adoption and repatriation workers, as well as counsellors and therapists, as a starting point for exploring identity issues. Although it should not be used to supersede discussions of racial issues, it can complement racism interventions.

Racism and Identity

Cultural identity is clearly a significant aspect of an adoptee's journey, and cultural identity programming in child welfare services is very important. Indeed cultural continuity in foster and adoptive contexts would mitigate many of the problems that adoptees face whether those are related to identity or racism. The purpose of this chapter has been to uncover racism from a cloak of silence. The issue has had tremendously detrimental affects on children in care, and racism must no longer be obfuscated by the focus of attention paid to the cultural identity conflict paradigm. Interventions must start to include a focus on racism.

In Canada, there are currently thousands of children in long-term care as the result of the 1985 Manitoba moratorium on Aboriginal adoptive placements. Moreover, institutional care, including foster care, in Canada is primarily non-Aboriginal in terms of staffing. The issues for Aboriginal children in long-term care will likely be similar to those of adoptees. The field of social work, so involved in Aboriginal life, needs to be prepared to deal with these issues because a vast majority of these children will emerge from care as adults raised in non-Aboriginal substitute care. A recent court case may have implications for increased adoption of Aboriginal children in the near future because there is a huge push to register children for adoption who are currently in long-term care.[11] Saskatchewan Justice Ryan-Froslie struck down the Saskatchewan provincial government policy that prohibited the adoption of First Nations children without band consent. Justice Ryan-Froslie argued that the policy violated children's Charter rights to security of the person because their access to a permanent adoptive home is being denied them. The Judge noted that First Nations are not constitutionally authorized to speak for their children. Ultimately, the judge deemed that First Nations status was the only reason children were not being placed in adoptive homes (Judgment 2004, Dec. 10, 2004). Hence, there is some urgency to pay attention to the voices of adults who have experienced being transracially adoptive. They have insights and understandings that only come from experience.

Despite the tribulations of being Aboriginal children adopted into foreign environments that created sometimes impossible social, emotional and psychological contexts, the adoptees whose stories form the foundation of the information for this chapter, are kind, generous and insightful adults, each of whom has achieved a measure of success in their lives. Their voices, it is hoped, will be heard and will ultimately contribute to relevant and efficacious adoption strategies that will serve the best interests of Aboriginal children.

Notes

1. Indian" means a person who pursuant to this Act is registered as an Indian or is entitled to be registered as an Indian" (Indian Act R.S., 1985. c. 1-5).

2   For a discussion of the federal government's use, abuse, and manipulation of
    .financial resources with respect to Aboriginal people that is beyond the scope
    of this work, two sources are highly useful: Hugh Shewell's (2004) *Enough to
    Keep Them Alive: Indian Social Welfare in Canada, 1873–1965*, and Dean Neu and
    Richard Therrian's (2003) *Accounting for Genocide*.

3. Section 91(24) of the Canadian Constitution details that the federal government
    has "responsibility for Indians and lands reserved for Indians."

4. The position paper asserts, "Unless a child learns about the forces which shape
    him; the history of his people, their values and customs, their language, he will
    never really know himself or his potential as a human being." See <http://
    www.afn.ca/article.asp?id=830>.

5. For a comprehensive look at Aboriginal child welfare literature, see Bennett,
    Blackstock and De La Ronde's (2005) literature review and annotated bibliography
    available at <http://www.fncfcs.com/docs/AboriginalCWLitReview_2ndEd.
    pdf>.

6. Adoption "breakdown" generally refers to the child leaving the adoptive home
    either through child welfare intervention, running away or being asked to
    leave.

7. Pseudonyms are used to identify the participants in my study.

8. Ryant was citing Fanshel (1972) and Simon and Alstein (1977) that adopters
    were on average of high social status.

9. Locust (2000) conducted interviews with Aboriginal American adoptees and
    developed the "Split Feather Syndrome," which comprises five psychologically
    traumatic factors common to Aboriginal adoptees, referred to as "Split Feathers,"
    the first of which is "loss of identity."

10. Palmer and Cooke's fifth recommendation was teaching children about posi-
    tive First Nation attributes; this has been adapted here to be more involving of
    Aboriginal culture rather than incorporating mere symbols of the culture.

11. First Nation finalized adoptions in Saskatchewan — four in 2002/3; seven in
    2003/4; seven in 2004/5; ten in 2005/6; and nineteen in the first six months
    of 2007 (Adoption Worker, Adoption Registry, Saskatchewan Department of
    Community Resources and Employment, personal communication, July 13,
    2007).

Chapter 6

Beyond Audacity and Aplomb
Understanding the Métis in Social Work Practice

Cathy Richardson (Kinewesquao) and Dana Lynn Seaborn

The Canadian Métis are an Aboriginal people who celebrate their Aboriginal-European mixed ancestry and identify within a unique Métis culture. In order for social workers to engage appropriately with Métis families, an understanding of Métis people and their sacred concerns is crucial. Historical factors influence the current position of Métis cultural marginality in a colonial landscape and relate to the fact that many Métis children become involved with social workers. As one of Canada's founding Aboriginal peoples (Department of Justice Canada 1982), the Métis exist at the periphery of the Canadian historical, cultural and social landscape. This social positioning may be attributed to oppression, racism and anti-Métis discrimination, particularly after the mid-1850s, when the Métis were attacked by the government and displaced from their land through the scrip process (Adams 1995, 1989; Tough 2002). Métis people have been accused of a number of crimes in Canada, including the audacious attempt to defend their homeland in the late 1800s, of being racially inferior due to hybridity and of wanting to preserve culture and identity for Métis children in child welfare settings. Indeed, the Métis are making ongoing efforts to articulate their perspectives and sacred concerns to a listening audience. Today, the Métis are starting to write themselves into larger historical and social sciences narratives, reclaiming their right to inclusion and belonging after generations of living without the safety necessary for public cultural expression. In this chapter, we present some of the socio-political conditions that set the context for Métis identity development and that relate to social work practice. We then discuss ideas of cultural safety for the Métis in relation to developing a "third space" of relative safety and belonging within the larger colonial Canada. We discuss the significance of the third space in relation to the Métis sense of self and wellbeing, and conclude with some recommendations for social work practice with Métis families that honour Métis culture and identity.

Some of the key concepts in this chapter include aplomb and audacity, as well as identity or the sense of Métis self. We refer to the assessment and negotiation of social safety and tactical responses to situations of social violence and exclusion (de Certeau 1984; Wade 1995). Aplomb refers to the adoption of an outer face of disregard or a quiet lack of concern or emotion in situations of social risk. Audacity refers to activities that are seen as inappropriate or outrageous by others, such as requesting that the system provide what it promises in accordance with laws, treaties and former agreements with the Crown. Audacity refers to challenging racism and imposed definitions of centrality or normality, or resisting a governmental practice of trying to undermine solidarity between Aboriginal peoples. These processes are enacted in a context of landlessness and displacement for the Métis, who tended to go to Canadian industrial or urban centres in order to secure employment and avoid stigmatization in prairie communities. Tactical responses were, and are, performed by Métis people, who are trying to balance their need for safety and inclusion with a need to live as cultural beings in a European Canada. The responses are termed "tactical" as opposed to "strategic" because of an important distinction related to unequal power relationships between oppressor and oppressed in colonial societies. Political strategies and strategic responses tend to be developed for long-term use by those in political positions of relative power, whereas tactics tend to be developed "on the move," as quick responses to attack and political oppression. For example, General Middleton implemented military strategies to defeat the Métis, while Louis Riel and Gabriel Dumont applied tactics in response to Middleton's attacks. Métis families use tactical responses when engaging with social workers who attempt to assert power and control over their lives with undemocratic, non-collaborative practices.

History: Rupertsland and Beyond

The Métis are people of mixed-race — European and First Nations ancestry — who self-identify as such and celebrate their "mixedness." The cultural mixing could have occurred at the time of contact, during the fur trade or more recently. Michif is the traditional language of the Métis, who are often multilingual. The Métis emerged as a nation in Red River, Rupertsland, in 1816, in response to orchestrated land theft, facilitated by the Saskatchewan Valley Land Company in alignment with the interests of the federal government (O'Keefe and MacDonald, 2001; Tough, 2002). This sense of nationhood was strengthened over the next fifty years, as the Métis resisted the Government of Canada's repeated appropriation of their lands and refusal to acknowledge their right to representation. Métis people were driven off their homeland and generally live as a visible/invisible marginalized group in Canada. The brutal force of empire behind the colonizing project cannot be underestimated if one is to understand the events to which the Métis were responding. Imperial figure Charles Lyell (1832), a contemporary of Charles Darwin, reminded his contemporaries:

> If we wield the sword of extermination as we advance, we have no reason to repine the havoc committed. (Crosby 2004: ix)

Métis lives have been interwoven with many historical events on this land, some directly and deliberately, others as part of a general oppression against Aboriginal people. Many Métis found themselves in uncomfortable positions of having to negotiate safety within a myriad of strange and violent events. For example, while on the one hand attacking militarily and dispersing the Métis, the federal government then took the Métis constitution and used it as the basis for the *Manitoba Act* when Manitoba became a province. Manitoba's first premier, John Norquay, known as a "mixed-blood," was a Métis leader from Red River. Although minimally involved in the Red River resistance, he took up politics shortly after. In 1872 he was defeated by Cunningham, an ally of Louis Riel. During this time, the Métis required strong leadership to take on the violence directed at them. In 1885 the Canadian government sent its army to clear the Métis from the prairies at Batoche. After the Métis defeat, 1.4 million acres of land were transferred to the Canadian state. Federal oppression against Aboriginal people has deliberately undermined relationships between the Métis and the First Nations, through strategies such as assigning arbitrary identity categories, policies and funding processes that promote unhealthy competition in conditions of deprivation.

While the Métis community embraced both English- and French-speaking people with equality, as well as having close ties with the many First Nations to which they are related, linguistic and class tensions in European Canada were exploited in the trial, legal process and then state execution of the Métis leader. Louis Riel's trial was moved from Manitoba, and Canada hanged him for treason against the British Crown. This act served multiple functions: to humiliate the Métis and intimidate those remaining who contemplated ongoing resistance, either overtly or in ways that defended the Métis' right to exist.

With a few notable exceptions, such as the Pauly case, regarding hunting rights in limited areas, human rights violations against the Métis have not yet been addressed. The land theft process has been documented extensively in the University of Alberta archives by Frank Tough and his staff. Scrip documents stored there may support collective legal action concerning this theft (Goyette 2003; Tough 2002). While the history of the Red River Rebellion is presented in Canadian schools, the analysis seldom acknowledges the concerns of empire and colonial violence on which this attack and land theft were predicated. After Batoche, many Métis were forced to flee in response to ongoing anti-Métis sentiment in the area. Those who could went "underground" and did not identify openly as Métis, often using a familial name that evoked "Englishness" to resist being locked out of the economy.

Many Métis moved away, some following industrial development westward. English protestant settlers from Ontario moved into the area and perpetuated views of European superiority over the local "halfbreeds." The Métis who remained in the area tried their best to negotiate the harsh social climate and find a way to hold their ground and maintain their dignity. Many families settled on the edges of prairie towns and were dubbed "the Road Allowance people." Their children were forbidden to attend the local schools because the families were not tax-paying citizens. Settlers often mistook the Métis for gypsies, unsure of their origin or their destination (Adams 1995, 1989). While giving a talk on the Métis at a workshop, I was approached by a participant who recounted the story of a childhood visit to her grandmother in Saskatchewan. The participant had accompanied her grandmother to the edge of the community, where they presented food to the starving people living there in shanties. She remembered thinking, "I wonder who these people are," and decided they must be gypsies.

Authors O'Keefe and MacDonald have documented (2001) land theft through the guise of a treaty process, capitalist ventures and the brokerage of land deals that resulted in great private wealth for capitalists and members of the Canadian parliament alike. These swindles constitute some of the corruption and profiteering that deprived First Nations and Métis communities of their homelands. As is common for much colonial discourse, Aboriginal peoples' experiences are absent in the account. Historically accurate accounts of deliberate theft and violence have been systematically deleted or obscured in the colonial discourse found in Canadian education, media and popular representations of Euro-Canadian life.

The Ground on Which Métis Identity Is Created

Due to historical oppression, Eurocentrism, racism and a general lack of understanding of Métis culture, many of our grandmothers and grandfathers went "underground" culturally. It has become clear that whenever people are mistreated they resist in some way. "Alongside each history of violence and oppression, there runs a parallel history of prudent, creative, and determined resistance" (Wade 1997: 11). As a tactic of survival and safety, many, when the hue of their skin would permit such assimilation, tried to "pass" and conform to Victorian values and Euro-Canadian ways. The term "aplomb" has been used to describe acts necessary to resist violence, such as "moving under the radar," withholding outward expressions and putting on a public face that does not reveal one's true response to violence or indignity (Richardson 2004). In a western tradition of thought that expresses itself in terms of "either/or," the Métis were told they must be either White or red. Cultural demographics assigned us to our "worlds" — the world occupied by the Europeans/Euro-Canadians or the world occupied by the First Nations.

In conversations with Métis people, many share the sentiment that they do not feeling completely at home, or completely welcome, in either of these worlds (Richardson 2004). Indeed, it is difficult to feel at home when your land has been taken and you are living on space claimed by others. As well, connections to land and opportunities to sustain life through hunting, fishing and gathering were compromised by forced displacement and capitalist industrial intrusion. While many Métis have experienced spiritual pain at the erosion of their life and livelihood, personal and familial survival meant that they often dared not "speak truth to power" aloud, but rather performed resistance on the inside. Land is life and being landless impinges upon opportunities for collective cultural survival. Unlike the Euro-Canadians and some of the First Nations, the Métis have no recognized homeland. Much of the Red River settlement is now filled with shopping malls.

As Métis, we have found that our identity lies in a third alternative — a psychological homeland. Métis people travel in and out of a given cultural "no man's land," by situation or by choice, looking for somewhere to belong. For the Métis, identity is constantly being created through ongoing interaction with the various worlds. One Métis, Martin Dunn, has said, "It may be closer to the truth to think of Métis as a process or a verb, rather than a static noun. In French the appropriate word is *Métissage*. I am not aware of a single-word English translation" (Dunn n.d.). The salient point here is that we construct our identity through the ongoing mixing of our ancestral cultures and influences. When we are strong in our sense of self, we also gain the strength of community, because our Métis family exists behind us in our past, with us in our present and in our future with our grandchildren yet to be born. Our birthright does not disappear because history has erased the names of our forebears.

Particular challenges, concerns and considerations exist for those engaging in social work in a Métis context. While many of the historical events described earlier relate to the current struggles of many Métis, ongoing identity challenges must be attended to in professional practice. Métis families may experience immediate issues in their lives related to compromised human rights, but issues of dignity, identity, acknowledgement and belonging are at stake. These sacred concerns must be taken into account in each interaction and intervention of the social worker. Practices that attempt to restore dignity may form the substance of presence and conversations, acknowledging that economic and cultural marginality may constitute forms of social humiliation for families. One of the deepest forms of humiliation involves being prevented from caring and providing for one's family. Métis activist Duke Redbird referred to people experiencing this as being locked out of the economy. Métis people still tend to negotiate cultural safety when deciding to tell other people that they are Métis. Many report experiencing negative repercussions after disclosing their ancestry, both from other family members and in the social world (Richardson 2004). Métis families must assess risk in situations where racial diversity and historical claims may not be celebrated and honoured. Where dignity and cultural acknowledgement (e.g., social justice) are at stake, families will often seek to preserve their dignity in ways that are available. Where racism and abuses of power exist, outward appearances may be deceiving. This latter point is particularly relevant for social workers.

When interacting with the system, families are often placed in situations where they must defend their dignity, which may draw energy away from the task that is being imposed. Métis families commonly experience imposed values and directives by social workers. In cases where social work practice is non-collaborative, pathologizing and authoritarian, the family may organize around the attack or humiliation. In such situations, it is next to impossible for families to be judged positively by workers on their parent-child or intra-familial relationships, and children are typically removed because risk has been inaccurately assessed or intensified by the social worker's intervention. This situation is pervasive for families who must attend to colonial practices in their most intimate spaces.

The site of the social work intervention tends not to reflect Métis culture. In professional settings, pan-Aboriginal accoutrements may serve to decorate the surroundings, but they contain no meaning for Métis families. The absence of meaningful cultural planning where Métis children are removed from their families has created great suffering for Métis children (Carrière, 2005). Where families are separated through child welfare interventions, Métis children tend to move through the system without information about their birthright, their entitlements or the family traditions that once encircled our people in a blanket of survival. Audaciously, Métis advocates continue to assert the importance of cultural planning in social work as a means of warding off assimilation. Whenever a Métis child is destroyed spiritually, through suicide, hatred, self-mutilation or violence, they represent another of colonialism's victims. We are attempting to stand up to colonial policies that would rid Canada of all Aboriginal peoples and its obligations to them.

Although Métis families may not even be immediately identifiable as Aboriginal people, as this chapter has outlined, we are often quite distinct from the White, middle-class family. Our people have been informed by a unique historical experience that makes us the first "new" race of people to be born in Canada, insofar as the construct of race can be said to exist at all. This formulation has been helpful for some Métis in their identity strengthening process because it offers a possibility of holism. We are unique as a mixed-race people whose collective identity centres around the "mixedness" rather than being seen as bi-cultural as are those in many colonized countries. We are a pre-Canadian people who came into existence shortly after the first Europeans sailed up the St. Lawrence River. For these reasons, Métis people carry a different legacy than the Canadian of the colonist or immigrant variety. This leads to a simple, but important, fact. Métis people are different from other people. Social work professionals need to become educated about the unique history, culture and contemporary challenges facing Métis people in order to effectively work with Métis families and children. Without this specific knowledge, the social worker runs the risk of replicating dominance and oppression. This chapter provides an initial foray into the topic of Métis identity and provides insight on the historical and contemporary challenges facing Métis people with respect to issues of identity.

Métis Identity

Métis identity is created through a process of social interaction and dialogic relationships between the inner world and the external world. Relations of unequal power serve as foundational influences negotiated by Métis individuals in the creation of a sense of "Métis self." It is important to acknowledge that whenever an Aboriginal group is deprived, when something is withheld from them, their loss constitutes gain for another group, most typically the Euro-Canadian state and those most reflected and represented within its colonial container.

Particularly helpful for understanding Métis identity creation is Wade's (1997) articulation of human beings as sentient "responding" agents, rather than as passive bystanders who are affected by their surroundings. While humans are responsive in every cell of their body, in every expression of their being, we are said to be affected by our context, a formulation that does not give expression to our humanity. This reformulation of humans as responding agents dignifies people who have been pathologized and blamed for their suffering, as they are in most psychological theories. Advancing earlier groundbreaking formulations of systemic communications (Bateson, Jackson, Haley and Weakland 1956), a major contribution to the understanding of "self and identity" is situated in the belief that we change ourselves through a process of social communication with the outside world while continuously assessing safety and the "room to move."

Métis identity creation is enacted on a foundation of two life-affirming beliefs, which are also foundational to both response-based ideas (Wade 2000) and systemic communication theory (Watzlawick, Beaven, Bavelas and Jackson 1967): first, *that people possess pre-existing ability*, and second, *that people know how to be well*. Although these beliefs may appear relatively basic, they have been strikingly absent in psychological theories and in depictions of victims of violence and colonized populations. Clearly, the Métis have been presented historically as deficient and pathetic. As Métis writer Howard Adams noted:

> The books I read at school said that my ancestors were cruel, sadistic savages who had not even reached the early stages of civilization, and I felt that I was constantly being reminded of the direct link between myself and my "Barbarian" ancestors. My first reaction was to pretend that there was nothing Indian about me. (1989: 15)

Métis poet Andrea Menard documents her experience of going "underground":

> I was born the privileged skin
> and my eyes are bright, bright brown.
> You'd never know there is Métis blood
> raging underground.
> Let me tell you a story about a revelation,
> it's not the colour of a nation that holds a nation's pride
> it's imagination
> it's imagination inside. (2001: 32)

Another example can be found through the popular representation of Métis leader Louis Riel. He is generally not acknowledged for his extraordinary education, accomplishments as a political leader or visionary abilities, but rather as a delusional man suffering from mental health issues. As well, his own personal experience with violence and loss, and the ensuing grief, are further obfuscated in the Canadian portrayal of him (Adams 1995; Storey, personal communication 2005). This is part of a broader strategy, facilitated by particular use of colonial discourse, to decontextualize the violence, in this case on the part of the Canadian state, from the suffering of the attacked, to blame victims for their suffering (Coates and Wade 2004).

In a study of Métis identity, "Becoming Métis: The Relationship Between the Sense of Métis Self and Cultural Stories" (Richardson 2004), Métis people demonstrated both pre-existing ability and knowledge of how to be well, as well as an acute analysis of social power. They were keenly aware of the various risks and disadvantages of having relatively less power than European Canadians, particularly if they had dark skin. Through stories and testimonials, the Métis acknowledged that, as marginalized people, they possess few political or civil rights. Many responded to social injustice by trying to maximize their sense of dignity with the "small acts of living" that indicate resistance on physical, spiritual, emotional and intellectual levels. Creating safe spaces for Métis children, and thus ensuring continuity of Métis identity and nationhood, has become a preoccupation of many. This is why many Métis community agencies are in favour of taking control over their child protection and social services.

Experiencing wellbeing and creating a vibrant and evolving sense of Métis self is dependent upon the enactment of prudent and tactical responses in a climate where reprisal and punishment are possible. Through the engagement of the responses identified in this chapter, we can observe how the Métis apply their knowledge of how to be well while simultaneously creating a sense of their Métis self.

In the Absence of Cultural Safety

The Medicine Wheel contains an overview of Métis responses to oppression and racism, actions that are initiated at the various levels of being. Many of these actions serve to keep people safe in times of danger and may be enacted at a conscious, intellectual level or at a more subtle intuitive or physiological level. Although most responses do not stop the violence or danger, they often constitute a form of ethical or political opposition to the injustice. Henry, Tator, Matis and Rees (1995) defined a particular aspect of White/Aboriginal relations in Canada: Canadians are said to value equality and therefore cannot address outstanding issues of racism and oppression against Aboriginal people if it entails treating certain Canadians "unequally." Here, the term "unequal" refers to a Canadian perception of treating Aboriginal people with favouritism or as distinct societies based on historical treaties and commitments. When historical realities are not acknowledged in mainstream culture, events are distorted through a discourse of equality to further disadvantage Aboriginal Canadians. This perceived dilemma decreases cultural safety for Aboriginal Canadians, including the Métis. For example, when caught in situations of oppression, Métis individuals may face increased danger when they speak out or act directly against violence or exclusion. Therefore, many Métis apply "aplomb," defined by as "keeping calm in situations of danger, to prevent an escalation of danger and promote safety" (Richardson 2004: 145). Aplomb is thus explained as acting prudently in the face of danger, while simultaneously responding internally to the oppression or injustice.

Métis people speak of experiencing censure, danger and discrimination in many different ways and enact a number of tactics for self-preservation and the preservation of dignity. As in other forms of oppression, open defiance was the least common form of resistance by victims (Burstow 1992; Coates and Wade 2004; Kelly 1988; Scott 1990). Many Métis responded by trying to keep themselves, their families and their culture alive, but within a cloak of secrecy. One Métis woman said that "being Métis means keeping your mouth shut" (Richardson 2004: 112). She said that her mother told her to not talk about "the family" when she was outside of the home. Her family members used a Scottish surname when applying for jobs and avoided using family names that were identifiable as Métis.

Although much of the discrimination was enacted in the mainstream society, the Métis also experienced racism in non-White communities. Racism within families also manifested, sometimes in response to the fear of social attack. Families were often sworn to silence about their ancestry and experienced reprisals for talking aloud about being Métis. Howard Adams reported: "One of my maternal aunts has refused to allow me in her house or to speak to her because I stated publicly that my mother was of Cree ancestry" (1995: 145). Another Métis woman said: "Prejudice is such an evil thing, and as Métis we often get it from both sides of the blanket. A feeling of never quite belonging anywhere haunts me" (Richardson 2004: 5). She was referring to being seen as neither White enough nor red enough for her European or First Nations communities.

Métis writer Joanne Arnott wrote about her experience of racism and ancestral denial:

> I am a person of mixed Native and European heritages. Fundamentally what I have inherited is a good deal of information about the various European traditions from which I come, and racist denial of the existence of my Native ancestry. (1994: 1)

The experience of being persecuted as both different and undeserving is typical for many Métis people. In this cultural context, disclosing one's identity is unsafe and imprudent. Being treated with dignity and respect takes precedent over the need to be culturally visible. By asserting a social presence that affirms "mixedness," cultural safety is created for others in future. As with all social initiatives, the ones who step forward first tend to face more risk and harm, paving a way for others who follow. Métis child welfare activists speak about Métis-centred services as a way of ensuring the holistic wellbeing of today's Métis children, and those yet unborn.

The Tactic of "Passing" as a Response to Racism

Many Métis people have made strategic decisions to try to "fit in" or "pass" in the dominant culture in order to promote personal or family safety and opportunities for economic and emotional wellness. In the Métis context, passing refers to the act of appearing to belong to another culture, without being noticed as different. For the Métis, passing meant presenting themselves as either White or First Nations in order to escape social ostracism. In colonial society, possessing dark skin has lead to discrimination and positioning as the "other," while light skin has concealed an invisible Métis-ness. Skin colour has been problematic for many Métis people because it has confounded their attempts to protect themselves from racism and hide their Indigenous origins. This leads to the Métis being called "the invisible people." "'Passing' is one of the very few options for survival of a mixed-race people in a virulently racist society" (Arnott 1994: 59). However, passing does not protect the individual from the internal wounds received through witnessing racism towards other Métis people, particularly other family members and loved ones.

Complicated dynamics of racism have been experienced within Métis families where the "colourism" present in mainstream society means lighter people are valued over darker people. However, Métis people have experienced another aspect of this dynamic: being rejected in First Nations communities for being "too White" or "wannabe Indians." On what has been called "the other side of the blanket," one Métis woman talked about her sadness in being excluded from the First Nations world:

> I'd like to say I feel more [in the First Nations world] but that isn't always the case. Now that I am older and am seen as an Elder it is better, but when I was younger I faced a lot of prejudice from Natives because I am very light-skinned. I still feel a bit nervous when I am around "full-bloods" that I don't know well. They don't always treat me like a Native figure. I'm just another "wannabe." That used to hurt most of all. (Richardson 2004: 128)

Other Métis women also shared this nervousness in the First Nations context. One said, "Sometimes I'm nervous round being a Métis person [in a First Nations setting] 'cause I feel like that's [being Métis] frowned upon" (Richardson 2004: 127). Another reported feeling insecure at a powwow, thinking that others were saying, "Why is that White woman here?" (127). A third Métis woman reported that she dealt with being in First Nations settings by "not relaxing," referring to her need to plan what she will say about herself and how she will respond if told that she is an imposter: "Well, I feel like I'm going to be looked at as a White person unless I self-identify, at which point I assume I'm going to be looked at as a Wannabe Indian" (127). She also shared the following experience of helping a Métis man find employment in Vancouver:

> Métis history is amazing. And painful! I mean with all the pressure that Métis people have gone through. For example, one of our members, he's trying to find a job. He's in one field but he wants to move into another field of work. You know, he puts on his resume that he is Métis. His friends have told him, you know, not meaning to be mean or anything, you should drop the Métis from [your] resume. Still, stuff like that is happening! (Richardson 2004: 113)

One Métis man believes that "the worst kind of racism is that which occurs in one's own family":

> When it comes entirely from my family — that is kind of the worst form of discrimination, you know. That's funny because I had an aunt who was very racist, and didn't want anything to do with it [her Métis culture and ancestry], and I guess I just have to accept that. (150)

Detectable in his comment about having to accept racism in families is the message that he does not accept racism of any sort and that he finds racial discrimination morally repugnant. The sadness experienced at moments like this by Métis individuals can be construed as an emotional response to injustice and violations of human dignity.

Métis poet Marilyn Dumont did not have the option of "passing" and writes "all the bleach and soup bones in The Red & White couldn't keep our halfbreed hides from showing through" (1996: 17). Typically, Dumont's Métis friends and family would be placed in the situation of having to decide how to respond to racism; whether to speak out in defence of other Métis and risk being attacked, or whether to say nothing and experience a form of shame or survivor guilt. Both choices were unsafe and unsatisfying and ultimately constitute limited options for action. In a context where social justice is absent and where victims may place themselves at increased risk when they address the injustice, social violence is often used against those with lesser social power. Victims are seldom able to stop the violence that is being perpetuated upon them. To be well emotionally, at the level of integrity, Métis people may look inside themselves to see if they have acted in ways similar to the oppressor. Nick Todd, a therapist who works with male perpetrators and abused women, says that victims of abuse tend to take responsibility in inverse proportion to the perpetrator; hence, he has ironically called this conscious scouring the "law of inverse moral proportion" (Coates, Todd and Wade 2003).

A Métis woman named Sarah demonstrated an application of this law by analyzing her White privilege as an invisible Métis who accessed post-secondary education with ease due to her lightness of skin:

> You know, basically I've always been in the White world. So, you know, I have gotten the advantages of, you know, being White. Going to University, getting my PhD, you know, if I was darker, or looked more Native, it could have been a lot more different. (Richardson 2004: 126)

Sarah and many other Métis who pass as White in the dominant culture have had to sacrifice aspects of their cultural pride, or their right to be "who they are," in order to access the same rights and privileges as other Canadians. The difficult choice of accessing opportunity or risking the denial of that opportunity constitutes another form of the double bind.

The double bind, a term for a lose/lose situation, investigated by anthropologist and communication analyst Gregory Bateson, was recognized as a kind of trap that sometimes constituted a context for schizophrenia after extended periods with no respite. Being caught in a lose/lose situation is reminiscent of the Métis experience of being neither this nor that (e.g., neither White nor First Nations) and being told that you don't belong. The Métis devised tactics to transcend and overcome this Cartesian duality, and these tactics were identified by some Métis people as integral to their health and wholeness. One woman articulated wanting to learn about ways to transcend the limitations of duality: "Being neither one thing nor the other, I would like to explore more of how to take these two traditions and bring them together in a new way of being. But for me it is still a discovering process" (Richardson 2004: 113).

Third Space Possibilities and Sharing Métis Stories

The tactics discussed in this chapter coalesce around the notion of creating a "third space," where Métis-ness, Métis community and Métis knowledge can be shared. In this space, history can be retold from a Métis perspective; a Métis-centred analysis can be honed. Groups who are oppressed, marginalized or who have been harmed in similar ways experience support in joining together to share, discuss, analyze and develop strategies for action (Bhabha 1998 and 1988; Goffman 1963; Reissman 1993). By spending time in Métis-centred situations, "colonial interpretations can be appropriated, translated, rehistoricized, and read anew" (Ashcroft, Griffiths and Tiffin 1995: 184). Métis cultural tactics for how to be well become central to cultural activity, and belonging is implicit. Indeed, the act of visiting can be considered traditional social work practice, in a spirit of natural helping (Carrière, University of Victoria, personal communication, 2009). Visiting entails checking in on people, bringing food, talking, seeing what's going well and what is not. Visiting involves helping people with practical tasks and making sure people are invited to social events to ward off isolation and loneliness. Social work's goal is to extend and preserve a sense of wellbeing for people by facilitating community networks, safety nets and positive social responses that hold people up in times of adversity. It is important to remember that most people who become involved with social workers have experienced violence or oppression in some form. Coates and Wade (2004) have shown that wellbeing after violence is linked directly to the presence of social justice and an accurate account of the nature of the violence, in addition to what has been called a positive social response (Donalek 2001). Goffman (1963) noted the importance of oppressed people coming together to strategize and develop a counterhegemonic discourse to the "dominant story." Similarly, Maori researcher Linda Smith (1999) identifies "the act of witnessing and sharing testimonials" as one way to promote wellness for victims of violence and oppression, and King (2003) invites us to live differently because we have heard important, life-altering stories about the experience of Aboriginal people in North America. Stories have the potential to incite social justice. So how do Métis people enact their knowing how to be well in the absence of social justice? When one Métis woman was told by her university instructor, in a class analyzing issues of race, "Well, you look White, so you are White!" She chose to speak aloud her opposition, stating, "No, I am Métis!" She linked her frustration and anger with her instructor's comment with the fact that "she herself does not identify with the colonizer and does not want to be told she is the colonizer." She added, "I constantly need to fight to prove who I am, and I'm not liking that at all!" (Richardson 2004: 123).

While some Métis people live in the dominant culture and practise "White ways," they think "Métis thoughts" in the privacy of their mind. The resistance of the mind has been documented as "the private, hidden space of consciousness, the 'inside ideas' that allow [women] to transcend the confines of oppression" (Scott 1990: 124). One of the ways to transcend oppression is to tell stories from life-affirming perspectives that help us to feel whole. Stories remind us of how to be well. As cultural psychologist George Howard (1991) says, a culture is a group of people who share the same stories. Métis people share stories about how to be well in spite of having to become culturally invisible and live in non-Métis cultural worlds.

Thomas King says that "stories are a form of medicine" (2003: 92) and, like many good medicines, they fight illness and death. A number of Métis I have spoken with identified the act of sharing stories as a process of soothing in times of difficulty, which could be seen as a way to create a third space — a Métis space. One woman shared numerous stories told to her by her dad. Her family stories served the function of making people feel better in challenging situations. One of her dad's stories was told to help comfort her younger brother when he got in trouble at school:

> When my brother was having trouble at school, [my dad] told a story about when he went to an English school for the first time. He didn't know how to speak English; he only knew how to speak French. And so everybody would come up to him and say things like, "Hey, do you wanna fight?" And he'd be like, "Yeah, yeah sure!" [because he didn't understand what was being said]. And we thought that was just hilarious, like the idea of our dad not knowing how to speak English, or he used to say he was kicked out of Catholic

school because he was too smart for the nuns. And just the idea of that it made it good for my brother because he really struggled with school. I think it made it good for my brother because he'd think to himself, "Well, I'm too smart for my teacher anyway!" (Richardson 2004: 116)

Another Métis man says that he finds hope in sharing stories and he experiences a strengthening in his Métis cultural identity and pride:

By telling the story, I hope that it inspires people and that there's not going to be any feelings of shame for anyone about being open about their heritage.... It does create hope. It also creates a sense of ownership. These are my stories; these stories affect me. It brings me closer to feeling pride in my Métis community — the feeling that I am Métis. It's not just a label. This is what I am. It's more of a validation that I am part of a race of people. (Richardson 2004: 157)

Sometimes, people need a safe space where stories can be shared and respected as cultural knowledge. For Métis people, Métis-specific cultural spaces are important for preserving the sacredness of stories and they use stories as discursive strategies for propagating a particular point of view (Coates and Wade 2004); in this case for advancing the view that is it good to be Métis and that it is safe to be Métis. Such conditions help in the strengthening of Métis cultural identity.

Creating a Third Space Community

A third space offers a place where hybridity, or being mixed-race, can be experienced holistically and celebrated as central to Métis culture. A third space offers an escape from Cartesian duality and polarized thinking of Métis as being a White person with some Indian blood or a Native person with some White ancestors. Guyanese writer Wilson Harris identified this opportunity as accompanying an "assimilation of contraries" (1973: 60). Homi Bhabha conceives of the third space as a holistic place where

unity is not found in the sum of its parts, but emerges from the process of opening a third space within which other elements encounter and transform each other. It is not the combination, accumulation, fusion or synthesis, but an energy field of different forces. (1998: 208)

This energy field of different forces constitutes a place that feels qualitatively different than other cultural spaces for many Métis. One woman described it as the pleasure in being together with other Métis people, in Métis settings, in contrast with her experience in the Euro-Canadian world: "When you are together with other Métis people, it's a pleasure. But otherwise you're always ashamed. It's really true… always have that feeling that you're inferior, and you don't believe it, but it's true" (Richardson 2004: 129). Similarly, there can be a sense of recognition when one is together with other Métis people:

> There was a room full of Métis people and people who really — it was strange — it was like almost sometimes like the same sense of humour as my own family, and sometimes really reinforcing for the way I was brought up, and for my background and things that happened. (129)

Another stated that she feels most clear and articulate in Métis settings:

> I think I'm more confident in the Métis world, like I feel better that I am able to articulate who I am and what the issues are for Métis people as well as myself, as a Métis person, better than in any other setting. (130)

Individuals described first finding this sense of Métis community in a variety of locations, such as a Métis community agency, a Native treatment centre, on a grandmother's porch, on the prairies, and together with Métis family and friends in homes and outdoors (Richardson 2004). They also experienced intuitive processes that offered clues or insights about Métis ancestry. These experiences help Métis people find a sense of "home" and help connect them to other Métis people. Intuitive experiences included possessing an affinity towards other Métis before knowing they were Métis. Many Métis have perceived incongruence in their family history when Métis culture was kept hidden. Sometimes contrasting information would emerge, creating holes in the official family story. Métis children who had been adopted into other families or raised in foster care were sometimes not told about their Métis ancestry. It is not uncommon to have an intuitive sense of one's origins, even before evidence is produced.

Métis children are often born with "Mongolian blue spots" or have had "Native" dreams, visions or visitors from the spirit world. Many Métis report mystical experiences in nature that hold some meaning for their identity (Richardson 2004; Scofield 1999; Trudeau 1999). Métis people often report having epiphanies or "aha!" moments when they discover they are Métis, and feel that they knew (at some level) all along (Richardson 2004: 32–35). Métis ancestry and hidden identity tend to live within the realm of family secrets and are often revealed on the deathbed of an Elder (36). Family secrets often constitute the double bind, where people may suffer if they talk about the family secret through losing the affection of a loved one, and they suffer if they don't talk about it by being denied the "truth" about themselves and their culture. Information and family stories are instrumental in finding one's way to cultural identity. Spending time together with other Métis, in third space Métis settings, may involve a process of gathering genealogical information and finding relatives. Through the sharing of stories, Métis people gain a stronger sense of who they are and what it means to be Métis.

When we initially asked Métis people to tell us some of their Métis stories, participants commonly replied that they didn't have any stories. When they related the story of their life and their journeys towards a greater sense of Métis self, we would then retell the story to them. Participants were commonly astonished that they had "a Métis story" — often a story of not knowing what it means to be Métis after generations of keeping Métis culture underground, as well as the process of finding their way back home.

Métis psychological wellness is strengthened through the experience of being a whole, rather than "part" Indian: As a political and cultural strategy of opening a space of possibility and opportunity, "the application of a third space thinking... quite properly challenges our sense of the historical identity of culture as a homogenizing, unifying force" (Bhabha 1998: 208). In the process of forward motion, the Métis create new possibilities for identity and cultural expression. Métis people can place themselves back in the centre of their cultural universe. The enactment of a wide range of strategic responses, at the intellectual, physical, spiritual and emotional aspects of self, serves to promote social justice, community safety and awareness of the Métis in the Canadian cultural landscape. While we continue to experience violence of various forms, we are required, in our beings, to compartmentalize and make tactical decisions about the aspects of self that we put forward in the world. Social justice creates a ground on which Métis people, and others who have been de-centred, neglected and abused, may begin to demonstrate their sacred concerns in the outer world. Dana Lynn Seaborn, a Métis songwriter, captures a longing for wholeness and sacred connection in her song "When will we learn?":

> When will we learn to see the sacred;
> How can we know we're not alone;
> Where will we find a way to heal our mother earth;
> When will we find our way back home?
> Oh Eagle of the east bring inspiration;
> Great bison of the south, the strength to be;
> Orca of the west bring integration;
> Great Bear of the north, the mystery.

Implications for Social Work with Métis People

This chapter outlines some of the historical and ongoing challenges facing Métis people and provides a glimpse into their experiences in Canada. It is offered as an educational tool for those working in the helping professions to better understand Métis identity and Métis reality. It is important for social workers in particular to understand the people they work with, and given that Métis life has been well hidden, this work offers important cultural and social understanding of Métis experiences. It articulates Métis responses and tactics of resistance to oppression. These tactics include acting with aplomb, passing, sharing stories and creating community in a Métis third space as means to support Métis-ness and Métis culture.

In terms of practical recommendations for social workers who are entrusted with the lives of Métis children and the wellbeing of families, there are a number of points for guidance. Interaction must begin by identifying a set of dignifying practices that restore and acknowledge Métis children in terms of Métis culture. Dignifying practices include restoring to families what has been taken from them, either literally or symbolically, in child protection encounters.[1] This means understanding that many Métis families have lived underground culturally for some time and may have delicate and carefully negotiated relationships with Métis identity; they may be selective of how and with whom they discuss family history. It means understanding that there are still risks to "coming out" and identifying as Métis in Canadian and First Nation contexts, where Métis are still largely misunderstood and misrepresented.

Social workers need take a position of advocacy and "hold back the walls" that close in on Métis children and families, to create as much safety as possible and to combat oppressive practices. Finally, being sensitive to Métis children means taking an overt position that notions of racial superiority are evil constructs and that diversity of all forms is to be celebrated and cherished. There is no such thing as "pure race" outside of the bounds of eugenics and hate literature. Louis Riel's vision for the Métis homeland — Métisoma — was to create a place of peace and refuge for the Métis as well as to extend an invitation to others who were fleeing oppression and in search of peace and justice. At the time of his execution, Riel had a letter published in the *Irish Times* condemning the barbarism of the British empire worldwide and inviting those who believe in justice to not forget the Métis. It is this same spirit that Métis advocates invoke in our interaction with child protection services. Preserving children and culture is equated with preserving peace (non-violence), justice and families. "Decolonization itself is contained within a larger wheel that is grinding the earth to dust (Bruyere 1999: 177). Like the original saboteurs, we must continue to insert our clogs into the machinery to keep our children from harm and assimilation. We must facilitate a strong identity for the Métis child, upholding or restoring connections to family members, to cultural practice and to Earth. This work cannot be done alone, but requires relationships of solidarity based on a shared longing for social justice. Under these conditions, we will best be able to see the sacred in ourselves and one another. Then, Métis people will take their place alongside others in recognition of their rightful place on Turtle Island.

Note

1. Dignifying practices are currently being articulated and highlighted by Allan Wade and Cathy Richardson in the "Islands of Safety" work, based on a child and family safety planning model in cases of domestic violence in Métis and urban Aboriginal communities.

Chapter 7

Evolution and Revolution
Healing Approaches with Aboriginal Adults

Cyndy Baskin (On-koo-khag-kno kwe)

Indigenous people are said to be leading the largest healing movement throughout Turtle Island. This is consistent with the Seven Fires Prophesies of the Anishinaabe, which tell us we are currently in the time of re-learning our cultures. My understanding of Indigenous healing approaches with adults is that they are based on holistic worldviews that see individuals in the context of their families and communities. These approaches also need to include consciousness-raising — assisting Indigenous adults in understanding that much of their circumstances are the direct result of colonization rather than individual failing or pathology.

This chapter explores the evolution of my involvement, and that of other Indigenous social workers/helpers, in healing with Indigenous adults over the past two decades. Healing is achieving wholeness, which focuses on the health and wellness of our bodies, minds, hearts and spirits. I follow the Canadian Collaborative Mental Health Initiative's definition of healing, which includes the following:

> Living in harmony with and being able to provide for our families and communities;
>
> Knowing who we are, where we belong, that we matter and are accepted;
>
> Feeling at peace with the Creator;
>
> Caring for others, being cared for, feeling pride in ourselves and having others believe in our abilities;
>
> Learning from our successes and mistakes and accepting the challenges that life offers;
>
> Knowing our history and cultures; and
>
> Being responsible for our actions and understanding that our actions can shape our futures. (2006)

The chapter takes up the following questions: What do Indigenous and western approaches to helping Indigenous adults look like? Do Indigenous culture-based healing programs exist or are they combined with western approaches to social work? and What Indigenous approaches are of benefit to all of humanity and are they showing up in non-Indigenous services?

Why Do Indigenous Peoples Become Involved with Social Workers?

Indigenous people come to social work services sometimes on their own but more often at the mandate of social control systems such as justice and child welfare. For some, conflict with the law includes a directive to complete alcohol and drug treatment or an anger management program. Parents involved with the Children's Aid Society (CAS) tend to be ordered to complete programs such as parenting courses and individual counselling in order to keep their children in their care or have them returned to their care. Thus, adults may be coerced into accessing services rather than coming to them voluntarily.

In my years of experience as a front-line social worker, the majority of adults who came to me for services were pressured in one way or another to do so, either by the courts, the CAS or a partner giving an ultimatum, "get help or I'll leave you." However, such experiences are not necessarily negative. Most adults who came to me were resistant or at least guarded at first, and rightly so. Small acts of resistance, such as sitting sullenly or not answering questions, are ways of holding on to one's personal power. And yet, most of these adults quickly decided that the services were helpful to them and continued long after the required number of sessions or circles were completed.

The presenting issues that most Indigenous adults bring to the attention of social workers are depression, suicide attempts, alcohol and drug misuse, sexual and physical abuse and family violence. Many of these adults had been victimized sexually and physically at the hands of several adults throughout their lives. This violence has created out-of-balance adults who in turn may perpetuate the cycle of abuse with their partners, children and other family members. The many traumas that Indigenous people have faced have created this spiral effect, which stems from unresolved guilt, disenfranchised grief and internalized self-hatred — the legacy of colonization. The guilt, grief and self-hatred are all symptoms of what has come to be referred to as the "historical trauma response" (Yellow Horse Brave Heart and DeBruyn 1998: 61). Indigenous adults tend to access social work services when these responses have grown out of their control or are no longer working for them. It is at this time that most social workers will see an Indigenous person — when they are mandated and/or most emotionally fragile. Because of this it is crucial that helpers of Indigenous adults understand the colonization process and the effects it has had on the last several generations.

Unresolved guilt has occurred due to generations of genocidal practices that have left present day Indigenous adults feeling that they do not deserve to be alive when so many of their relations were raped, tortured and killed. The atrocities that Indigenous populations have been subjected to have not been properly mourned, as many of the traditions around death and dying have been taken away through colonization, leaving our people without culturally appropriate ways to grieve and recover. In addition, the western idea of the stoic Indigenous person has hampered the grieving process by creating an environment where expressions of loss cannot be openly acknowledged or mourned (Yellow Horse Brave Heart and DeBruyn 1998).

Traumas that have been faced by generations of Indigenous people are now part of our collective memory. These painful and destructive memories, passed from one generation to the next, perpetuates the cycle of unhealthy interactions and relationships with family members, community members and the self — struggles that need to be addressed as a whole. The effects of disenfranchised grief (named as anger, guilt and helplessness) have created shame within Indigenous people. This shame of their own culture and community has spurred internalized racism and hatred that must be worked through even before the guilt and grief. According to some authors, resolving these reactions to the colonization process is not an individual endeavour. Rather, healing needs to begin at the community and nation levels before it can progress towards work with families and individuals (Wesley-Esquimaux and Smolewski 2004).

Aaron R. Denham (2008) suggests that "historical unresolved grief" and the "historical trauma response" can be healed through using stories and narratives to reframe trauma or the wound into an act of resistance. This is a means to acknowledge the strength and cultural power that Indigenous individuals, families and communities possess even though they may not be conscious of it. He suggests that it is by finding the connections to a lived experience and passing that knowledge on to the next generation that Indigenous people can heal, decolonize and strengthen communities, families and individuals. This can be done within the context of an Indigenous person's life as they can use their own personal story, which might include sexual abuse and drug and alcohol misuse, to explain the effects of colonization upon themself.

Western Approaches to Social Work with Indigenous Adults

Many social work academics, researchers and practitioners — both Indigenous and non-Indigenous — have referred to social work as an arm of colonization (Baskin 2005; Carniol 2005; Hart 2002[1]). This criticism has particularly been emphasized in the front-line services of child welfare and mental health (Bellefeuille and Ricks 2003; Gair et al. 2002; Hurdle 2002[2]) and within social work education and research (Baskin 2005; Battiste and Youngblood Henderson 2000; Holmes 2000[3]). Both historically and today, the partial aim of social work has been social control.

One of the main problems when non-Indigenous helpers work with Indigenous adults is that they overlook the Indigenous person's culturally held beliefs and values, instead using an approach to social work they assume to be universal. The role that worldviews and cultures can play in problem identification, manifestation and causes, and ideas around solutions to problems, tends to be disregarded by helpers of non-Indigenous descent (Weaver 2004). Approaches within western ways of helping that may not fit with Indigenous worldviews include the following:

- individualistic rather than a community-based;
- offering counseling services to an abused partner while leaving the abusive partner out;
- strictly talk therapy instead of holistic methods, which deal with all the parts of a person;
- adhering to strict professional boundaries rather than more flexible ones; and
- ignoring spirituality instead of seeing it as a strength.

Furthermore, as Maria Napoli and Edwin Gonzalez-Santin 2001: 317) stress "a knowledgeable professional who does not fit a personality profile with which the community feels comfortable will not be able to successfully deliver services." Just because a social worker is Indigenous, this helper might not be the best person to work with any particular Indigenous community or group of people. It is imperative that the community feels comfortable, respected and have a part in decision-making when it comes to choosing individuals to work within social services in that community. In my work, I usually said to a first-time potential service user, "I am not the only option for you. When you leave today, think about whether or not you want to continue seeing me. If you're sitting here thinking, 'I can't stand this person,' then you have the choice to decide to try someone else."

Indigenous Worldviews in Social Work

Indigenous social workers and other helpers who strive to assist individuals, families and communities from the perspectives of their worldviews, tend to emphasize the following areas: culture-based, holistic, positive identity and help for the helpers.

Culture Based

An Indigenous approach to social work and being a helper is one that seeks harmony and balance among individuals, the family and community (Baskin 2002a). In using the teachings that have been given to Indigenous peoples, the worldviews strive to re-balance all aspects of an individual, family, community and society. This is done with the recognition that when the physical, emotional, psychological and spiritual aspects within an individual are out of balance, the rest of the family and community are also out of balance (Baskin 2002a; Hart 2002). This is one of the most fundamental teachings and is the basis for learning to work from an Indigenous worldview.

In my work with Indigenous adults, I always strove to incorporate techniques that addressed all four aspects of a person. Believing that emotions and traumatic memories can be stuck in the body, causing physical illnesses and unexplained pains, I implemented ways of assisting adults to release these emotions. Releases took place through, for example, body movements such as shaking, stretching and punching a pillow, meditation, visualization, yelling and crying. The emotional aspect was attended to by inviting adults to talk about their emotions and experience, both those on the surface and those that had been buried for many years. To work on the psychological level, adults created safe spaces where they could tell their stories without judgement, remember deeply buried past experiences and then re-tell the stories from a place of greater understanding. The spiritual aspect was addressed in such ways as prayer, smudging, participation in ceremonies and dream interpretation.

Holism

I also emphasized in my work the inter-connectedness of individual adults to their families, communities, other adults, Mother Earth, all of creation, the Creator and all of the spirit world. It is important for adults in pain to realize that they are both affected by and have an impact on everything and everyone around them. They also need to see that their connection to other people, the earth and the spirit world can be a powerful source of healing for them; that they can communicate with and gain clarity from their ancestors in the spirit world; that holding a rock can give them strength; and that water can soothe and calm them.

At times, my work with adults around achieving harmony and balance with family and community members or people from their past was literal, for example, bringing family and other community members together for healing circles and ceremonies where unresolved issues could be raised and worked through. At other times, when gathering people together was unsafe, unwanted or not possible because those from the past were no longer living, we worked on achieving harmony and balance symbolically. For instance, adults could write letters, which they later burned in a sacred fire; they could imagine the person from the past sitting in the room with them and talk to that person; or they could speak with the spirit of a person who had passed on while in a sweat lodge ceremony or at a feast for the dead. These activities, which help to free people from the holds of the past, bring balance for the individual adult, which then ripples outward to have positive effects on their relationships with others.

Positive Identity

There are many ways in which Indigenous cultures and the sense of a positive identity as an Indigenous person are important to maintaining health and wellbeing. When urban Dakota and Dene peoples in Winnipeg were asked to state certain indicators that they felt revealed poverty levels and personal struggles (Ten Fingers 2005), both groups identified lack of education and training, underemployment and poor living conditions. Changes to these structural issues were seen as important, but all participants also included the need for family and community involvement, along with cultural teachings, spirituality and ceremonies as necessary in their lives.

A group of fifty Indigenous adults in British Columbia explained a time they needed help or healing and what approaches worked or did not work for them (McCormick 1995). Seventy percent of the participants in this project mentioned that "expressing oneself" emotionally was healing while 66 percent cited "establishing a connection with nature," "anchoring oneself in traditions" and "participating in ceremonies" (287). This study not only showed the resilience of Indigenous peoples but the resilience of, and belief in, Indigenous culture as sources of help and healing.

Research by C. June Strickland, Elaine Walsh and Michelle Cooper (2006) corroborates these findings. Their work was conducted with Elders and parents of youth at risk for suicide. Both groups recognized that, although the theft of cultures and traditional practices through the process of colonization were huge problems, communities are able to re-build their strengths and support their members in healthy ways through the revitalization of traditions and healthy identities.

In my helping work with adults over the years, I came to firmly believe that not having an identity strongly grounded in their cultural teachings is at the root of the problems people came to me about. All the counselling, therapy and healing in the world are not going to truly help an Indigenous adult if they do not come to a place of being intensely proud of their identity. There are many things that we can change about ourselves, but blood is not one of them. Mere acceptance of being an Indigenous person is not enough. All of us must embrace, cherish and celebrate our Indigenous identities in order to be whole and healthy. Whole means, of course, including all aspects of our Indigenous identity — sexual orientation, gender, abilities, and so on.

Needless to say, internalized racism has made it difficult for many Indigenous people to feel proud of who they are. Thus, my work with them on how they saw themselves and other Indigenous people and where these beliefs came from, was crucial in their healing journey. The internalized stereotypes were gradually replaced with knowledge and understanding through discussion, questioning, challenging, research, spending time with other Indigenous people, attending events and ceremonies, learning about pre and post colonization, role modeling and mentoring.

A significant way in which adults come to be proud of their Indigenous identity is through reclamation of inherent markers such as their clan and name. These aspects of each of us help define who we are and what our purpose in this life is. In my work, I assisted many adults claim what they ought to have been given at birth. This process involved supporting adults to go to family members, visit their home communities, offer tobacco to Elders, ask spirit for help through prayer and ceremonies such as fasting, in order to know the clans they belong to and receive the names that tell them who they are.

Help for the Helper

Another significant area of Indigenous worldviews that relates to social work with adults is the focus on the helper and the relationship between the person giving help and the one receiving it. What is typically referred to as "help for the helpers" means that social workers not only need to practise self-care, but they also need to be supported and nurtured by their family, community and agency. The elements of self-care are individual to each helper and involve whatever healthy, positive methods that person uses to ensure holistic balance. This can range from physical exercise to participating in ceremonies to listening to music.

However, the notion of help for the helpers is much more than self-care and support networks. Social work with adults can be emotionally and spiritually draining. It is helpful to have updated knowledge in many areas, such as how the system works and where to find specific resources. In addition, keeping abreast of new knowledge through ongoing professional education can assist in building confidence and maintaining optimism in one's practice. In these ways, continuing education is a form of self-care and, therefore, part of help for the helpers. Social workers need to be fully equipped to challenge oppressive social and political systems, advocate for people and work towards social change.

Another aspect of help for the helper is the notion within Indigenous worldviews that each of us learns from many different people and situations.

Helpers can learn a great deal from those who are receiving their help, the ones bringing forth their stories and experiences to share. Helpers are privileged to receive such learning, which is not likely to come from a textbook or a classroom.

The teachings within Indigenous worldviews contain the information about what being a helper entails. This is expressed through the values of collectivity — the importance of working together for the wellbeing of the group; reciprocity — the insurance of consistently giving and receiving; honouring those who do what must be done — the recognition of those who work with humility for the people; and respect for Elders — the ones who are our biggest helpers and who carry our teachings so they can share them with those who do the helping. Indigenous social workers require spaces where they can come together to share their pain and joy, exchange ideas and take care of one another. When one is tired, the rest of us need to work a little harder. And when one of us cannot meet the high expectations that are placed upon us, or stumbles or even falls, the rest of us need to care for that person, rather than pass judgment upon them, knowing that one day, we will likely be in that place of need as well.

Support for social workers/helpers also needs to come from their community and agency. This can take many forms, such as providing appropriate resources, adequate pay, manageable case loads, hearing their suggestions for improvements, honouring their strengths and assisting them to learn new skills, ensuring access to Elders and ceremonies and involving them in decision-making. Such an approach conforms to the values of Indigenous worldviews, which emphasize collectivity, consensus and that each person has something important to contribute to the whole.

For several years, I had the privilege to work at an agency where my supervisor's approach truly supported my work with adults. This supervisor carried the responsibilities of her position while never making me feel like a subordinate. She provided plenty of direction, was process oriented, involved me in decision-making, was secure enough to ask for my guidance at times and consistently made me feel valued. We supported each other and cared about one another's wellbeing. We worked as a team. Because of her support, I was assisted in being the best I could be, which had positive impacts on my work with adults. To this day, this woman is a friend and mentor, and I credit her with helping me become who I was meant to be.

Relationships in Indigenous Social Work

Within Indigenous worldviews there is a strong emphasis on relationships. The relationship between a person giving help and a person receiving it is seen as a natural part of life. If you need some help, because I can, I will help you. Tomorrow, next month or next year, when I need help, you will help me because you can. When relationships are built on reciprocity, there is no stigma attached to requiring assistance. This view of helping relationships makes way for a more personal situation between a service provider and a service user. Boundaries between the two tend to be flexible, and appropriate self-disclosure on the part of the social worker is viewed as a teaching method. Service providers and service users may participate in ceremonies and other gatherings together. Often, there is a family connection or friendship between the two. This applies not only in small communities, but it is also relevant in large urban centres, such as Vancouver or Toronto, that have Indigenous communities.

My own social work experiences reflect these circumstances. Both past service users and students have become colleagues and friends. My step-children have referred their friends to me for services. Colleagues have become service users. I have conducted ceremonies in which service users, family members and friends have all participated. My relationships with Indigenous service users and students are different from those I have with non-Indigenous people because I feel differently towards them. The work I do with Indigenous individuals and communities is not my career — it is my life. It is all about who I am and what I am meant to be doing here.

A final point can be made about helping relationships and being helped. How many of us Indigenous social workers have not been impacted by colonization? How many of us have not gone through the circumstances that adult service users come to us with? How many of us have not coped with these experiences in similar ways? How many of us would be where we are today if someone had not been our helper for a while? When I sit with an Indigenous adult, I remember to give thanks for what has been given to me and for the opportunity to give back. I also see a person who will one day be a helper because giving back comes in many ways.

Indigenous Social Work in Practice

What does Indigenous social work look like in practice?[4] What is currently offered is a combination of Indigenous worldviews and western approaches. Indigenous controlled services — from healing lodges for federal offenders to child welfare to addictions treatment — now exist across Canada in First Nations communities and urban centres. Typically, in describing their culture-based approaches to service provision, agencies and centres refer to "programs that reflect Aboriginal culture," "a space that incorporates Aboriginal peoples' tradition[s] and beliefs" and addresses needs "through Aboriginal teachings and ceremonies, contact with Elders…and interaction with nature" (Okimaw Ohci Healing Lodge 2006).

Correctional Services Canada has become involved in providing

Indigenous specific programs. Some healing lodges/residential centres are set up for families. One such lodge for women in Saskatchewan describes its residential units as containing "a bedroom, a bathroom, a kitchenette with an eating area, a living room, and, in those units that are built to accommodate children, a playroom" (Okimaw Ohci Healing Lodge 2006). There is even an onsite daycare facility. Services are described as addressing what is needed "emotionally, physically, and spiritually to heal." This includes programs for mothers and their children, outdoor programs and those that are "Aboriginal-specific... such as language...." Another centre that stands out is located in Alberta and was developed in consultation with the Samson Cree First Nation. According to the website, this centre adheres to many of the perspectives within Indigenous worldviews:

> Pe Sakastew Centre is a federally owned minimum-security facility, located on land owned by the Samson Cree First Nation and leased to the CSC [Correctional Services Canada]. Consultations with community Elders on the values and beliefs of the Samson Cree led to an architectural design that reflects the Aboriginal world view. Six circular buildings are arranged in a large circle on the 40-acre site. Symbols significant to the Samson Cree First Nation, such as the medicine wheel, the four directions, and the colors red, yellow, white, and black, were integrated into the centre's design. The programs at Pe Sakastew Centre are based on the belief that Aboriginal spirituality is central to the healing process for Aboriginal offenders. Elders from surrounding Aboriginal communities instruct inmates in traditional values and spiritual practices, while offering counseling and serving as role models. Aboriginal values and beliefs inform the programs, whether they are specifically Aboriginal in subject or not. Thus, inmates who are unfamiliar with Aboriginal practices have a chance to learn about them, while those who are familiar with them are re-exposed to the traditions that will aid them on their path to healing.

A scan of services for Indigenous adults also reveals many non-Indigenous approaches to helping/healing. Many of these agencies focus on training service providers. For example, one such centre in Ontario and another in British Columbia explain their services as being "holistic programs that educate and train individuals" in order to "start a spark that will unite our minds, bodies and spirits." This includes "holistic counseling, reiki[5] training, emotional freedom technique," and "under the guidance of Elders, we offer Medicine Wheel Facilitator training... [which] consists of an introduction to the Medicine Wheel concepts, smudging ceremony, sharing circles, residential schools, stories, legends, and an opportunity to facilitate a Medicine Wheel presentation…. This workshop is not found anywhere else in North America" (Universal Energy Training and Learning Centre 2006; Kakakaway and Associates 2006).

Whitepath, an Ontario agency that offers training for social services workers asserts that it has "a new approach that works," which includes "a culturally appropriate assessment tool" (Wesley-Esquimaux and Smolewski 2004). This organization focuses on "Aboriginal programs in Addictions, Violence Prevention, Emotion Management and Pre-Employment." Its website states:

> In association with Trent University's Emotion and Health Laboratory, Whitepath conducts extensive qualitative research that includes facilitating focus groups, developing culturally-appropriate data collection instruments, analyzing data, conducting feasibility studies, creating and delivering needs assessments as well as formulating and supporting the implementation of research recommendations. Whitepath's success in connecting the disconnected to the community at large is the result of its programs of prevention, intervention and reintegration. Whitepath's goal is to integrate its unique personal training approach, TheRedPath model, in every Aboriginal community, in both urban and rural settings.

In addition to how agencies describe themselves in their mission statements, mandates, websites and brochures, it is also important to hear what both service providers and users have to say about the services and programs being offered and implemented. Do agencies do what they say they will do? What does "culture-based" look like in practice? How are Indigenous values and teachings implemented?

What Service Providers Say

To get an idea about culture-based practice from both service providers and users, I located a dozen across Canada and asked them to anonymously answer the following question from their respective points of view: What does social work/helping look like in practice at this agency?

Responses from service providers seemed to be along a continuum of how much influence comes from Indigenous ways of helping and how much from western approaches. Several practitioners alluded to the tokenism of Indigenous approaches within programming and services. As Carrie (not her real name) stated, "In the agency where I work, culture is represented by smudging with our clients. It's all superficial — not culture-based."

Many responses to the question put out to service providers came from practitioners who work at family and children's services that were once voluntary but that have become mandated child protection agencies, meaning they have been given the legal responsibility by the government to protect children, including apprehending them if they believe this is needed. Typically, Indigenous voluntary agencies in child welfare focus not only on child protection, but also incorporate programs such as individual counselling, substance misuse treatment, family violence interventions and family therapy. Mandy (pseudonym) eloquently articulated the stressful transition from voluntary to mandated services:

> In the past, I believe my agency worked with adults in a very healing way. Social workers focused on developing a positive, healthy relationship [with adults] based on trust and the work started where the client was at. Once the agency became mandated in the area of child protection, the focus changed as did the agency's philosophy. The mandate of child protection is very rigid in many ways and is based on a Eurocentric framework. Efforts to include cultural practices in case work is encouraged but there is little training. The worker is now the expert on the [client's] situation and the adult must conform to certain requirements.

Steve (pseudonym) offered similar feedback, saying "while the agency purports to be culturally based, there is no overall framework developed or implemented for integrating cultural knowledge into day to day work with clients. Such decisions are left to individual workers with varying results from positive outcomes that promote healing to acts of racism."

Some service providers who work in urban centres critiqued Indigenous services and programs for perhaps relying too much on them to assess how much adults were interested in their cultures and for implementing the practices of one particular nation upon all Indigenous peoples. Rob (pseudonym) described these issues this way:

> We [service providers] are expected to navigate where clients are at in terms of their cultural identity and desire or distaste for culture-based care. [Another] issue is that there is so much diversity of Aboriginal clients in [big cities] and yet most services are presented from only one specific [Aboriginal Nation's] perspective or practices. [Both of these issues] raise the question of whether or not this is a fit with what clients are seeking.

Interestingly enough, practitioners working in Indigenous agencies serving adults who are involved with the justice system responded more favourably in terms of their agency's Indigenous practices. The following response from Elsie (not her real name) is representative of service providers who work within this context:

> Adults in the agency where I work are helped through community driven programs. This process is based on Aboriginal values of respect and kindness and mimics the way issues have been dealt with historically. Rather than take the person charged out of the community, our agency volunteers seek to bring our people closer to their community in order to restore balance and to help begin the healing process. In addition, those we work with are recipients of service that is mindful of the impacts of colonization and our agency serves as advocates to change the systemic discrimination that exists.

Obviously this small sample cannot be taken as representative of Indigenous social workers everywhere. Nevertheless, it appears that approaches in working with adults may be connected to the type of agency and how it is perceived by the community. In the case of a mandated child welfare agency, community members may view it, and its social workers, as agents of social control or policing, given that they have the power to apprehend a community's children. However, an Indigenous agency that advocates for adults involved in the criminal justice system may be seen more as an agent of social change or assistance. Thus, Indigenous child welfare may be viewed as working for the system whereas Indigenous justice agencies may be viewed as working against the system. The point along the continuum of social control and social change where agencies are positioned is likely to affect how much they are able to implement Indigenous worldviews and cultures into their services. Hence, we have the predominant situation of agencies implementing a combination of Indigenous and western approaches in their services for adults.

What Service Users Say

Indigenous people who use social services also had diverse responses to what practices look like at these agencies. Again, I remind readers that these responses are not meant to be representative of Indigenous service users. Some service users responded to the question by talking about how they were treated at agencies based on their physical appearance (namely skin colour). As Jess (not his real name) mentioned, "I feel respected in any Aboriginal agency that I have accessed even though I have white skin." However, Georgina (not her real name) had the opposite to say:

> I have experienced racism in seeking services from Aboriginal agencies, based on the whiteness of my skin. This has certainly affected

my help-seeking behaviour as a client. I see this as an issue of serious concern.... [For] mixed [race] or pale [skinned] clients, such experiences, when they are extremely vulnerable and requiring help, could be very damaging, if not dangerous.

How do we account for the extreme difference in the experiences of these two service users, plus many more to whom I have spoken over the years? My guess is that some Indigenous service providers assume that White skin equals belonging to the White race and, as most Indigenous social services agencies are meant for Indigenous peoples only, this is a reaction about who is eligible for services. In a time when many Canadians are claiming some Indigenous heritage and agency resources are scarce, caution around eligibility needs to be taken. Perhaps once it becomes clear that a person is Indigenous regardless of skin colour, acceptance will follow. Nevertheless, service providers, guided by the agencies they work for, need to be mindful of their assumptions and biases and ensure respect towards all. Respect, after all, means "to look twice."

Samantha (not her real name) made another significant comment about service provision:

When I began my healing journey years ago, I ran into two influential Aboriginal people with social work degrees who worked with me in a client-centred way and allowed me to be my own healer, while giving me some tools I desperately needed to be where I am today. I credit both of them for contributing to the way I work today and some of the little things that make me a better social worker. I am now colleagues with both of these women, but I still find myself learning from them. They make me proud to be in the social work field.

This quote, which addresses relationships between Indigenous service providers and users, reinforces what I wrote earlier in this chapter. This service user clearly views service providers as mentors who greatly influenced their decision to go into social work. It is an example of relationships being fluid and boundaries less rigid.

Challenges to Implementing Indigenous Worldviews into Social Work

While analyzing the stories of service providers and users of Indigenous social service agencies and, reflecting on my experiences, a number of challenges come to light. These challenges around implementing Indigenous values, teachings and cultures into practice include questions such as: Who makes the important decisions? How are community members involved?

Where does the funding come from, and how and by whom is research and evaluation conducted? It becomes clear that the overall question is "Who has control?"

No doubt there are enormous restrictions placed on Indigenous social services agencies. Although they have control over certain policies and procedures within their agencies, they have to comply with government legislation, social policies and dominant ideologies, which are mandated and funded by federal and provincial statutes. Eurocentric social policies and legislation, which do not address the colonization of Aboriginal peoples, inevitably influence and restrict models of service provision. Researchers in the area of Indigenous child welfare, Marilyn Bennett, Cindy Blackstock and Richard De La Ronde, write:

> Up to this day, provisions, in both federal and provincial legislation dictate how child welfare will be governed, administered, and, often, delivered by the over 120+ Aboriginal Child and Family Services Agencies in Canada. This would not be so controversial if the provincial and federal systems were meeting the needs of Aboriginal children and youth but the evidence overwhelmingly indicates that the current legislation, policy and practice of child welfare are not making meaningful differences in supporting the wellbeing of Aboriginal children and youth. The question is thus raised why Canadian governments have not recognized tribal authority that sustained child wellbeing for millennia. (2005: 45)

It is a daunting task to take an institution, such as child welfare, that has left behind such a deplorable legacy, and turn it into something healthy and appropriate for Indigenous individuals, families and communities. Though perhaps helpful for some service providers and users, merely adding a few cultural practices here and there is clearly not enough. What is needed is a framework that addresses the negative impacts of colonization on Indigenous peoples and emphasizes our strengths. Legal and political discourses regarding self-government and Indigenous rights and treaties are grounded in notions of nationhood that originate from European history. Such discourses ignore and marginalize Indigenous worldviews. Inevitably, this approach continues to entrench Eurocentric-Canadian structural power imbalances, rather than creating positive economic, political and social change for Indigenous peoples. As these power imbalances trickle downward, they seep into all aspects of our lives, including how services are delivered within our social services agencies. Until constructions of nationhood are examined from both an Indigenous and a Eurocentric lens equally, developing self-government that creates inclusive and sustainable Indigenous communities and social services agencies will be impossible.

Isn't Social Work More Than This?

Social work with Indigenous adults must deal with the roots of issues rather than only the symptoms — such as substance misuse or depression. Such roots go much deeper than personal experiences of childhood sexual abuse or growing up in a family struggling with addictions. All of these issues have their roots in colonization, which in Canada is a political situation unique to Indigenous peoples. In recent years, a movement has begun to recognize and heal from the horrific violations stemming from colonization, which have marked the lives of Indigenous peoples, families and communities. This movement has been driven by Indigenous communities and nations through the work of Indigenous social workers and other helpers, such as Elders and traditional teachers (Denham 2008; Mussell 2006; Weaver 2004; Wesley-Esquimaux and Smolewski 2004[6]).

Some Indigenous social service organizations seem to be looking at the bigger picture and addressing areas of "economic, social and community development" (Otway 2006). In Quebec, for instance, there is a program that works "with Aboriginal offenders and the communities they will return to [which] includes the establishment of a healing and development centre… tied to an alternative/restorative justice strategy that focuses on the need to heal offenders… and not on punishment or other less effective measures" (Waseskun Network 2006). This program targets one of the most devastating instruments of colonization — the residential school system. According to the agency's website, its major goal is "to address the unresolved trauma of the physical, sexual and emotional abuse suffered by the residents in residential schools or in families or communities affected by residential schools, and to restore balance in people's relationships with their world."

Making this connection to colonization is critical to any work with Indigenous people. In order to heal, move forward into self-determination and create a more positive future for the next seven generations, each one of us needs to know about colonization and its impacts. We must raise our consciousness about the life of our ancestors prior to colonization, what happened during that time of the great struggle and how it has impacted us and continues to do so. We must also educate ourselves and others about our rights. Without this consciousness, there can be no healing because we will not understand the source of the problem. Without healing, there can be no restoration to how we have always been meant to be.

In my work as a helper, I constantly strove to assist Indigenous adults in connecting their "individual troubles" to those of other adults and then to the history of colonization and today's circumstances. This is the beauty of working with people in circle and through ceremony — bringing them together to learn about how many of our people have survived residential schools, been taken away by CAS due to neglect, which is, in reality, poverty, and had family members so full of hopelessness that they saw no other way out than to take their own lives. Knowing "it's not just me" leads to "why so many of us then?" which eventually turns towards "who am I really?" That is when the healing truly begins.

The more experience I gained in helping others, the more I came to see the greater value of bringing people together rather than working with them individually. Through healing circles for women with abusive partners, for instance, I watched women not only support one another in circle, but more importantly, learn how to help each other in the community. They developed safety plans that included each other and helped each another with grocery shopping and childcare. In circle with others, women learned how to speak up for themselves, advocate for their children, communicate their feelings and needs, and negotiate in ways that took everyone into consideration.

During healing circles for men who had abused their female partners or committed sexual offences, it was not only the facilitators who challenged them on their attitudes and behaviours — this came from the other men as well. Such methods are crucial to this work because it is much more difficult for these men to manipulate, minimize and deny their behaviours to other men than to the facilitators. As a group they can also explore what it means to be an Indigenous man in today's world and come up with concrete ways to live according to their roles and responsibilities.

Indigenous approaches to helping/social work attends to the immediate needs of adults within the larger context of why these needs exist and how we will eradicate or, at the least, lessen them through self-determination for all. It is first finding food for a single mom when she has none in the fridge and diapers for her youngest who is wearing the last one in the pack. Seeing this in the context of the bigger picture does not mean engaging this mother in a discussion of how Indigenous women have been devalued by colonization when her children are hungry and she is crying. However, this discussion must occur at some point, along with those about restoring Indigenous women to their rightful places. This is the work I have been privileged to be a part of, and I have seen it spark fires in people to make positive changes in themselves and for others.

Politicizing the current situation — living with the impacts of colonization — for Indigenous people and raising consciousness that leads to positive actions is a critical piece to helping work with Aboriginal adults. Over the years, I witnessed this happening in many diverse ways. Often, the spark that ignites led to post-secondary education, employment within Indigenous agencies, becoming helpers to well respected Elders, re-learning how to dance, sing or be part of a drum, speaking publicly in classrooms or at conferences about one's experiences, taking up leadership roles, and holding the church and state accountable for past wrongs. Adults that I saw in helping processes told me years later that these positive actions came about because they first took the steps to reach an awareness of themselves as Indigenous people and heal past traumas.

Value of Indigenous Social Work to All People

I have no doubt that Indigenous approaches to social work/helping are of great value to all people of the world — particularly to those in the West who seem to be searching for something meaningful in life. This is evident by the growing interest in the spiritualities of Indigenous peoples worldwide. There is much in Indigenous worldviews that applies to all people — a holistic way of looking at health and wellbeing, healing rather than punishment and community responsibility when some members are not coping well with life's difficulties. It is also of interest to note the teachings of the Seven Fires Prophesies, which tell us about pre-contact time, colonization and the present day of healing and reclamation. Some Elders make reference to an "Eighth Fire," which is the future. They teach that some day, the "White race" will turn to the Indigenous peoples of the world for assistance on how to survive, thus coming full circle to when their ancestors first came to Turtle Island and needed our ancestors' help to live.

Certainly, Indigenous peoples do not have a monopoly on spirituality, story-telling or forms of justice that are meant to restore balance. Yet, the tools currently being implemented by social work and other helping professions, such as spirituality in social work practice, narrative therapy, family conferencing and restorative justice, all have their origins in Indigenous worldviews. This is not to say that these techniques should not be adapted and incorporated into western forms of social work. However, when such practices are used, acknowledgement needs to be given to their origins, which lie in Indigenous approaches. For example, the term "ecospiritual" is a clear appropriation unless there is acknowledgement that this is merely a renaming.

Appropriation is the new-age tool of colonization. Indigenous peoples have been remarkably resilient in surviving the impacts of colonization, and spirituality has been primarily responsible for this. It has been our major act of resistance and, in many circumstances, all that is left of pre-contact times. To appropriate Indigenous spiritualities or other practices into western forms of social work without consultation of Indigenous people and without acknowledgement of Indigenous knowledge is no different than the theft of our lands and resources centuries ago. The question then arises of how to incorporate Indigenous approaches to social work/helping in western perspectives without appropriating them. This topic, however, I am leaving for another time.

Meanwhile, here is an example of a helping place that combines several practices, including Indigenous ones, in its approach. At a lodge located in

Ontario, "guests sleep in a teepee, go on a drum journey, canoe, swim, fish, and participate in an introductory sweat lodge" (Jalbun Lodge 2006). As the website states,

> A couple — one Indigenous and one non-Indigenous… opened a Spiritual Retreat… [which] is a small refuge… that offers traditional Native teachings, drum building workshops and Sacred ceremony in a teepee setting. Currently… the lodge runs one weekend a month from April to October offering workshops of self exploration through "stirring the pot" with movement, sound, and meditation, alternatively to mixed groups and to women. Through the winter… a series of six bodywork workshops [are offered, called] "begin with the Body" [which is] an introduction to Rebalancing….

You decide — is this lodge an example of the value of Indigenous social work/ helping to all people or is it an appropriation of Indigenous approaches?

Social Workers Are Also Warriors

Over the past twenty years, I have seen the creation of many Indigenous social service agencies across the country and I have had the privilege to assist several of them in their attempts to incorporate their particular culture into their programming. There are so many wonderful Indigenous social workers/ helpers in these agencies and they have been catalysts in assisting thousands of Indigenous adults become who they were always meant to be. These workers have managed to do this despite the challenges imposed upon them not only by the agencies themselves, but more importantly, by the structures, policies and legislation that govern these agencies. Today, a new generation is on the way, and I am privileged once again because I am one of their teachers within social work education. These new social workers are also warriors, who have benefitted from the mentoring of Indigenous teachers within the academy and the lessons learned from helpers in the trenches before them. They have a far greater understanding of the history and impacts of coloniza- tion, are not afraid to speak out strategically and are much more politicized than those of us who did similar work years ago. They have the potential to create a true revolution by carving out spaces for themselves, not only within Indigenous social services agencies but also within research, policy-making and self-government. Evolution is, fortunately, endless.

Notes

1. See also Baskin 1997; Blaeser 1996; Lynn 2001; Morrissette, McKenzie and Morrissettee 1993.
2. McKenzie, Seidl and Bone 1995; Morrisseau 1998; Morrissette, McKenzie and

Morrissette 1993; Shilling 2002; Timpson et al. 1988; Waller and Patterson 2002; Weaver 2000.

3. See also Baskin 2002b; Bishop 1998; Bruyere 1998; Cavender Wilson 1996; Gair et al. 2002; Graveline 1998; Hurdle 2002; King 1997; Mihesuah 1996; Mihesuah 1998; Smith 1999.

4. Based on the literature, a scan of social services agencies, dialogue with service providers and service users, and my own observations and experiences.

5. Reiki is described as a form of energetic healing using the palms of the hands.

6. See also Angell 2000; McCormick 1995; Napoli and Gonzalez-Santin 2000; Yellow Horse Brave Heart and DeBruyn 1998.

Chapter 8

For Indigenous People, by Indigenous People, with Indigenous People
Towards an Indigenist Research Paradigm

Michael Anthony Hart

Recently I was supporting a student as she was completing an assignment for a post-graduate course on research. For her research project she proposed to interview students at an Indigenous training institute regarding their experiences. She was thinking of using a phenomenological methodology along with Indigenous ways-of-knowing. While assisting her it became clear to me that she was going to include a phenomenological methodology mainly in name as she was primarily interested in Indigenous ways of research. As she was focused on an Indigenous organizations and would be interviewing Indigenous students, and since she is Indigenous, I suggested leaving phenomenology out of the research proposal and following an Indigenous methodology. We agreed that I would support her in developing her proposal along such lines. Approximately two months later she came back to share her experiences with me. She had completed her assignment by outlining a methodology that was based in Indigenous ways of coming to know while dropping the phenomenological perspective. The feedback she received from her professor was that she was off track, and she was clearly told that there are *no* Indigenous methodologies. She had to rewrite the assignment with a focus on phenomenology while dropping much of her material on Indigenous ways of coming to know.

Not only was I feeling terrible for influencing this student and encouraging her to walk along a path that led straight into the thick of the continued oppression we face as Indigenous people, but I was angry that in this institution of higher learning, which claims to be the institution of choice for Indigenous peoples, colonialism continues to be blatantly supported. Whether by ignorance or by choice, the professor was not supportive of our emancipation. Instead, she remained tied to the status quo, and while she did acknowledge a wide spectrum of worldviews in her work, she apparently remained enmeshed in an Amer-European construction of the world. This enmeshment was being transferred to an Indigenous woman working with

Indigenous participants from an Indigenous institution on an Indigenous research project.

Whether we are talking about colonialism generally, or in regards to research specifically, such an event is not new. As Indigenous people we continue to face such oppression on a regular basis. This chapter counters this oppression in research by describing one means of moving research towards what is more relevant to Indigenous peoples. I begin with brief points regarding Indigenous worldviews. These points act as the basis for the following discussions of Indigenous research as a paradigm and the Indigenist stance from which I approached my research project. I close the chapter with a commentary on research and Indigenous people.

Setting the Groundwork: Indigenous Peoples' Worldviews

As Indigenous peoples we have existed for millennia, developing and relying upon our own ways of coming to know. Indeed, all peoples of the earth had and have abilities to search for answers, learn and grow. To say otherwise locks them into mythical portraits of people who are in ignorance and without vitality. What is different between peoples is how we view the world, the understandings that stem from our views and how we develop such understandings. As Indigenous peoples of Turtle Island we have our own worldviews. Our worldviews have divergences from one another, but they also share commonalities that are distinguishable from an Amer-European "Enlightened" worldview. For example, Kuokkanen (2007: 39) explains that, "culturally, socially, economically, and spiritually, Indigenous peoples, as collectivists, continue to depend directly on the natural environment that surrounds them. Such thinking is still central to Indigenous philosophies."

It is apparent to me from a previous review of the literature on Indigenous worldviews (Hart 2007) that Indigenous peoples share a strong focus on people and entities coming together to help and support one another. Reiterating Terry Cross, Thomas Crofoot (2002) called this a relational worldview. Taken together, spirit and spirituality are a key emphasis within this relational worldview. Directly tied to this spiritual emphasis are the concepts of communitism and respectful individualism. Communitism is the sense of community tied together by familial relations and the families' commitment to it, where family is understood broadly and multi-generationally (Weaver 1997, 2001). Respectful individualism is a way-of-being where individuals enjoy great freedom in self-expression, since it is recognized by the society that individuals do not act on self-interest alone but take into consideration the needs of the community (Gross 2003).

Relational concepts are often reflected in Indigenous authors' discussions of research. For example, Maggie (Margaret) Kovach (2006), in her doctoral dissertation entitled "Searching for Arrowheads: An Inquiry into

Approaches to Indigenous Research using a Tribal Methodology with a Nêhiýaw Kiskêýihtamowin Worldview," asserts that Indigenous methodologies are being used by doctoral researchers and that these approaches are relational, flow from an Indigenous worldview, are congruent with specific cultural ways and protocols of the different nations, encompass an inclusive, broad range of knowing that demands a holistic interpretation of ethical considerations, and include decolonizing theory and action. As another example, Kathy Absolon (2008), in her doctoral thesis entitled "Kaandosswin, This is How We Come to Know! Indigenous Graduate Research in the Academy: Worldviews and Methodologies," explains that the roots of Indigenous research are embedded in Indigenous worldviews and paradigms. She identifies that Indigenous locations, histories, experiences, values, traditions, languages and consciousness are central to Indigenous research methodologies. Further, concepts such as interrelationships, holism and reciprocity are integral to the research journey Indigenous learners embark upon.

Similar concepts are reflected in Eva Marie Garroutte's (2003: 101) approach to American Indian scholarship, which she names "radical Indigenism." She explains that "it argues for the reassertion and rebuilding of traditional knowledge from its roots, its fundamental principles." Radical Indigenous scholarship privileges Indigenous intellectual traditions, including their spiritual and sacred elements. It takes the stand that such elements are absolutely central to the coherence of our knowledge traditions and that if the spiritual and sacred elements are surrendered, there is little left of our philosophies that will make any sense. Garroutte also explains that radical Indigenous scholarship allows questions to unfold in ways that lie within our Indigenous philosophies, values, goals, categories of thought and models of inquiry.

These points on worldviews and the discussion of the relationship between worldviews and research as explained by Kovach, Absolon and Garroutte were the foundation for the development of the Indigenist research paradigm that I relied on for my research project.

An Indigenist Research Paradigm

When I embarked upon my doctoral studies, I paid attention to the ideas expressed by Linda Tuhiwai Smith (1999), who identifies the need for a modern Indigenous peoples' research paradigm that resists the oppression found within research. I knew I must work from a place that supported Indigenous perspectives, voices and ways-of-being, but recognized at that time there were not many options for how to put this stance into action around research in the academy. I first determined the orientation that best suited my research and relied on Garroutte's (2003) point that Indigenist research must stem from Indigenous peoples' roots and principles. I decided to seek out an Indigenous paradigm. However, not finding any such paradigm, I was driven to develop an Indigenous research paradigm to act as the foundation for my research design. In relation to social sciences, a paradigm is "a comprehensive belief system, worldview or framework that guides research and practice in a field" (Willis 2007: 8). I followed Shawn Wilson's identification of four components that, together, make up a research paradigm:

> Ontology is a belief in the nature of reality. Your way of being, what you believe is real in the world…. Second is epistemology, which is how you think about that reality. Next, when we talk about research methodology, we are talking about how you are going to use your ways of thinking (your epistemology) to gain more knowledge about your reality. Finally, a paradigm includes axiology, which is a set of morals or a set of ethics. (2001: 175)

It is important to recognize at the very beginning that even this explanation of what makes up a paradigm is steeped in Amer-European worldviews. I am not aware of terms parallel to ontology, epistemology, methodology and axiology in my own Cree language, which admittedly may be equally a reflection of my limited ability to speak the language of my family and ancestors as it is a reflection that such terms do not reflect our worldview. By using these terms, I may be reshaping Indigenous ways-of-being so that they fit into another worldview. While I take the position here that I am attempting to move towards a more Indigenous way of coming to know, we must recognize that the movement is only a small step compared to what is needed. Indeed, others may effectively argue that this step is not really a move towards Indigenism at all but is really an entrenchment of Amer-European colonialism within Indigenous ways of coming to know. I can only encourage you to keep this caution in mind while reviewing the following outline of this particular Indigenous paradigm.

This Indigenous paradigm has an ontology, the dominant aspect of which is the recognition and acceptance of a spiritual realm and that this realm is interconnected with the physical realm (Cajete 2000; Rice 2005). It accepts that there are influences between the spiritual and physical. For example, Gregory Cajete (2000) explains that Indigenous science integrates a spiritual orientation; human beings have an important role in the perpetuation in the nature processes of the world; and acting in the world must be sanctioned through ceremony and ritual. Another dominant aspect of this ontology is reciprocity, or the belief that, as we receive from others, we must also offer to others (Rice 2005). Reciprocity reflects the significance of relationships, as in a relational worldview, and the understanding that we must honour our relationships with others, including other than human life. Since all life is considered equal, albeit different, to human beings, all life must be respected as we are in reciprocal relationships with them. These two key factors of an Indigenous ontology form part of the foundation of the Indigenous paradigm I relied upon.

Another part of the foundation is its epistemology. Maggie Kovach (2005) presents the thoughts of several Indigenous authors who note characteristics of Indigenous epistemology. It is derived from teachings transmitted from generation to generation by story-telling, where each story is alive with the nuances of the story-teller. It emerges from Indigenous languages, which emphasize verbs, and is garnered through dreams and visions, since it arises from the interconnections between the human world, spirit and inanimate entities. Another aspect of Indigenous epistemology is perceptual experience, where perception includes the metaphysics of inner space (Ermine 1995). In other words, perception includes a form of experiential insight. Willie Ermine presents an excellent overview of this means of perception. He explains that an Aboriginal epistemology is a subjectively based process, *mamatawisowin*, or the "capacity to tap the creative life forces of the inner space by the use of all the faculties that constitute our being — it is to exercise inwardness" (1995: 104). Through inward exploration, where creative forces that run through all life are tapped into, individuals come to subjectively experience a sense of wholeness. This exploration is an experience in context, where the context is the self in connection with happenings, and the findings from such experience is knowledge. Happenings include events, thoughts, feelings and actions that have occurred, are occurring or are believed will occur within and around an individual life being. Happenings may be facilitated through rituals and ceremonies that incorporate dreaming, visioning, meditation and/or prayer. The findings from such experiences are encoded in community praxis as a way of synthesizing knowledge derived from such introspection. Hence, Indigenous peoples' cultures recognize and affirm the spiritual through practical applications of inner-space discoveries. In this process, "the community became paramount by virtue of its role as repository and incubator of total tribal knowledge in the form of custom and culture. Each part of the community became an integral part of the whole flowing movement and was modeled on the inward wholeness and harmony" (Ermine 1995: 105). Key people for this process are Elders and practitioners who have undergone processes to develop this ability. Thus, an Indigenous research paradigm incorporates an epistemology that includes *mamatawisowin* for knowledge development and a reliance on Elders and individuals who have or are developing this insight.

The third part of this Indigenous research paradigm is its methodology. Cora Weber-Pillwax (2001) explains Indigenous methodologies as ones that permit and enable Indigenous researchers to be who they are while they are actively engaged as participants in the research processes. This way-of-being not only creates new knowledge but transforms who researchers are and where they are located. This point is connected to Shawn Wilson's suggestion that an Indigenous methodology includes relational accountability, that researchers are accountable to "all my relations," meaning that researchers, in their research process, must fulfill their relationship with the world around them as part of their research. Wilson (2001: 177) explains his thoughts on relationality this way:

> An Indigenous paradigm comes from the fundamental belief that knowledge is relational. Knowledge is shared with all creation. It is not just interpersonal relationships, or just with the research subjects I may be working with, but it is a relationship with all of creation. It is with the cosmos; it is with the animals, with the plants, with the earth that we share this knowledge. It goes beyond the idea of individual knowledge to the concept of relational knowledge... [hence] you are answerable to all your relations when you are doing research.

This accountability relates to another key characteristic of Indigenous methodologies, that being the collective. As explained by Maggie Kovach (2005) researchers have a commitment to the people and hear this question being whispered in our ears as we move forward in our research: "Are you helping us?" A final point I noted for this methodology is Garroutte's (2003: 114) identification of a particular aspect of radical Indigenism, an emphasis on practicality — "one seeks knowledge because one is prepared to use it." In other words, an Indigenous methodology includes the assumption that knowledge gained will be utilized practically.

The fourth component of this Indigenous paradigm is axiology. I relied on Shawn Wilson's (2003) outline of Atkinson's identification of certain principles for Indigenous research. Expanding this outline, I identified the following values to be held and actions that would reflect these values:

- Indigenous control over research, which can be demonstrated by having Indigenous people themselves approving the research and the research methods;
- respect for individuals *and* communities, which can be demonstrated by a researcher being knowledgeable and considerate of the uniqueness of communities, their diversities within and between each other, and the gifts and contributions that citizens of that community have and do bring to their communities;
- reciprocity and responsibility, which can be demonstrated in the ways a researcher relates and acts within a community, such as openly sharing and presenting their research ideas and experiences with the intent of supporting the community. Note that the nature of the support is determined by the community;

- respect and safety, which can be evident when the research participants feel safe and are safe. This includes addressing confidentiality, openness and anonymity in a manner desired by the research participants;
- non-intrusiveness, where the researcher is quietly aware, watching and participating only when invited;
- deep listening and hearing with more than the ears, where the researcher carefully listens and pays attention to how their heart and sense of being are emotionally and spiritually moved;
- reflective non-judgment, where the researcher considers what is being seen and heard without immediately placing a sense of right or wrong and considers what is said within the context presented by the speaker and the worldview of Indigenous peoples;
- honouring what is shared, which can be translated to fulfilling the responsibility to act with fidelity to the relationship and to what has been heard, observed and learned;
- awareness and connection between the logic of mind and the feelings of the heart, where both the emotional and cognitive experiences are incorporated into all of the researcher's actions;
- self-awareness, where researchers listen and observe themselves emotionally, physically, mentally and spiritually, as well as in relationship with others throughout the research process; and
- subjectivity, where the researcher acknowledges that they bring their subjective self to the research process and openly and truthfully incorporates their subjective self in all aspects of the research.

Cora Weber-Pillwax (2001: 168) reflects some of these values, particularly the importance of relationships, in the following statement about values that need to be considered for Indigenous research:

> I could also make a value statement and say that whatever I do as an Indigenous researcher must be hooked to the "community" or the Indigenous research has to benefit the community.... The research methods have to mesh with the community and serve the community. Any research that I do must not destroy or in any way negatively implicate or compromise my own personal integrity as a person, as a human being. This integrity is based on how I contextualize myself in my community, with my family and my people, and eventually how I contextualize myself in the planet, with the rest of all living systems and things. Without personal integrity, I would be outside the system. If I am outside the system, I don't survive. I destroy myself. I am isolated. All these are important aspects connected to research in general and would almost certainly

be an important consideration of anything I would be claiming as Indigenous research.

Respect is perhaps the most cited value of Indigenous peoples. While I have noted several definitions of respect (Hart 2002), Patricia Steinhauer (2001: 79) explains that respect is reflected in the Ininew term *kisténitámowin*, which directly relates to my research. She defines *kisténitámowin* as "to take care never to mistreat any form of life." It is not tied to the idea that respect is something earned, as is the respect people higher up on the economic or political ladder often receive in the Amer-European "Enlightenment" worldview, but something that is given automatically since we are all worthy beings who come from Creator/Creation and carry gifts — abilities — that come from the Creator that can benefit all life. In turn, whenever we are disrespectful to another life, we are being disrespectful to all life, including ourselves, our families and our communities.

I understand these values in relation to research as meaning that I must respect and honour myself for what I know and do not know; that I must respect and honour others for what they know and do not know; that I must respect and honour the relationship between me, others involved in the research, others influenced by the research and others generally; and that I must conduct myself in a way that supports and/or helps Indigenous people individually and collectively.

To summarize this research paradigm, its ontology is relational, with the interconnections between life entities, including the spiritual, being paramount. This is evident in the phrase "all my relations." Its epistemology focuses on the widely understood perceptual experiences of "happenings" as the means to developing insight into the whole, which are then shared and encoded, particularly by and/or with Elders, in community praxis, a process referred to as *mamatawisowin*. Its methodology is a subjective process of interactions between the researcher and participants as whole human beings, as opposed to functional entities. The researcher fulfills their obligations to the world around them, including the collective, in a manner that is accountable and practical to "all my relations." The axiology of this paradigm emphasizes many values held by Indigenous peoples, particularly reciprocity, non-judgement, honour, self-awareness, respect and integrity.

An Indigenist Research Project

Relying on this Indigenist paradigm, I designed my research project to include the following elements: appropriate Indigenous protocols; my subjective self, which includes self-reflection and insight; established relationships; Elders and knowledgeable participants; an open "interview" structure; Indigenous understandings of trustworthiness; and ceremonies. While an Indigenist research paradigm also includes elements such as the significance of context; awareness of the potential influences of other than human beings through more than conscious means, such as dreams, vision and ceremonial experiences; and additional values, space permits only the former elements to be addressed here.

Appropriate Indigenous Protocols

The research project I undertook using this paradigm was focused on Cree peoples, and I therefore followed Cree protocols. Perhaps most significant is the Cree protocol of *pakitinásow*, which is the offering of something in exchange for help, support and/or direction. I presented each person involved in the research project with *cistémáw* [tobacco] and *wípinasona* [ceremonial cloth] prior to the interview. From an Indigenous perspective, acceptance of these items indicated consent to participate in the study. For the knowledge keepers, this approval for participating was recognized as a commitment to themselves as holders of the knowledge sought, to me as the person wanting to learn about the knowledge and to the spiritual realm. All individuals given offers accepted the *cistémáw*, *wípinasona* and gifts. These individuals included the Elders who supported me and who participated in the "interview" processes, Cree social workers who participated and people who led ceremonies that I partook in. I also offered tobacco and cloth to individuals who supported me in the academic processes, namely representatives from the universities. There was a balance in this last point as the host university has very clear limits on gifting. These limits are reflective of the dominant societal ethics in Canada; members of my research committee were not allowed to receive gifts.

Another aspect of this protocol defined how I approached people with the tobacco and cloth. It required me to demonstrate humility, to honour what is held by the person being approached and to respect the person being approached, myself and the spiritual aspect of the relationships within the individual, between us and between the individual and their relations.

My Subjective Self and Subjectivity

I was an active participant in this research project, meaning in order for me to learn through this project I not only connected with participants, herein referred to as knowledge keepers, I also considered my own insight gained through my interactions and relationships with these people and through my own participation in traditional Muskéko Ininew means of learning, such as ceremonies. In other words, as I could not shed my values, beliefs and experiences, they became part of the research project in all aspects. In particular, I approached the project with values that I learned from my family, other Cree Kété-ayak [Elders] and traditional Cree ways of living. As such, I had some ideas of what might be shared with me when I was about to talk and/or hear from the knowledge keepers. I attempted not to focus only on those ways that had been shared with me in my past. On the other hand, those ways that I had not considered stood out to me when they were presented to me. I attempted to remain open to hearing about, seeing in practice and/or participating in activities that would demonstrate other values and beliefs, since I recognized that Cree people hold an assortment of values and beliefs.

I also recognized that my life experiences prior to taking on this research project have likely influenced it. I recognize that I have not lived any large part of my life on a First Nation; have lived in various territories, albeit mostly Cree; have an education based in Amer-European society; spent extensive parts of my life learning from Cree Kété-ayak, as well as Kété-ayak from other nations; faced many oppressive comments and actions regarding our peoples and our practices; met many people who want to support our peoples to meet our aspirations; and have generally lived my life in a manner where there is a division between my traditional and academic learning. These, and many other experiences, influence how I look upon the world.

I tend to work in a manner that reflects a belief in the good of Cree ways of living, including Cree ways of helping, a hope for the re-emergence of our ways as the means to guide our liberation from the colonial oppression we continue to face and a commitment to supporting Cree ways-of-being. I approached the knowledge keepers with this manner in my heart. Through our interactions during past years and their observation of me during that time, they know my commitment to further our people and our ways. Indeed, some people agreed to participate in this study because it was I who asked them and they believed I would respect them, the understandings shared and Cree people.

In relation to the knowledge keepers, when research is addressed from an Indigenous research paradigm, subjectivity is expected to be present. Indeed, the Kété-ayak that I have been privileged to accompany and learn from have often said, "I am not here to offend you. I am here to share with you what I have come to understand" and "Take what is useful to you and leave the rest." These comments speak of the specificity of what they know. These comments also speak to the idea that what they know may or may not be applicable to others. In academic terms, it speaks to location. It means the person hearing is given the opportunity to partake in this knowledge if that person deems it applicable to their life. This dynamic is well-captured in a common passage shared by Thomas King (2003: 119) in several of his personal stories:

> Take Louis's [or any another other person he may have addressed in the story] story for instance. It's yours. Do with it what you will.

Cry over it. Get angry. Forget it. But don't say in the years to come that you would have lived your life differently if only you had heard this story. You've heard it now.

Self-Reflection

Another key process of an Indigenist research paradigm and undertaken within this research project is self-reflection. To give understanding of what I mean by self-reflection, I present two scenarios I have experienced on several occasions. First, I have spent many years with and learning from Kété-ayak. I spent much of this time developing a relationship with them, and I have been honoured with the responsibility to hold particular knowledge. At times this knowledge was given directly and clearly. I knew the nature of this knowledge and how it was to be passed on to others and put into practice. However, I was still left to figure out how it was to shape my life. Second, there were times when Kété-ayak gave me information, usually through stories, and I was left to ponder, "What does that have to do with what we were previously talking about? What does that have to do with my question?" I took me a while to realize that each time this dynamic occurred, I was actually given the task to reflect on what was said by the Kété-ayak. Rather than being given direct answers, I was to make the knowledge my own by taking what was said and running it through my mind, my heart and my experiences. The passing of knowledge from the Kété-ayak to me as a learner in this manner supports knowledge maintenance and development. In both of these situations deep self-reflection was required, meaning becoming or being aware of myself, the Kété-ayak, what is shared and the relationship between me, what is shared, the Kété-ayak and the spiritual realm. This awareness is necessary so that I will able to understand and incorporate the knowledge in a manner that respects and honours all involved, including the knowledge that was shared.

Self-reflection was incorporated into this study throughout the research process, from when I first considered entering the PhD program to the completion of the project. It included my previous experiences that I determined to be relevant to the research. This inclusion reflects the principle that I was to be part of this research and as such, that my life experiences were part of and have likely shaped the research. It fits within the previously outlined Indigenous research paradigm, which requires the total involvement of the researcher with their environment (Colorado 1988) and has been implemented and supported in other studies by Indigenous researchers, including Shaun Hains (2001), Mary Hermes (1998), Patricia Steinhauer (2001) and Roxanne Struthers (2001).

Established Relationships

As explained by Kovach (2005: 30), "In Indigenous communities (both urban and rural), a relationship-based approach is a practical necessity because access to the community is unlikely unless time is invested in relationship building." I incorporated Cora Weber-Pillwax's (2001: 170) understanding of interviews from an Indigenous perspective, which reflected my intentions and expectations regarding the "interviews":

> To address methods in the framework of Indigenous research, I will share some points on one practice that I follow in doing my research. I talk to people all the time, purposefully and with as much awareness as I possess. I could refer to my method as interviewing so that it might be more easily recognized. Interviewing, however, is to be seen as a process of total involvement. I connected with people that I had known for years, not in terms of knowing their personalities, but knowing their connections. They also knew my connections. We were part of a network that was safe and trusted and established. The trust in some cases was not necessarily vested in me as an individual, but in me as a part of my family…. I met a lot of people, but a meeting with one Elder provides a good demonstration of the process that I followed in my work. To meet this Elder and to have him share with me, three people spoke for me, indicating to him that it was all right for him to talk to me. Further, they advised me and supported me by active participation in the planning and carrying out of a particular event. If something had occurred to put anyone in the community in a "bad" position, I would have been held accountable, and rightly so. However, the three people who stood beside me would also have been held accountable, whether in fact they had been responsible or not.

I already knew all the knowledge keepers I approached to participate in the research project. One has known me all my life. Most I had known at that time for at least nine years. While the relationship I had with one of the knowledge keepers was limited in that we only had conversed on occasion, we shared a relationship with a third person, who had spoken encouragingly about me, him and the project. By having a relationship with the knowledge keepers prior to the implementation of the research project, we had already established a strong sense of acceptance, trust, mutuality and respect. As was noted in the paradigm, this sense comes with a high level of relationship accountability. It also provided the knowledge keepers with awareness about my commitment to our people in terms of my spoken word and actions.

Elders as Knowledge Keepers

The thrust of this project was to understand Cree ways of helping. In following the Indigenist research paradigm, this required a reliance on those who hold such understandings, namely Cree Kété-ayak. In addition, as the project focused on these ways in relation to social work, I relied on those who hold at least some knowledge of Cree ways of helping as well as social work, specifically Cree social workers learning from Cree Kété-ayak. The part most relevant to the project was the Kété-ayak, who came from a cross-section of Cree territory and dialects. The territory was that of the Western Cree, which spans from the areas now known as Alberta, Saskatchewan and Manitoba. It is made up of rocky muskeg, muskeg, boreal forest and plains. The Cree dialects included the Néhiýaw (two speakers), Néhithaw (two speakers) and Muskéko-Ininew (two speakers) dialects. The Kété-ayak I learned from in this project understood the concept of *mamatawisowin*, had partaken in this process on many occasions, if not regularly, and have shared their experiences with their community, particularly their Kété-ayak, who have guided them. Each of the Kété-ayak had been given the responsibility by their respective communities to carry their knowledge and learning further and have guided others in this process. The social workers, while not Kété-ayak, have begun participating in this cultural learning process under the guidance of their Kété-ayak.

An Open "Interview" Structure

While the term "interview" was used to describe the interaction between me and knowledge holders, the reality is that it was more than an interview. As mentioned, I had been in relationship with the knowledge keepers for years and I had included my subjective self in this research project. It would be most accurate to say that the research incorporated, at least indirectly and many times directly, our whole relationship over the many years we had been connected.

Still, there were particular times that were established for us to have a discussion on the questions I had. Five out of the six interviews conducted with the Kété-ayak occurred in their homes. For the sixth interview, the Kété-ayak was in a city away from his home, and he chose a restaurant in his hotel as the venue for the interview. Most of the interviews, which commenced with my arrival and ended at the completion of our discussions, took several hours. An exception was the discussion between me and two Kété-ayak that took place over two and half days.

The first interview occurred at the home of two of the Kété-ayak and the process started soon after I arrived. I sat with the Kété-aya I had initially spoke with over the phone and her *oskápéwis* [Elder's helper] in the dining room. The husband of the Kété-aya, their daughter and their grandchild were in the adjoining living room. We talked over tea about our families, our present wellbeing and our recent activities, a dynamic that occurred at the start of the interviews with the other four Kété-ayak as well. The more formal part of the interviews began when I offered the *cístémáw* and *wípinasona* to the Kété-aya, to whom I had previously explained about the research and what I was requesting. She agreed to participate. The *oskápéwis* then set up the necessary items for a pipe ceremony in the living room, which was lead by the Kété-aya. At this time the daughter left the room. The husband of the Kété-aya participated in the pipe ceremony, which included the *oskápéwis*, the grandchild and me. The discussion on consent, confidentiality and the questions I brought forward then took place. The Kété-aya signed the consent form before the recording of the interview. The husband of the Kété-aya demonstrated his willingness to be part of the process by immediately participating in the discussions as one of the Kété-ayak. He signed his consent form after the interview. I had not initially offered him a consent form as I did not realize that he was intending to participate. At the end of the interview I offered this Kété-ayak a gift and took the first Kété-aya and her *oskápéwis* out for supper, as the second Kété-aya decided to remain at home.

At the home of another Kété-aya, I was offered a meal before we started. After we ate the meal he prepared, I offered the Kété-aya the *cístémáw* and *wípinasona* and explained about the research and what I was asking from him. He agreed to participate. He also signed the consent form, noting that he understood the requirements of the university as well as his desire to help me through that part of the process. He also explained that there was no need to identify him, hence his identity has been kept confidential. Upon completion of the interview, I offered him a gift.

The interview of the fourth Kété-aya occurred in a restaurant. As he immediately saw that I was carrying the *cístémáw* and *wípinasona*, I offered him these items soon after we had discussed our families, personal wellbeing and activities. We were interrupted by the serving personnel several times, and this interview was the shortest, likely due to the venue and our relationship being based on only occasional visits. At the end of the interview, I offered the Kété-aya a gift and paid for our meal.

The final two interviews took place over two and half days. For these interviews, I travelled to the residence of the Kété-aya with whom I had spoken. I spent two nights and two and half days staying with him and his life partner. His life partner became the sixth Kété-aya to be interviewed. On the first day of this visit, most of our conversation was an update about our families, lives and activities. The bulk of the interview began on the second day, starting immediately after breakfast. The first Kété-ayak and I moved to the living room, at which time he began talking. After a while I realized he was addressing topics related to my research. In following Cree protocol, I did not immediately interrupt the discussion with the offering of the *cistémáw* and *wípinasona*. These items were still packed in my bag and I would have had to leave to get them. The second Kété-aya joined our discussions in the latter part of the morning. We broke our discussion in the early afternoon when the second Kété-aya asked us to eat lunch and then complete a chore. This chore took approximately three hours and included some travel through the reserve. Afterwards we sat down for tea. In the meantime a visitor had arrived to ask the Kété-aya to facilitate a *matotisán* [sweat lodge] ceremony later that day. After the guest left, the Kété-aya reinitiated the conversation for a short period of time, and once again, the conversation started before I could offer him the *cistémáw* and *wípinasona*. Later, we partook in the *matotisán* ceremony, after which he began speaking about the matters once again, but without the presence of the second Kété-aya. On the morning of the third day, I brought out the *cistémáw* and *wípinasona*, and before we began our discussion, I offered them to both of the Kété-ayak. They mediated/prayed over the items before continuing on with their sharing, which took most of that day. Before leaving their residence, I offered my words of thankfulness and presented them with gifts.

The Value of Trustworthiness

In an Indigenous research paradigm, trustworthiness is about relying on understandings stemming from people who are living in way that reflects their understandings, such as community acknowledged Elders; one's own understandings, which have grown from the process of *mamatawisowin* and the practical applications of one's inner-space discoveries; and/or relationships between people, where both parties are respectful as defined by all the people participating in the project, committed to helping to one another and their community and supportive of each other's actions as a means of personal and community growth. This third point is about one's place in relation to the community, where the community trusts the person's intent to move forward in a way that will reinforce the community's wellbeing. As such, it requires an individual to be well-situated in the community. Accordingly, I relied on Elders and people I knew to be following Cree ways of helping in their social work practice to inform me, included my own inner-space discoveries and relied on relationships with people in the Cree community, as well as openly conducted myself as a member of the community.

Ceremonies

As explained previously, ceremonies play a feature role in an Indigenous research paradigm and have been incorporated throughout this project. *Wípinason* and *cistémáw* were ceremoniously offered to the people interviewed as part of the process. Also included were fasting, pipe and sweat lodge ceremonies.

Fasting relates to the process of self-reflection, and people fast for various reasons at different periods in their lives, for varying lengths of time. When and where a fast occurs is dependent upon the person doing the fasting, the directions they may have been given, the experiences they are undergoing and logistical parameters. One of the reasons for fasting is to figure out an answer about something (Hains 2001). I fasted at one point in the research process for this particular reason.

Pipe ceremonies relate to many matters, including the establishing of an honest, faithful, respectful, kind and mutually supportive relationship. A pipe ceremony affirms participants' commitment to the relationships of the people involved, including the spiritual relationships. The pipe ceremonies included in this research fell within these lines and thus established a level of commitment by me to the participants that went beyond any academic requirements.

Sweat lodge ceremonies are held for many reasons, including cleansing one's mind, body, spirit and emotions; re-balancing of oneself; and preparation before a particular deed. With these reasons in mind I participated in sweat lodge ceremonies before and during the research process. These ceremonies prepared me for the research, supported me during the research and supported me in my reflections, analysis and synthesis. They helped me to ground my mind and heart in Cree culture. This grounding helped me to keep focused on the Cree aspect of the study, as opposed to discourse around postmodern and critical theories and theorists, which had initially captivated my attention.

Closing Thoughts

Research is a political act whether we want it to be or not. When we choose *how* we are going to come to know, meaning when we pick a research methodology, we are privileging particular ways-of-being in the world. When we give this choice little thought, the likelihood is high that we will unconsciously contribute to colonial oppression by bringing non-Indigenous ways-of-being into our relationships with Indigenous peoples and expecting them to at least accommodate our position. The knowledge that emerges will likely entrench non-Indigenous perspectives of life and will certainly not be a full Indigenous perspective. Whether this is understood as assimilation, marginalization or exclusion, the effects are similar: We as Indigenous peoples leave out some aspects of who we are in order to access the means and power for survival. This is what happened to the student who was forced to let go of the Indigenous ways of coming to know in order to complete her course "successfully." We cannot let this continue. As Indigenous peoples, we need our own ways of coming to know to be available to us so that when the time comes to do research with our people, we have the option to go forth in a manner consistent with our worldviews and ways-of-being. We need our research to be "for Indigenous people, by Indigenous people, and with Indigenous people."[1] In this way, we will maintain who we are as Indigenous people while contributing to the development of Indigenous knowledge.

This chapter outlines one way of going forward in a manner that is consistent with Indigenous worldviews and ways-of-being. It provides explanation of the relationship between worldviews and Indigenous research, which needs to be taken into consideration by people conducting research with Indigenous people. It presents a research paradigm that holds Indigenous perceptions, understandings and practices up front, with the intent that the knowledge gained from following such a paradigm will be more consistent with Indigenous ways-of-being than if other paradigms were used. While arguably limited, the paradigm acts to support the power of Indigenous people, whether they are in the role of researcher or research participant, so that our understandings will continue to be fertile ground for the developing knowledge of coming generations.

Notes

1. This term is partially borrowed from our Indigenous relatives, the Maori of Aotearoa, who coined the concept, "For Maori, by Maori." I added the phrase "with Indigenous people" to reflect the stance of many Indigenous people and recognize the communal focus where we do not act or go forward alone.

Section III — Traditional Knowledge

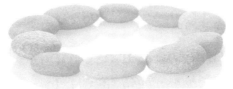

The Spirit of Dreaming
Traditional Knowledge for Indigenous Social Work

Gord Bruyere (Amawaajibitang)

> In the time of the Seventh Fire, a New People will emerge. They
> will retrace their steps to find what was left by the trail. Their steps
> will take them to the Elders who they will ask to guide them on
> their journey. But many of the Elders will have fallen asleep. They
> will awaken to this new time with nothing to offer. Some of the
> Elders will be silent out of fear. Some of the Elders will be silent
> because no one will ask anything of them. The New People will
> have to be careful in how they approach the Elders. The task of
> the New People will not be easy. If the New People remain strong
> in their quest... there will be a rebirth of the Anishinaabe nation
> and a rekindling of old flames. The Sacred Fire will again be lit.
> (Benton-Banai 1988: 91)

A friend who works in the field of community economic development among
the Nishnawbe-Aski Nation of Oji-Cree people of northern Ontario once
said to me that we are the contemporary manifestations of our languages,
cultures and ancestors. I hope that is true, and if it is true. I hope that we
represent them well and that our ways of life demonstrate an unbroken line
back to our creation.

Kathy Absolon, Michelle Reid and Jacquie Green offer powerful proof
that we are indeed picking up what was left by the trail, and they demonstrate that social work practice, even though a foreign construct, may be
reconceived and enacted through values, beliefs and practices uniquely
Indigenous. They illustrate that Indigenous social work practice is inevitably imbued with spirit and that what helped our ancestors to be sustained
and thrive may find expression in contemporary contexts. Together we can
dream of lighting that fire.

Chapter 9

Navigating the Landscape of Practice
Dbaagmowin of a Helper

Kathy Absolon (Minogiizhigokwe)

Giiwenh...
Geese teach us to share leadership
Amik (beaver) build dams and their agendas can divert waterways
Mukwa (bear) are protective; they are also healers
Birch trees, M'tig (trees) teach us about layers of being and they
stand together
Wabizhazhi (marten) teach us about being warriors and
strategists...
So marten up... our teachers are watching! (K. Absolon 2006)

Dbaagmowin [stories] of an *o'shkaabewis kwe* [woman helper] articulate a critical, compassionate, challenging and caring journey across landscapes of practice. Indigenous social work is a vast landscape encompassing prevention, intervention, post-intervention, administration, management, crisis, treatment, education, program development, community practice (healing and wellness) and organizing. Indigenous social work practice occurs with individuals, families, groups, communities, organizations and government and is cross referenced with the practice of many other health and social service professionals. It includes approaches based in Indigenous knowledge and traditions. Applications of practice that are culturally relevant and community-based must still interface with practitioners and services based in Euro-western theories. At times, finding a balance in the blend poses challenges. The terrain is as broad as the prairies and as diverse as the Canadian landscape from east to west, and north to south. Indigenous social work *o'shkaabewisuk* [helpers] seek positive transformation within the vastness of landscapes we navigate and negotiate. In becoming a social worker, we are essentially choosing to work as an *o'shkaabewis* [helper] within the realms where challenges, pain, trauma and turmoil exist. Such landscapes are rugged and turbulent, and navigation requires pertinent skills and knowledge. The landscape of practice is also full of inspiration, hope, possibilities and vision.

In this chapter, I locate myself, the land and the holistic context from which I practice. I introduce my philosophies as an Indigenous practitioner. My stories are about preparation, working with many strong people and communities, navigating rugged practice areas, identifying gems and thriving as a holistic *o'shkaabewis*. My overall goal is to share experiences and lessons and reflect on dynamics that, at times, I felt unprepared for. My hopes are that other *o'shkaabewisuk* may benefit and find validation and direction as they navigate their own landscapes and practice journeys.

Aki, The Land I Come From

Locating who I am establishes a context from where I write and speak (Absolon and Willett 2005; Monture-Angus 1995). Indigenous people always want to know who you are and where you come from. Location also establishes who I am not. I only represent myself and my experiences and do not speak on behalf of all Indigenous people.

Boozhoo. My Anishinaabe name is Minogiizhigokwe and I am from Flying Post First Nation in Northern Ontario. I grew up at a CN railway posting called Cranberry Lake, near Pickeral River. My mother is Anishinaabe and my father is British. My maternal grandparents were Shannon and Elizabeth Cryer (Pigeon); both were Anishinaabe language speakers and knew how to live off the land. My mother was sent to the Chapleau St. John's Anglican Residential School.

The land has many healing medicines. That is where I draw my strength from. Today my mind remembers being on the land and travels there when I need solace, healing and direction. My brother and I travelled in the bush, exploring, playing, making birch bark tea, trapping, fishing and being free. We loved going out on the land, and I found peace, comfort and safety among the trees. I often felt close to the animals and knew that the spirits around me would protect and watch me when I was in the bush alone. There were no streetlights, sidewalks, stores, malls, theatres or people. Trees, swamp, railway tracks and brush surrounded our house. I have much love, gratitude and connection to the uncolonized landscapes where I grew up.

Our Creator has given us beautiful life teachings that exist within Creation. Once again, we need to become aware of what those are. The bush offered central teachings, which I received as early as I can remember. My parents, especially my mother, ensured that we knew how to find our way home and that we had essentials for survival. We never went into the bush unprepared and we were taught how not to get lost. We made markers, remembered our trails and always had our pack of supplies. These early teachings and bush socialization remained in my consciousness as I entered into urban settings to live and work, and into universities to learn, teach and research. I have also carried my teachings and worldview into my practice as a social worker and community *o'shkaabewis kwe* [woman helper]. When I use the term *o'shkaabewis* [helper], what I mean is I am one of many of the Creator's helpers doing the Creator's work for our people. *O'shkaabewis* is Anishinaabe and loosely translates into the work of doing and being a helper. When I add *kwe*, it denotes woman, and *o'shkaabewisuk* is plural. Herein I use both English and Anishinaabe words. Being a social worker and educator is how I am an *o'shkaabewis kwe*, and I have learned some valuable lessons about being one.

Undoubtedly, my worldview is informed through my connection to the land. I search the earth's teachings for direction and guidance in my teaching, research and practice. I still recognize and remember that our true helpers and medicines come from the earth and if we are to regain our balance we need to reconnect to our life source. My social work education did not teach me that. For instance, the act of helping people doesn't always occur only in an office. For years our ancestors and relations lived outside, and healing ceremonies occurred in tandem with spirit helpers and with elements of the earth. Taking people on the land is good for their spirit, heart, mind and body. Medicines are all around. The elements give us the space we need to breath, yell, scream, feel, weep or laugh. In a sweat lodge ceremony, the water applied to hot rocks evokes a cleansing steam while we humbly sit in our mothers' womb. Spirit helpers are summoned and the doorway helpers call upon those keepers of medicine in each of the doorways. The wind, rivers and lakes can help us let go of grief, anger, pain and other baggage as they carry and release what is being let go. Earth is strong and I would encourage people to stomp on the ground and give their anger to her. Rocks can carry our burdens, so I would encourage people to pick up stones and toss them as far as they could to facilitate letting go. Facilitating healing with some people would occur outdoors with a fire and offerings of tobacco, prayers and rituals. Sitting on the water's edge provided grounding energy to sharing, listening and releasing. Sharing would then not only be with me, but with all of Creation. I took many people on walks among the natural healing properties of Creation so they could diffuse and process their experiences. During those times, I believe, the elements such as the wind, water, earth, trees, animals and birds became the helpers and healers, and the environment's harmony fostered balance and healing within. Because of my connection to the land, Spirit is also central to my practice. I recognize that each of us is a spirit being and that our spirits must work together using the principles bestowed upon us through our sacred teachings. These are teachings that address balance, humility, truth, respect, sharing and love. Upon the earth there are many *o'shkaabewisuk* [helpers] and their healing medicines come in many forms. We must try to recognize them and bring them into our practice as holistic helpers.

Preparing and Learning to Be That
Mino o'shkaabewis [Good Helper]

Our personal wellness and healing determines our capacity as *o'shkaabewisuk*. Years ago, I journeyed within my own personal landscape critically reflecting on my internalized colonialism and knew that "something wasn't right and something didn't fit." I felt that my experiences were not what the Creator intended for us as a people. My only explanation for knowing this comes from growing up immersed in the bush with Creation where Spirit was all around me. From this place, a small spirit within with a tiny voice began to tug at me and I started to listen. A transformational and paradoxical shift occurred when I became conscious of my own feelings of incongruence. From the outside I heard messages stating that I was inferior, subordinate, stupid, unworthy and incapable. I heard us being called drunken dirty Indians. Yet, inside me there was a tiny voice urging me to make my way out of the darkness of chaos (hooks 1993). Deep within me I felt my *cocomish* and *shaumish* (grandparents) urging me to seek our truth.

When I was twenty-five I began my journey out of internalized shame, blame and racism toward love and acceptance of myself as an Anishinaabe *kwe*. On this journey, I remembered my ancestors, grandparents and mother. I learnt from other Anishinaabe teachers and Elders. I learned to listen to my inner voice and tend to the wounds within. Anishinaabe relations and non-Aboriginal allies encouraged and supported my journey. There have been many *o'shkaabewisuk* along the way. I went to ceremonies and gatherings, and as I learnt about the beauty of my culture, people and identity, I heard and saw myself in those teachings. Today, I am committed to practising our ceremonies and learning Anishinaabemowin (Anishinaabe language). I am proud to belong to the Midewiwin Lodge. The dominant messages of inferiority no longer matched what I was learning and I had the tools to critique colonizing knowledges. I studied colonization and history from Indigenous perspectives and began making sense of my family experiences. A process of unlearning racist messages and representations began. Listening to other Aboriginal mentors and tending to my spirit fuelled a strengthening of my own inner fire and mind. The dismemberment between my heart and head was being remembered and reconnected. The stronger my fire grew, the more I could identify colonizing experiences. This listening and learning quenched an unbelievable thirst for understanding and validation. A critical analysis along with cultural healing and learning occurred. The journey has continued for many years now and has been what guides me as I continue to travel the landscapes that are beautiful, rugged and rough. My personal learning and healing is holistic and goes in tandem with becoming a strong *o'shkaabewis*.

I am critical of my western education because of the colonial legacy to assimilate our minds into Euro-western knowledge. Negotiating the academic landscape of my western education was time consuming and required extra effort to explain, articulate and present my worldview, history and experiences as an Indigenous social work student. Extra research was required because Indigenous literature was omitted and faculty did not have the resources I needed. I became self-directed and self-determined. I had to search harder for Indigenous-based practica and pushed to include Indigenous methods in my thesis. To the credit of some of the faculty, I felt supported and encouraged along the way and experienced the significance of allies in the academy. I am thankful for those allies. It wasn't until my doctoral studies that I had the incredible opportunity to experience classes taught by Indigenous professors with choices of explicitly Indigenous courses. The experience was extremely positive, validating and full of tremendous learning. For the first time in my education I experienced a sense of normalcy, the presence of cultural mirrors, peer dialogue, relevant knowledge and contextual validation. Indigenous education by and with Indigenous people possesses a capacity for transformation, Indigenization and decolonization. Because some Indigenous people have received both a cultural and colonial education we tend to translate knowledge back and forth toward a bi-cultural competency, which I think is still unacknowledged by the academy. I continually challenge western academics to achieve the level of bi-cultural competency that we, Indigenous scholars, have achieved. Bi-culturalism is a product of having to master western approaches while simultaneously being Anishinaabe and having an Anishinaabe orientation.

As I searched for relevant knowledge, I encountered critical Indigenous educators, social workers and cultural teachers who eventually became a part of my circle of mentors. They educated me about our cultural and colonial history, while helping me to develop a working theory and analysis. I was hungry for contextual relevance, understanding and knowledge. When I was introduced to the works of Howard Adams (1975), Paulo Freire (1996), bell hooks (1990, 1993, 1994), Franz Fanon (1963) and other critical educators and writers, I devoured their work.

Determining a full sense of which western theories and practice methods would stay in my repertoire of tools took a long time. Critical analysis and reflection were central to the process of deciding what I would accept and utilize. I currently prefer holistic circle work as a primary methodology in practice. It facilitates connectedness, which counters colonial alienation. For Indigenous people it fosters a group memory, power, togetherness and hope. Empowerment theories[1] facilitated understanding of powerlessness and regaining one's power. A strengths perspective[2] resonated with my goals in lifting up our strengths versus enshrining our pain and suffering. Resistance knowledge[3] provided an approach to reframing experiences of trauma, pain and despair into stories of resistance and empowerment. It moved us from victim to survivor to living. Trauma theory[4] and intergenerational trauma theory helped me to understand the impact of residential schools, land dispossessions, relocations and community oppression at the hand of a racist and colonizing government. Intergenerational trauma theory helped me to see the impact of events that happened to my great grandparents, grandparents, parents and me. They helped us to see how colonial trauma affected our ancestors, families and communities. Liberation theory[5] helped me to understand the movement from a place of oppression to freedom. Liberation can occur at all levels of the spirit, mind, heart and body. This theory is very useful in understanding that the oppression experienced by Indigenous peoples are systemic and structural and that differences in class, social location, education and employment are a result of structural inequalities and institutional oppressions. These theories helped me to place my experiences as an Aboriginal woman in the context of colonialism, racism, classism and sexism. Theories that help Indigenous individuals, families, communities and nations understand the root causes of the social, health, economic and systemic problems are very useful. Furthermore, a structural approach fit because it moved problem definitions away from marginalized people to structures and institutions. Thus, change is not directed toward oppressed or marginalized people, but towards institutions and structures in society that oppress and marginalize. A structural social worker aims to change structures and how they interface with people. For example, I have tried to change how social workers are educated in relation to Indigenous issues, and schools of social work and the social work curriculum are the focus of change. We can improve the lives of people by making resources and structures more accessible and less oppressive. In my search for relevant practice approaches, I knew that the problem definition was not based on individual deficits or limitations. I diligently continued searching for relevant explanations, approaches and tools so that I could build a knowledge bundle of Indigenous peoples' history, experiences and ways of helping.

Community-based approaches, participatory and action oriented methodologies, liberation theory and anti-colonial practices are relevant in developing a knowledge and application base for working within Indigenous community contexts. These approaches are inclusive of people, foster identifying resources, draw on existing knowledge and wisdoms, and position control in the hands of the community. I have such gratitude to people at the community level because they are the people with whom and for whom I worked; they are also my teachers, helpers and friends. From them I received lessons, strength and support.

Today, the genealogy of my *kandossiwin dkobjiganan* [knowledge bundle] is rooted in the land, the teachings of the Midewiwin Lodge and being Anishinaabe. My *kandossiwin dkobjiganan* is combination of an Anishinaabe cultural orientation (Absolon 1993; Benton-Banai 1988, 2001; Graveline 2000, 2004; Gross 2002; Hart 1997, 2002; McCormick 2005; Nabigon 2006; Nabigon, Hagey, Webster and MacKay 1998; Poonwassie and Charter 2005), decolonizing theory and methodologies (Absolon and Willett 2005; Alfred 2005; Battiste 2000; Brown and Strega 2005; Calliou 2001; Duran and Duran 1995; Henderson 2000a, 2000b; hooks 1993; LaRocque 1991; Little Bear 2000; Mihesuah 2003; Monture-Angus 1999; Simpson 2001; Smith 1999; Stevenson 2000; Young 2003) and empowerment-based practices (Absolon and Herbert 1997; Antone, Miller and Myers 1986; Pinderhughes 1989). I have utilized empowerment approaches, such as the spiral model, where existing experiences are acknowledged to foster a process of reflection and action. Eclectic best describes the blending of Indigenous knowledge and traditions with progressive contemporary approaches to practice. I continue to draw on group work and community work as allied methodologies of practice, although today I draw primarily on my own holistic teachings and practices. When I personally feel weak and tired I often go into the bush or to the water to replenish my spirit and to be with the Creator.

> On the rocky shore of the beautiful Georgian Bay
> Rocks beneath me are smooth and as ancient as the earth
> Solid, grounding and testimony to her strength
> Sparkling, shimmering water nourishes the land
> Asema, I hold in my left hand
> Looking over the water
> Chi'miigwech to the ancestors and to G'chi' Manidoo;
> Praying for guidance and strength — am I alone?
> I offer a song and sing into the wind —
> Five (maangak) loons slowly appear one by one
> They offer their song and call back to me — I am not!
> Life's circle affirming presence and connections
> Maang is my spirit guide and friend… Miigwech.
> That was a good day! (K. Absolon 2008)

Dbaagmowin of Strength, Spirit and Resistance

I begin with reflections of the practice landscape that are filled with *dbaagmowin* [stories] of spirit and strength. Integral to the outcome of any story is the perspective from which it flows. Indigenous people have had enough approaches and perspectives that problematize, pathologize, patronize and paternalize us. The landscape of practice is full of gems and rarities. People in communities are diverse. What I mean by that is there are people who have survived residential school assaults, child welfare authorities, missionary enthusiasts and the assimilationist violence of Canadian Indian policy. There are people who, despite living in conditions of poverty, violence, unemployment and inadequate housing, continue to believe in who they are and know more about their language and culture than I ever will. They are our teachers. There are people who work toward *mino-bimaadisiwin* [the good life] at a variety of levels and in a variety of ways. Collectively, efforts towards community healing and wellness are evident at the spiritual, emotional, mental and physical levels. Further examples of healing and wellness initiatives exist at the political, economic, health, education, justice and social levels, where worker's individual efforts are interrelated and interdependent toward more holistic and broader community and nation levels. Many resources can be identified and brought together. The vision and lens from which we practice must, first and foremost, enable us to see those spirits, strengths and resources. Indigenous traditions are holistic, based on cyclical and circular teachings. The use of circles has become recognized as powerful in teaching, healing and learning processes.

Using circles and groups engages many minds, hearts and bodies to work, learn and grow together. Information about the pragmatics of facilitating and working with groups or circles already exists (Graveline 2000; Hart 1997, 2002; Nabigon 2006; Nabigon et al. 1999). These authors discuss affirmative circles and group processes that are beneficial within Indigenous contexts. Circles facilitate a re-membership and reconnection with other people. It helps counter isolation that many people feel; there is strength in circle. When initiating a circle, the size isn't as relevant as those who actually show up. Responding to critical issues in groups lends itself to developing peer support networks, especially with intense issues such as suicide. In my experience, at the community level, we would organize a group meeting to deal with the increasing episodes of suicide and a few people would show up. Great, a process has begun! Validate those people who put the time and energy into attending a group meeting because they are your beginning and they will be the strength of the circle. Those who attend a circle are the strength and the resource. Lift them up and give them your time and energy, and work collectively with those who are present. Those people who do attend have a reason and that's where you begin.

Sometimes people are reluctant to share what they know or think. This is not just an Indigenous cultural characteristic of being shy. Some people have internalized fear and lack self-confidence in expressing what they think or feel and hold back their views, ideas and feelings. Critical education and community action works to consciously evoke the thoughts, experiences and knowledge of people via education, dialogue, reflection and action (Absolon and Herbert 1997). Dealing with internalized fear means spending time acknowledging and educating groups about the history of colonization and its effects on our voice and confidence. Facilitating opportunities for people to share their stories and knowledge creates portals for opportunities of learning, healing and remembering. Through critical educational processes, people can develop an understanding about racism, colonization and oppression and their effects on how we think and feel about ourselves. The answers exist within the process of finding our voices and our way.

For some people, finding the power within and expressing themselves is difficult. Because of their internalized inferiority and fear, people need encouragement and support to feel safe enough to share their thoughts and feelings. Facilitating voice can be done by allowing people time to collect their thoughts, honouring silence and waiting for responses. Ask specific questions and be persistent in seeking people's ideas. Patience is required, along with the belief and faith that the answers lie within the people. Share the facilitating by having others take responsibility for various aspects of the process, such as the opening, scheduling, facilitating, praying, singing, drumming, recording and organizing. Create a collective process. Effort is needed to reassure, affirm and validate what people have to offer and to create a safe space for people to explore hearing themselves share openly within a group. The experience of speaking up can be intimidating and exciting for people who are typically silenced. Initially that voice sounds like a squeaky mouse. Affirmations, validations, acknowledgement and gratitude counter internalized fear of expression. It is truly amazing to witness people who have not shared their voice with others begin to experience the sound of their own voice. At times the integrations of story-telling, drumming or singing are examples of how voices are expressed. Having tea and bannock is a non-threatening way to bring people together to share. As people begin to trust themselves and one another, they start to express what is on their mind and in their hearts. Innovative ideas emerge. Ideas are shared and enthusiasm grows. Birthing an idea begins with a sound of a voice. I saw people's eyes shine with pride. I saw people come out from their timidity and uncertainty to a place of being catalysts and leaders in community-based initiatives. I saw groups who were hesitant to establish their authority move to accepting their position and knowledge as they made changes to their programs, goals and mandates. These changes occurred, in part, as a result of confronting internalized oppression and inferiority. They also occurred because of community support, cultural teachings and a will to create positive change. In the next section I share a couple of stories, one of an individual and the other of a community process.

Akiikwe

As a helper, I walked with Akiikwe for only a short time during her life. From her I carry an incredible story of resilience and resistance. Her story is not uncommon as I have witnessed this resiliency and strength in others too. I had been working with Akiikwe, an older woman, who had spent most of her life on the reserve. Like me, she had lived in the bush. Her eyes were worn, wrinkles evident, and her body reflected life's harshness, yet she still smiled and joked around. She presented herself as a tough survivor of life and was somewhat guarded. She was seeking help with post-traumatic stress and depression and had been in her sobriety for a few years. She was still in recovery. Other issues that concerned her were finances, relationships and family matters. She did not have a high income and was working part-time as a hotel chambermaid. We walked among Creation and spent many hours together, and in those moments I encouraged her to tell me the stories of her life experiences, of which she had many. This woman had lived a thousand lives and was still walking around smiling, laughing and shining. I truly enjoyed listening to her and being her helper. One day she came to see me. We had tea and just began talking when she unveiled a particular time in her childhood that was pretty daunting and traumatic for her. This is a close variation of what she told me. I call her Akiikwe [Earth woman] because she is so strong and amazing.

Akiikwe told me of her life growing up in the small house on a reserve in remote Northern Ontario with her younger sisters and brothers. Akiikwe was the oldest of six children. She described being sexually abused by her uncles while they were intoxicated. Her parents could not help her because they too were alcoholics and were usually passed out when her uncle came and forced himself upon her. She was sexually abused throughout her growing up years. She described her childhood house as a typical reserve bungalow with a small kitchen where they cooked and ate. A woodstove kept the kitchen and surrounding areas warm. The bedrooms and living room were also tiny. They had a bathroom with a sink and tub, and an extra outhouse. Accommodations were tight and they all shared bedrooms.

Akiikwe said that she hated Fridays and dreaded the coming of the weekend, unlike most people who look forward to the weekend. Akiikwe cringed in telling me that she would dread the weekend because that was when all the drinking and partying would take over her home. Given the size of the house, there was no place to hide or seek refuge from adults.

One weekend in particular her house was filling up with people and the drinking had begun. She was afraid for her sisters. While sharing this, she became quiet and the energy changed — she took a breath to pause. Water came and in tears, she recounted that day when she began to pack up her younger siblings and took them into the thick of the bush and swamp. She described a fort that she had previously built back there. She had stocked that fort with canned food and supplies and had snuck blankets to keep them warm. She had been preparing for this time. She told me that as the people in the house got drunker she got more afraid and took her younger siblings to the fort and kept them there all weekend until she knew that the drinkers would be going home. She cried and cried about being afraid and wanting to keep the others safe. When Sunday evening came, she knew that it would be okay to go back home and that her siblings would be safe. The memories of this story conjured up traumatic pain and suffering. Akiikwe recounted this story, telling me how ashamed and humiliated she felt about herself and her fear. Akiikwe was, at that moment, that young girl feeling afraid and powerless in the forces of family alcoholism, abuse and violence.

I listened to her story, asking for more details from time to time. As I witnessed Akiikwe share the painful memories of her past, I was astounded by her strength and beauty. Here sat with me a woman feeling weak, afraid and hurt, and all I could see was her resilience and resistance. As she was wiping the tears from her eyes and blowing her nose, I looked at her with a faint smile. She looked up at me with a wondering glare, searching for an explanation for my smile. I waited for her to ask and she did. I returned her question with a question and I said to Akiikwe, "Do you see how strong and resourceful you really are?" She nodded indicating no. I first told her that I was sorry she had experienced such pain in her childhood and that the memory brought her hurt to the surface again. But then I went on to share with Akiikwe what else I saw in her experience. She was very courageous and strong to have gone and built a fort for her siblings to keep them safe. She was really smart to have gotten food and supplies so that they wouldn't be hungry or thirsty. She was very brave to take them into the bush by herself, even though she felt so afraid. Finally, I shared with her that her siblings were so lucky to have her to protect them. I told her: "You must have really loved them. You are a beautiful person Akiikwe. Your story is amazing and it shows what courage, strength and resilience you had then and must still have today. Your spirit is strong. That is why, I believe, you are still smiling, laughing and working so hard to rebuild yourself and your own family."

Akiikwe had never thought of that particular experience as an indication of her own resourcefulness, strength, resistance and resilience. As we talked about her experiences further, she began to reframe — to re-story — her experience and to see herself in a different, more positive way. Re-storying is the process of restoring our history and ourselves. I will never forget that day with Akiikwe and that story she shared with me because it tells me that you never know what is beneath the surface of a person. Stories of survival are horrific and magnificent all at once. There are many strengths and gems within our people. Akiikwe is a gem that I carry in my memory.

B'saanibamaadsiwin

Community practice with Indigenous communities has to be culturally and contextually relevant, liberatory, participatory and involve capacity building. This next story comes from a time when I was coordinating

B'saanibamaadsiwin, a Native mental health program. Working with community was central to our philosophy and mission as a program. Much of what we did involved community-based efforts, whereby participants in programs and initiatives were identified by their community and worked for the benefit of their community.

In this particular story we were engaging in a broad community-based research project, which spanned two years with a goal of identifying the needs of our participating communities. A big emphasis of this project was capacity building, and structured into the design was community education and community-based participation throughout all stages of the research project. Eight communities each identified two researchers to participate. Another essential process in this project was community-based researcher education and support. Many of the community-based researchers had not done research before, indicated that they did not know how to do research and felt intimidated at the prospects of being in such a role.

Education about research theory and methods was the first priority of the project, and we drafted a curriculum for teaching the researchers. Community-based research also means that the community has control over the design and methodology, data, analysis and results. Hence, the community-based researchers were trained on the whole gamut of the research process. We had to go through stages of colonization of research toward decolonizing research and introduce the participants to possible methods for their communities. We emphasized the principles of respect and community diversity and that all community research methods would not have to be homogeneous. Needless to say, the process was in-depth, time consuming and not without its challenges. Peer support to the community-based researchers was imperative.

The community-based researchers grappled with their own confidence and self-esteem issues and abilities to do the project and to do the research in their own communities. There were community dynamics, political dynamics, family dynamics and critical incidents. For example, some communities were going through elections, which can positively or negatively effect community dynamics. Other communities were dealing with homicides and suicides. Other communities had frequent governance or staff turnovers, and relationship building was always necessary. Certainly, there were challenging dynamics across all the communities. Despite this, the community-based researchers were innovative, motivated and instrumental. The project's success was depended on the development of their capacity and confidence.

I clearly remember being in meetings with the group and hearing some of them express their trepidation at doing the research. Over time, as we demystified research methods, the participants grew in their understanding and confidence. In creating a step-by-step process the researchers slowly began to understand how to search for knowledge in their own community. They also realized that this was not new to them. Acknowledging their existing knowledge and skill was the foundation upon which we built. The process of witnessing their growth was far more rewarding than the actual results. Their problem-solving skills were tested and their ability to know what to do was supported. I remember receiving panic stricken phone calls about some research or community issue. Slowly we identified the obstacles, while supporting the community-based researchers to implement their communication and problem-solving skills. They experienced positive outcomes, which further empowered them. They learnt about various stages of research and participated in the design and implementation of methods. The community-based researchers collected their own data; we had workshops on data analysis and interpretation, and on final reporting. Educating about the various facets of research helped them to understand how we search for knowledge and acquire information. They could then become their own researchers in relation to program development, evaluation or needs assessments.

At the end of the process, some of the researchers were amazed with themselves. There were many smiles and stories about their experiences. We celebrated their accomplishments. We had sharing circles where we processed the experience and shared stories of what it was like to be a researcher in your own community. I distinctly remember one of the community-based researchers happily proclaiming with confidence, "I didn't know I could do this!" The experience over the two years was long and intense at times, but the changes in the researchers' capacities from not knowing to learning and understanding demonstrated the strength inherent within our communities. Education that is relevant, meaningful and purposeful strengthens community capacity and redistributes power and control of knowledge into the hands of the community. Cultural protocols and practices, when coupled with capacity-building initiatives, present powerful tools for community healing and wellness practices.

Community practice is dynamic, exciting, challenging and fun. My love for it also comes from all the amazing strengths and processes I was involved in. It was an honour to have worked with so many good people. Good stuff happens when Indigenous people's strengths and knowledge are built into the process. The communities are full of positive and heartwarming people who have beautiful spirits and whose resilience shines in their spirits. I began with sharing stories of resources, beauty and strength because that's where I needed to begin. The beauty of the landscape exists in the beauty of the people, whose strengths I witnessed and found to be exquisite.

Dbaagmowin of Gems

Hidden gems lie in the abundance of cultural and traditional knowledge that exists beneath a community's surface. This knowledge is not always evident. There are people who know about the land, language, medicines, rituals and who have stories of times past. They are the record keepers and sacred knowledge holders. There are cultural helpers who facilitate cultural healing processes. Gems are precious minerals often hidden beneath a rugged exterior. They possess healing properties and their energies are used to facilitate healing. Finding the gems beneath the surface requires knowledge that they do, in fact, exist. Respect for the existence of gems enables an *o'shkaabewis* to be patient and to watch for those gem-like qualities to emerge. Qualities of the Seven Grandfathers' teachings are an example of such gifts we carry. The following story is part of our Anishinaabe Creation story where O'Shkaabewis was sent to the earth as the Creator's helper to find someone who could be taught about how to live in harmony with Creation and who would deliver that knowledge to the people. O'Shkaabewis found a little boy and that little boy was the one who received the teachings of the Seven Grandfathers. Each of those gifts was presented to him in a vessel and he was to be a messenger for his people. The following story is about those gifts, which we all carry:

> The boy had been given a huge bundle to take to his people from the Seven Grandfathers, Ni-gig [otter] and the boy took turns carrying the bundle. Along the way, they stopped seven times. At each stop a spirit came and told the boy the meaning of one of the seven gifts that were given to him out of the vessel of the Grandfathers.
>
> 1. To cherish knowledge is to know WISDOM.
> 2. To know LOVE is to know peace.
> 3. To honour all of Creation is to have RESPECT.
> 4. BRAVERY is to face the foe with integrity.
> 5. HONESTY in facing a situation is to be brave.
> 6. HUMILITY is to know yourself as a sacred part of Creation.
> 7. TRUTH is to know all of these things.
>
> The spirit taught the boy that for each gift there was an opposite, as evil is the opposite of good. He would have to be careful to instruct his people in the right way to use each gift. (Benton-Benai 1988: 64)

The story of the little boy and the Seven Grandfathers teaches us to see beyond and beneath: to see the gifts/gems within people. Communities are made up of people who are visionaries, healers, teachers, leaders, helpers and others who are viable community resources. Communities today may have healing and wellness centers. Some of the people look rough on the outside, but are still community gems. For example, I knew an old woman who loved to feed others. She loved to prepare and share food. Her food and gatherings fostered community connections and broke cycles of isolation. An *o'shkaabewis* needs to have a belief in the people and a faith in our communities. We need to search for hidden gems, keep our eyes open, and when we see evidence of them, we need to genuinely invite them along. Here is another short story about what I saw in a community's efforts to develop its crisis response capacity:

Many community *o'shkaabewisuk* gathered on this particular day to organize a community crisis response capacity. Only a few people attended our planning circle to generate ideas. The low attendance did not stop us though. Some felt discouraged by this. A few others said we must continue with our work and do our best. So we proceeded to discuss the many concerns and issues of developing a community crisis response plan. The food was great, as was the laughter and team spirit. Throughout our discussions it became evident that a strong community capacity did exist. Our fire was getting stronger. We began to identify community members and how we saw them. Mabel down the road was an excellent cook and could provide meals if needed. Percy was the community healing and wellness worker and could provide support. Stan drove the bus and could provide emergency transportation if needed. Brenda was a nurse and could provide emergency first aid support. Walter was a roofer and had all kinds of tools, ladders and ropes. Judy made the best scone and pies. She also loved children and could provide a good safe house. There were other small business owners who could provide services such as firewood, emergency repairs, carpentry, electrical or mechanical support. The community had a firehall, recreation centre, health centre and school. As we searched and looked within, we started to see what was actually present in both the people and in the community's capacity. Over time through our planning circles we began to identify and articulate many resources and how they could be mobilized in a community crisis response. We were excited with the possibilities and saw these capacities as realistic. A community crisis response plan was emerging and the people who could be utilized were right in the community.

Absolutely, strengths and gems exist within people and their communities. The answers are in the process. People are needed for a process to emerge. Engage with the people and trust them. Have faith and work to make the invisible visible. Seek them out because Indigenous practice is not a practice that ought to be done alone. Now, that's only half the story. As with anything there is also another side to our story. A story characterized by a more rugged landscape, a landscape more tenuous to navigate, negotiate and far more tricky to practise in.

> I dreamt last night that I was caught in a dark tornado
> I saw the darkness off in the distance
> Omniscience filled the sky
> The gray and blackened clouds quickly approached my window
> I ran to warn the others, but…
> It grabbed me and I was left powerless
> Floating, turning upside down and around…
> What happened and where am I?
> I was not prepared for this! (K. Absolon 2006)

Dbaagmowin of Rugged Landscapes

Holistic, cyclical and circular concepts exist within Indigenous philosophies. Opposite or contrary concepts of positive and negative forces exist, and dualities are recognized and accepted. Contrary to spirits that live toward *mino-bimaadisiwin* [a good life] are those spirits that are opposite and are called *windigo* [the negative forces or dark side within]. Sometimes trauma has such a devastating effect on a person's spirit that anger, hurt, pain, sorrow and resentment take over. Our stories exist along a circular continuum within which dualities exist: at one point there is *mino-bimaadisiwin* and at the opposite side there is self-hatred and ultimately suicide. There can be both love and hate, greed and generosity, fear and courage or weakness and strength. Within that circle many other conditions exist. Landscapes are never smooth, and the journey is fraught with difficult terrain, barriers, harsh weather and unforeseen circumstances. Often our visions and goals for our practices are filled with hopes of having a positive impact.

Within First Nations contexts the landscape is characterized by rich cultural histories and oppressive colonial histories. Landscapes of Indigenous practice are riddled with minefields of externalized and internalized racism and colonialism. In education we talk about decolonization, yet resistance to liberation exists at all levels from the personal, to the organizational, to the political. Dealing with the reality of turbulent landscapes can be disheartening and disillusioning. Yet, there are various coping, decolonizing and empowering strategies of practising within colonized realities. Always keep in mind that these landscapes evolved from psychological, emotional, mental, spiritual and physical trauma of colonial abuse and violence. Navigating and surviving turbulent landscapes is about staying focused, having awareness, knowing what to do and acknowledging our tools and capacities. Our grandparents taught us how not to get lost in the bush — we will take these skills and translate them to the journeys and practices of today.

Dynamic Relationships

The reality of working in my home territory as an Indigenous social worker meant that I would have multiple relationships with people I worked with. At the community level, relationships are multi-faceted. Our relationship boundaries are diverse, and roles within the community may be diverse. For example, there were many people with whom I worked who I also knew as a child and went to high school with. Some of my clients and colleagues were longtime friends. They may have also been the sisters, brothers or parents of my close friends. I felt related to some of these people. I was also involved within the traditional community, went to pow-wows and participated in community-based events. I could have been in relationship with any one person in a variety of contexts. In other words, our clients may be a combination of our friends, relatives, relatives of friends, Elders, leaders or other helpers. When you live and work in the same communities you service, your relationships tend to overlap. The advantage to having multi-layered relationships is in our direct connection and history within those relationships. These relationships are already created and developed, and most people know who you are and hopefully feel good enough about you to work with you. Disadvantages exist in areas of overlapping boundaries and the discomfort that can arise when you know "too much" about people in your community and that changes how you interact and makes moving around the community a bit more complicated. Tact, awareness and diplomacy become important skills. Confidentiality is imperative and not divulging confidential information means that, at times, you safeguard knowledge without others knowing, wishing you did not know what you did or wanting to say something but knowing you cannot. Walking on such landscapes requires making conscious choices and sacrifices, and having respect for all those relationships. Occasionally, people may become angry with you for not rescuing them or they may not understand the boundaries you exercise.

When working "at home" the multi-layered relationships are a reality, and there is no such thing as objectivity or anonymity because everyone knows where you live and who you are. I often did not need directions to people's homes or descriptions of where they lived because I already knew this. In the evenings or on weekends I would have people knock on my door and I would serve them tea and talk about whatever was on their mind. I would not turn people away. Sometimes people would arrive on my doorstep late at night seeking support, a drive home or a safe place to sleep. Most of the people with whom I worked knew me personally, and our relationships were life long. We were interconnected in both formal and informal ways. I liked having history with the people and I liked the informality it offered. I liked having contextual knowledge. People trusted me because I belonged there too. Sometimes, though, it was difficult to find a balance and establish healthy boundaries for myself and family.

Diversity

Diversity across Indigenous peoples and communities in terms of governance, nations, languages, protocols, lifestyles, community make-up, religions and cultures is impressive. Within Indigenous nations, the degree of diversity determines the types of practice approaches. Negotiating diverse governance systems means understanding and attending to diverse community protocols related to policy and legislation, such as in child welfare. Band council structures are diverse and changes in governance can affect programming, funding priorities and service portfolios and protocols. People who make up the communities are diverse. Communities are comprised of traditional Knowledge Keepers, who carry responsibilities as traditional teachers, medicine healers, traditional helpers and ceremony conductors. People of Christian denominations also exist in First Nations communities. Some people are atheists. As a result of the mixture of colonizing religions and the revitalization of Indigenous traditions and ceremonies, some people are in the midst of figuring out for themselves what it all means to them and may be unsure and cautious about their place within ceremony. There are people who are assimilated and live more of a Euro-western Canadian lifestyle; people who retain their traditional beliefs and values and who speak their language fluently; people who retain traditional beliefs and choose aspects of Euro-western life; and people who are still lost and caught in place of turmoil and despair. Never assume to know who the people are until you talk to them and hear their stories.

Because Indigenous communities are not homogeneous, generalizing traditional or cultural approaches to an Indigenous community can be erroneous and may alienate you from the people. Also, espousing Eurocentric theories and practices and applying them to Indigenous contexts is colonizing and resembles missionary work. Finding a balanced approach is challenging and requires a consciousness of the community context. Additionally, communities are comprised of people who have moved along a continuum of turmoil and despair to healing and wellness. Along that continuum some people exist in survival mode and do not have the inner resources, time or external resources to "self-actualize." Along this continuum some people see a future, others live each day as it comes, and others are caught in the past.

The diversity of people's existence along this continuum are manifestations of a combination of rich cultures and a legacy of colonization, residential schools, *Indian Act* policy, reserve systems, racism, child welfare scoops, social welfare dependency and societal marginalization. Overcoming such a violent and oppressive history is complicated, and the process of recovery is taking an undetermined amount of time, resources, knowledge and methodologies.

Windigo

O'shkaabewisuk, too, can become traumatized by working in the front lines of the colonial aftermath. Just as a doctor can catch a cold from patients, an *o'shkaabewis* [helper] can experience secondary or vicarious trauma. That being said, I don't believe that vicarious is an accurate word for Indigenous social workers affected by critical incidents because we too, carry our own baggage of colonization. Traumatic events can simply trigger our own traumatic experiences. I believe there is a greater likelihood for an Indigenous social worker to be exposed and become as traumatized by critical events as the community. This likelihood, I believe, is increased when the *o'shkaabewis* is from or personally connected to the community.

The intensity of community crisis situations is overwhelming at times. For example, suicide attempts are critical and suicide fatalities are tragic. When innocent bystanders are involved in crisis situations the response must become broader. Communities deal with violent and volatile situations on a regular basis. Living in crisis for some communities is the norm, and these situations may be exacerbated when people cope by using drugs and alcohol. In some communities sexual abuse is rampant and multiple sexual abuse disclosures can create a community wide crisis in a very short period of time. Homicides and double homicides, or homicide/suicides, do occur and the effects on the people and crisis responders are traumatic.

Coping with and resolving such critical incidents takes an understanding of the crisis response process as well as knowledge of services and resources to aid in a response. Care of immediate responders involves providing debriefings and opportunities for helpers to recover from any residual effects they may be experiencing. Beginning with community strengths and resiliencies is imperative to working through traumatic community crisis back toward that place of resilience again. During the intensity of a crisis it is also important that the capacity of the community to respond, intervene and resolve the events be visible. Working with community strengths and resources enables the identification and mobilization of community-based capacities to enact crisis responses.

Disempowerment has manifested in many forms and with oppressed peoples we must be prepared to recognize the faces of disempowerment. The most common face is blaming. Blaming is endemic in our communities. I wondered why there is so much blaming. I witnessed workers blaming leadership, leadership blaming each other, community members blaming leadership and workers, families blaming families, and the list goes on. It all boils down to people giving their power away. I believe the blaming game is a form of disempowerment and disables us from taking power back and responsibility where we can. Within a power analysis, blaming reflects the epitome of someone saying, "you have power over me and I don't have any power." Blaming reinforces a dispossession of people's power and creates mental blocks that inhibit people from identifying what they have the power to do and then owning that power. For example, a referral is not made and a client misses the intake for a residential program. The client blames the worker for not being there. The worker blames the client for not showing up. Someone did not do the paperwork and the band clerk is blamed for not providing the forms. Everyone blamed someone else and ultimately gave away their power. When we blame, I see power being passed along to someone else. Blaming becomes a destructive means of resolving a problem, avoiding responsibility or denying one's power to make a change.

As a helper, blaming may be directed at you and you may incur a few hits yourself. So be prepared and recognize that blaming is a form of disempowerment and try not to take it personally. This blaming can come in the form of a complaint about your work, you may be accused of not following through, or you may be blamed for not being organized enough. You may also be blamed for not being available on demand. Blaming is common, and we need to talk about it and identify it as a symptom of disempowerment. Colonized people can strive for empowerment in dangerous ways and clients can make allegations or complaints against you. I have talked with police officers, mental health professionals, child welfare workers, social welfare workers, educators and justice workers. All of those *o'shkaabewisuk* are vulnerable to allegations and complaints. They all expressed concerns and have experienced the backlash of blaming and anger. I don't have any words of advice except to create awareness that a turbulent landscape of blaming exists.

Some people who have lived in oppressive and colonized conditions have learnt the masterful art of manipulation as a survival strategy. The reality of social work practice is that we work with people who have adapted to their hardships of abuse by becoming abusive and manipulative. In schools of social work, I rarely hear educators talking about clients who become abusive in their helping relationship or clients who attempt to manipulate their helpers to get their unhealthy needs met. Manipulations occur in distorted accounts of events, misrepresentations, denials and blaming. I have heard stories from other helpers of how their clients manipulated them to get more money or resources, or to not have to be responsible to fulfill their service agreements. We hear many excuses, reasons, stories and explanations from clients for not doing their part. People cry, scream, weep or become pitiful. We can feel sorry for them. They can even become angry with us, and for some helpers, experiencing intense emotional reactions in people is scary. As frustrating as it is, human helpers are not beyond the swindling master-minds of manipulators. People with addictions are a good example of master manipulators because when their addiction is out of control, they will say or do almost anything to feed it. Naïve and good hearted social workers are vulnerable to being manipulated. Do not take it personally. Manipulations are a survival strategy. I felt that I needed to talk about oppression and disempowerment, not in the political sense, but as an internalized dynamic because these situations are real in Indigenous social work contexts and our *o'shkaabewisuk* need to be prepared for the other side of reality. Social workers need to find means to deal with traumatization in their own lives and develop their own supports. If a worker experiences victimization by clients they need to confide in other helpers and seek the support and guidance of their Elders, peers and supervisors.

Kandossiwin Dkobjiganan [Knowledge Bundles]

Navigating rugged landscapes requires a strong knowledge bundle — *kandossiwin dkobjiganan*. A Euro-western education alone will not fully prepare you for the reality of being a social worker on the front lines in Indigenous contexts. You will require a commitment to ongoing training and education. You will require knowledge of culture, community, colonialism and decolonization. Knowledge of Indigenous healing practices and protocols will help you navigate the landscape of Indigenous contexts. Your personal, professional and cultural development is essential. Feed your spirit and learn about yourself and your roots. Understand your history and where you come from. Develop your own capacity in your spirit, heart, mind and body. The location of learning for Indigenous practitioners is different than for non-Indigenous social workers. Understand the location from where you practice and work from there.

O'shkaabewisuk must build *kandossiwin dkobjiganan* [knowledge bundles and practice approaches] to understand blaming and disempowerment as manifestations of power loss. *Kandossiwin dkobjiganan* need to be equipped with information about disempowerment and the need for power. Knowledge about internalization of racism, colonialism and oppression is essential as are knowledge bundles fuelled by a spirit and motivation to learn our languages, traditions and ceremonies, and knowledge on the healing and recovery power of our ceremonies. Our bundles could include mechanisms of self-care and support when working in rugged landscapes. These bundles ought to help us be aware of and prepared for the rugged journey ahead. *Kandossiwin dkobjiganan* must be cultivated and maintained.

Peer dialogue supports the development of our *kandossiwin dkobjiganan*. Dialoguing within peer circles is liberating. During my practice, I talked with colleagues and co-workers about our experiences in the field and we found comfort and support in one another. Creating supportive circles kept me connected and grounded. Their collective support and care provided guidance, networking, debriefing and inspiration. For example, at the community level we created a caregivers' circle. This circle was for helpers and service providers to debrief, share and connect with one another. We utilized ceremony and shared food while talking about ourselves as caregivers. Our focus was ourselves. If we find ourselves struggling in the landscape of rugged practice, we need to have the courage to ask for support and guidance. Despite the challenges, I see our beauty, resources and strengths. This lens is imperative. I could also see the murky waters and minefields, and even though I felt unprepared for some, I still had my tools and knowledge bundles. All this awareness though did not exempt me from experiencing vicarious trauma or becoming masterfully manipulated, but it did help me be mindful of the complex dynamics and talk about them with my peers and colleagues.

My work as an *o'shkaabewis kwe* is to try and understand how colonization has really affected us and to recover our truths. Understanding what colonization is and its manifestations today is part of developing your critical *kandossiwin dkobjigan* for educational interventions. For example, I remember community members putting other members down because they were "Bill C31."[6] I saw this as an opportunity to put on an education workshop on that *Indian Act* legislation. When I heard the division between the people, I recognized their disconnection as a consequence of the sexism and patriarchy of the *Indian Act* policy and its attack on our membership and identity. In this workshop I explained the history of the *Indian Act* and the history of Bill C31, where women had been eliminated from band membership and evicted from communities because of discriminatory and patriarchal policies. We talked about our families and the people we know. We made the links of how the policies diminished us and how we can change. I helped them to understand that if they continued to attack each other and apply racist policies, they in turn, are doing the work of the colonizer. I also believe that some people, on that day, understood the impact of foreign policy on their life. We talked much more, but the point is that we cannot assume that our people have a critical understanding of colonization and how we are affected. We need to teach this and engage in critical education at the community level.

Practising with a strong mind will help social workers not get lost in landscapes that are laden with difficulty and rugged terrain. My goal was to identify the more difficult landscapes, such as multi-layered relationships, disempowerment, diversity, internalized colonialism and colonial trauma. I wanted to share the rugged terrain to foster awareness in hopes that further dialogue and discussions would be fuelled. These issues are by no means exhaustive. As an *o'shkaabewis kwe*, I think I may have been better prepared if, in my training, we had identified the realities of working within the aftermath of the psychological, spiritual, mental and physical trauma of colonization. Working within our own communities is difficult, and I have the utmost respect and admiration for the workers who continue as helpers in the front lines.

> My mother always told us to be prepared before we go into the bush.
> Carry our matches, water, snacks and watch where we walk.
> Listen to the land and be conscious of your surroundings
> Do not get lost
> Remember where you come from
> Always look back from where you came
> This way you'll recognize the path home. (K. Absolon 2007)

Surviving and Thriving in the Landscapes of Practice

How have we survived such complexities? Humour and a strong capacity to laugh at ourselves have enabled us to look at the serious and foolish nature within ourselves. In Anishinaabe teachings, Nanabush or Waynaboozho is both a trickster and helper to the Creator. This being is both comical and powerful. Waynaboozho was the one in our Creation stories that gave all the plants and creatures their name and purpose. This being is also foolish and likes to play tricks. There are many stories of how Nanabush tricks the animals and Creation. There are always teachings in those stories, and through the stories of Nanabush, we see the value of humour. We learn to laugh at ourselves. Waynaboozho teaches us about being the Creator's helpers and also to embrace life's follies. We are learning to discern when to laugh and when to cry and when to do both. Communities of people listening, learning and rebuilding relationships with one another enable and make the journeys worthwhile. The spirits of the people are strong and resilient, and witnessing our resiliency is healing in itself. Our relations are critical in this process as it is not a journey meant to be taken alone. It is both individual and collective.

Despite governments' attempts to divide and pit Indigenous people against one another, a solidarity and nation building among Indigenous peoples and nations is emerging. Terms like reclaim, reconnect, recover and revitalize are used to characterize a desire and fulfill a vision of a grand healing that is occurring. We have survived the militant attacks and numerous attempts to create divisions in our nations, communities, families, lives and ourselves. Yes, there are many casualties, but today we are still here surviving and, in some cases thriving.

We talk to one another and show care. We have the power to dialogue.

The voices that we have and the distinct way that we have of telling our story provides us with doorways to free our minds, hearts, spirits and bodies from colonial shackles. Within our cultures we have practices where the sounding of our voices was instrumental in our wellbeing. Singing, story-telling, dancing, smudging, chanting and talking with one another are healing practices resonating with the sound of our voices and use of our bodies. Finding space and time for silence allows us to become re-centred within and to hear the inner messages. What we develop in concepts and theory form out of re-telling and re-interpreting our experiences and truths (Smith 1999). Rebuilding and claiming our minds, hearts, bodies and spirits from our own perspectives enables us to reconnect and remember each other and ourselves. The power is in the circle of dialogue and sharing (Graveline 1998).

Talking to one another and sharing our experiences in colonization builds a critical consciousness. I agree with the idea expressed by Brazilian social reformer Paulo Freire (cited in Cajete 1994) who explained that when Aboriginal people express and understand from our own perspectives our cultural and historical roots then our own cultural emancipation has begun. Through dialogue we begin to unload the meaning of our individual and collective experiences, and come out of isolation and alienation toward a re-membering and reconnecting. Critical discourses on colonial trauma are imperative among people seeking truth and freedom. Henderson (2000c: 59) states that "these critiques give rise to anguished discourses about knowledge and truths." We are responsible and we have the capacity to restore our history and tell or write about our histories in own voices. An anguished discourse about truth is far more refreshing than discourse based on lies and manipulations. Sharing circles and other cultural circles provide the mechanisms and tools upon which collective critical consciousness occurs (Cajete 1994; Graveline 1998, Hart 2002; Nabigon et al. 1998). Thus, dialoging about contradictions and forms of anguish we experience normalizes and validates our reactions to colonization and the struggles we are challenged with. "Through such a process the group can truly cease being objects for outside political, economic, or educative manipulation. Instead, they become subjects in making their own stories for the future and controllers of their own destiny" (Cajete 1994: 217).

My experiences as an Indigenous social worker are filled with many supports and *dbaagmowin* [stories] of strength. As an Indigenous *o'shkaabewis kwe*, I rely on my culture for strength. Learning about our teachings, songs and dances empowered me and gave me the health to walk through the thick landscapes. As a runner, I still travel the land and receive power from the earth. When I need strength I sing my songs. I cannot underestimate the beauty of our cultures. The medicines that we need to live a good life are embedded in our worldviews and philosophies, and the pathway to *mino-*

bimaadsiwin is in our teachings. The medicine wheel is called that because its teachings contain medicine for a good life.

An essential tool in any caregiver's self-care kit is to identify your support systems and use them. Create support systems where you meet, share and check in with one another on a regular basis. Talk to your peers and do not isolate yourself. Teamwork and circle work are great ways of developing community cohesion and contribute to the development of stronger support systems. Informal and format support circles were really important to me, and I have much gratitude to those helpers who walked with me in the rugged landscapes of our practice. I gave myself permission to share and process my experiences with others.

I have learned to walk in two worlds and navigate both. My preference is to walk within Indigenous contexts where I can be myself. Holding on and letting go and knowing when to do so are aspects of navigating a bi-cultural landscape. In almost every aspect of my life I have developed my skills as a negotiator. As a child, I negotiated racism in the classroom and schoolyard, and in sports. As an adult I negotiated many power relations to assert my place and location as an Aboriginal woman. At times, I choose not to negotiate, but act and do what I need to without permission or approval. When we negotiate we are entering into a relationship hoping that an agreement can be reached that satisfies both parties. But I have experienced that a negotiation will often constitute a loss of power in some form or another, and oppressors are often reluctant to negotiate knowing that a loss is at stake (Pinderhughes 1989; Smith 1999). Even more challenging are the negotiations we enter into with those who are also oppressed. The continuum of liberation or emancipation varies individually as well as collectively (Freire 1996; Noël 1994). Navigating the landscapes of being oppressed/colonized while decolonizing/Indigenizing requires an ambidextrous consciousness and an awareness of our own dualities; and our practices are bi-cultural. We occupy many varied spaces.

My hope is that social work education today provides materials that facilitate an understanding of the strengths and challenges of Indigenous social contexts. I also hope that my stories have compelled other *o'shkaabewisuk* to be prepared to navigate landscapes that are rich, beautiful, rugged and complex. An *o'shkaabewisuk's kandossiwin dkobjiganan* is essential to navigating the landscapes of practice. Today, I am proud to be a part of a master's Aboriginal social work program based in Indigenous knowledge and holistic healing practices.[7] I close this chapter with a story about the *wewe* [geese] because I love *wewe* and see them as still following their original instructions. They share leadership, fill the sky with their songs, they travel in flocks, and they are both comical and beautiful in the sky. I also love people because we are silly, foolish and inherently good. I love stories because they offer so much. So in ending this chapter I share this *dbaagmowin* about *wewe* and a silly girl.

Quacance doesn't want wewe (geese) to leave
She knows that boon (winter) is coming... boon is cold and tough
She doesn't want the cold to come... she wonders what to do?
She gets a big net and tosses it into the sky to stop them
"Boon'zid (Stop)" she yells, "don't leave yet"... but it doesn't work...
Next she makes a really big kite that fills the sky to block them
"Boon'zid" she shouts... but they all just fly around
Next, she tries to sing them a beautiful song to make them stay
"Stay with me" Quacance sings, "don't leave yet"...
Wewe honk and continue flying south... "nice song" they yell.
Next she offers them a feast to get them to rest...
"Hey"... the entire flock halts and comes down to the ground
Hundreds and thousands of wewe are feasting and sitting around
They can't fly now because they are too fat and heavy
The winter doesn't come because wewe haven't left
The earth is tired and she wants to rest
The trees want to sleep, but can't
The bears are still walking around tired and angry
Everyone in creation is getting grumpy and mad at one another
Life is no longer in balance and
They are getting mad at Quacance for keeping wewe fat and heavy
"Goon (snow) needs to come, seasons need to change, we need to rest,
you must stop feeding the wewe, they need to leave" the bears growl...
Now Quacance listens, plus she misses her cocomish and wants to hear her stories
Cocomish only tells certain stories in the winter
and Quacance misses goon
"Okay"... so she stops feeding the wewe...
Balance and harmony slowly get restored...
Eventually, the wewe leave and go on flying south...
They keep on flying and they won't stop now
Everyone gets to rest, the snow comes and
The earth, she gets to rest
The trees finally go to sleep,
The bears go into hibernation and...

Wewe keep on following their original instructions...
Quacance didn't know she had the power to create change...
Maybe, that's all she needed to know.
"Miigwech" says Quacance and she runs off to find her
cocomish. (K. Absolon 2008)

Notes

1. Empowerment theories aim to create change in a person's power and access to resources, which help to increase power in their lives. Empowerment theory does not blame individuals, nor is it based on a deficit model of functioning; rather it looks at inequality of society, structural barriers and oppression. This theory has helped Indigenous practitioners find strategies of making power shifts in people's lives by increasing their access to supports, resources and services so that their lives can be enhanced.

2. Working from a strengths perspective means that the helper works to identify, highlight and embellish the person's strengths and resources. This perspective aims to figure out how the cup is half full and helps people see their strengths and strives to nurture, develop and grow from strength and resources. This perspective has given me practice strategies that identify what works for us as people, communities and nations. Some of our greatest strengths and assets lie in our culture and traditional knowledges. Additionally, the fact that we are surviving assimilation assaults and colonial attacks evidences that our strengths are many. This perspective provides us with useful ways of practising from a more positive and resourceful place.

3. Resistance knowledge tends to focus on how people have used their strengths and resources to resist oppression, racism, colonization and other attacks on their life. It strives to identify what strengths and resources they draw upon in their resistance. This theory states that people will resist being harmed and hurt because of our human instinct to survive. It works on the premise that humans have the capacity to resist being disempowered or oppressed. Focusing on and highlighting when resistance occurs can turn many stories of oppression, despair and suffering into stories of resilience, strength and resistance. I really find resistance knowledge useful in turning stories of despair into stories of power and strength. My story of Akiikwe is an example of this.

4. Trauma theory recognizes the full impact of trauma on functioning. It began to recognize the impact of war trauma on soldiers and currently acknowledges a broad range of traumas such as sexual abuse, incest, family violence, earth disasters, crime, cultural genocide and colonization, among many others. Trauma theory acknowledges the impact of traumatic events on peoples spiritual, psychological, emotional and physical functioning and aims to facilitate healing and understanding by exploring these impacts. There is currently a vast theory and knowledge base to trauma theory. Trauma theory is useful in terms of acknowledging the full impact of racism, colonialism and genocide on a people. It helps to recognize and validate the impact that residential schools, land relocation, cultural oppression, Indian affairs, disease and warfare have on Indigenous peoples. The terms intergenerational trauma have helped to recog-

nize that the impact of trauma, if left unresolved, can be passed on from one generation to the next. Intergenerational trauma has helped with understanding the legacy of residential schooling and the impact of the colonial legislation on generations of families and communities.

5. Liberation theory aims at understanding oppression in society and regards the issues that individuals, families, communities and nations face as a direct result this oppression. Liberation theory would engage people in critical education about the systemic equalities and power imbalances and through this education process, empower people to engage in creating change for themselves. Liberation theory recognizes that being socialized into oppression is painful and that change happens collectively through education. Freedom out of an oppressive state is possible. This theoretical approach has been very useful in linking the social and health problems faced by Indigenous populations to the lack of infrastructural support. It debunks the blaming the victim model.

6. Bill C-31 was an *Act to Amend the Indian Act* in 1985. This Bill brought changes to the *Indian Act* by attempting to remove the sexual discrimination of the Act. It restored the status and membership rights of many people, primarily women and their offspring, prevented people from gaining or losing their status through marriage and opened doorways for bands to change their band membership regulations. There are other changes that this Bill introduced, but the big change was reinstating the status of many women and children.

7. Wilfrid Laurier University offers an MSW Aboriginal program with curriculum and learning processes based in Indigenous knowledge and holistic healing practices. For more information on this program go <www.wlu.ca>.

Chapter 10

Kaxlaya Gvilas
Upholding Traditional Heiltsuk Laws, Values and Practices as Aboriginal People and Allies.

Michelle Reid (Juba)

Indigenous peoples have always had diverse worldviews, values and cultur-ally and community-based ways of relating and helping one another, which constituted their own social welfare systems. This chapter outlines part of my own process of asserting Heiltsuk cultural and community-based values and approaches to helping and how I connected to my own social work practice as a delegated child and family service worker. I briefly discuss the social work profession and the delegated child and family service context in which I worked and why it is important to advocate for Indigenous approaches to be affirmed, legalized and resourced. The terms "helper" and "social worker" are used interchangeably to capture the nature of the role within Heiltsuk cultural and community-based perspective and approach. Additionally, I use the terms Aboriginal and Indigenous interchangeably. The term First Nations generally refers to on-reserve community-based peoples.

This chapter explores the experiences of working within my own Heiltsuk community and talking with my Heiltsuk father and my non-Heiltsuk mother, who are community helpers. This chapter examines the questions: What approaches, skills and practices does a community helper need to assist the community? What are the challenges? How should Heiltsuk traditional cultural stories, values, beliefs, laws and practices inform community work? The main challenging question for Indigenous social work is: Are people in Indigenous organizations and/or communities working in a manner that reflects interdependent, respectful and responsible relationships that are informed by cultural values, beliefs and practices, and in ways that are not reflective of internalized colonialism? First, we must always look at our own values, beliefs, practices and intentions for doing the work as helpers and social workers. To begin, I provide a brief overview of the Heiltsuk peoples.

The Haitzaqw (Heiltsuk) People
and Mainstream Social Work

The Heiltsuk people have lived on the central coast of what is now called
British Columbia for approximately ten thousand years. The Heiltsuk people
are a potlatch and communal society who have strong connections to their
lands, resources and culture. The strength of the Heiltsuk society is based
on *kaxlaya gvilas*: the ones who uphold the laws, customs and traditions of
our ancestors. These *gvilas*, traditional laws, are reflected within the Heiltsuk
cultural structures and ensured through accountable and responsible interdependent relationships that maintain strong cultural identities and natural
resources for future generations. Through the generations, our complex
cultural societies and practices have been maintained through the nurturance
of our children and youth who carried on the stories and practices they were
modelled and taught. In dealing with the ongoing impacts of colonization
the challenge remains for Heiltsuk community helpers and social workers
(both Indigenous and non-Indigenous) to continue to rebuild collaborative
working relationships with Indigenous and non-Indigenous people that are
informed by traditional values and practices.

The Heiltsuk people, language, values and practices have been greatly
altered by colonial laws and practices, both historically and presently in
Canadian society. The Heiltsuk people are continuing to advocate for human
and cultural rights at the same time as addressing the intergenerational impacts of colonization, which manifest in the many social and health issues of
Heiltsuk community members. Further, the Heiltsuk people are in the process
of reclaiming language, values and practices while trying to co-exist within
mainstream Canadian society and systems. This chapter is a testament to the
resiliency of my Heiltsuk ancestors, who continue to exist amid the ongoing
colonialism. I am one of approximately three thousand Heiltsuk people that
constitute the Heiltsuk Nation. There is no other place in the world where
people speak Heiltsuk and have the exact same cultural practices in terms of
ties to the land and other living beings. It is imperative that my generation
builds on the values, teachings and practices of the ancestors, who have sustained the Heiltsuk for thousands of years. As I write this chapter and speak
with my parents, I am engaged in a process of reclaiming and asserting my
Heiltsuk identity. From this perspective, I briefly contextualize social work as
a profession and why it is important for all Aboriginal peoples to have their
own culturally and community-based ways of helping and practising social
work respected, legally recognized and financially supported.

Mainstream social work received professional recognition in the late
1920s and began its degree programs in the late 1940s (Hick 2002: 45). Social
work is a relatively new profession, which is culturally based and constructed
on dominant mainstream values, laws and practices. Indigenous people,

educators and allies are still advocating to get Indigenous social work perspectives and approaches equally recognized within schools of social work and
the profession. There is an increasing amount of Aboriginal literature that
supports Indigenous social work and helping, using community and culturally based practice perspectives and approaches (Absolon and Herbert 1997;
Anderson 2000; Anderson and Lawrence 2004; Armstrong 2000; Baskin
2007; Battiste 2000; Brendtro, Brokenleg and Bockern 1992; Bruyere 2007;
Graveline 1998; Hart 1999, 2001; Howse and Stalwick 1990; Morrisette,
MacKenzie and Morrisette 1993; Morrisseau 1998; Poupart and Scharnberg
2000; Red Horse, Martinez, Day, Day, Sinclair 2004; Thomas and Green
2007; Weaver and White 1997). Blackstock states that social work has had a
role in the colonial process towards Indigenous peoples in Canada by perpetuating harm through the placement of Aboriginal children in residential
schools, past and present child welfare interventions and other activities that
impose mainstream laws, values and practices that maintain the status quo
(2009: 30–31). Indigenous people have had very difficult interactions with
social workers and have painful associations with the profession. When I was
growing up, social workers represented the dominant mainstream authority
that removed Heiltsuk children from their families and cultural society.

Some social work educational frameworks and practice approaches have
become more meaningful in regard to working with Indigenous peoples in
Canada, but overall, the profession, schools and systems still centre mainstream worldviews, values and practices. Social work as a profession has not
greatly benefitted Aboriginal people or brought about social justice for them
in any significant way. Indigenous people continue to be disproportionately
over-represented in the socio-economic margins and continue to face gross
human rights violations under the *Indian Act* and other Canadian laws.
Blackstock states:

> Social work or other helping professions as professions have not done
> a lot of internal reflection on what their role has been in perpetrat-
> ing the harm and our concordant responsibility to understand and
> reconcile the harm.... The social work profession needs to stop say-
> ing they are applying culturally appropriate services to Indigenous
> peoples by simply adapting social work mainstream models, values,
> beliefs and standards. (2009: 35)

The real need, Blackstock argues, is for the profession to "to affirm Indigenous
ways-of-knowing and caring for children" (35).

Delegation Enabling Agreements

The challenges of providing child welfare services under mainstream models and legislation has been documented (Absolon, Mitchell and Armitage 1996; Armitage 1993; Awasis 1997; Blackstock 2000, 2001, 2009; Brown, Haddock and Kovach 2001; Bruyere 2003; Carrière 2007; Durst 2000; Durst, Mcdonald and Rich 1995; Johnson 1983; Kline 1992; Lee and Associates 1992; MacDonald 2000; Mckenzie and Hudson 1985; Richardson and Nelson 2007; Sinclair 2007a; Wotherspoon and Satezwich 1993). Indigenous peoples are in the process of defining how their traditional values, beliefs and approaches to helping apply within the various social work areas, while working within mainstream laws, values and practices and advocating for human and cultural rights as Indigenous people. The child welfare delegation process is one context in which the Heiltsuk are trying to incorporate traditional values, beliefs and approaches. I was working as a social worker and community helper in that process.

The Heiltsuk tribal council, with approval of a majority of the Heiltsuk people, entered into the child and family service delegation process in order to access funding under the federal government and to acquire delegated authority for individual social workers who completed training. The Heiltsuk Nation saw the delegation process as the only means to access resources to provide more services to the Heiltsuk community. The challenge is to truly deliver the services in a culturally and community-based way.

> The delegation model is founded on the [paternalistic and racist] notion of "giving" [provincial] authority to deliver child welfare services, rather than recognizing First Nations' inherent authority to care for their children… [and]… imposes… mainstream beliefs, concepts and practices. (Brown, Haddock, and Kovach 2001: 46)

The Delegation Enabling Agreement (DEA) speaks to the level of delegation agency social workers will receive and the terms under the delegated authority to be exercised pursuant to the provincial legislation. The provincial government, through child and family services (CFS) legislation, provides the delegated authority to First Nations CFS agency social workers to carry out specified powers, duties and functions (Reid 2005: 26–28). First Nations child and family service agencies have a choice to take on partial or full delegation and provide support, guardianship and child protection services. The federal government provides the funding under the Directive 20-1 funding formula to the First Nations on-reserve agencies to provide provincially delegated child and family services. Unfortunately, the federal government will only fund First Nations agencies that provide services pursuant to provincially delegated authority, which negates opportunities to affirm self-governing models. The DEA is a complicated process because of the jurisdictional disputes and the lack of coordination between the federal and provincial governments. This results in First Nations children and communities being faced with huge inequities in funding and services (Reid 2005: 26–28).

Colonialism continues to be prominent in DEAs, with the provincial and federal governments' assumptions that it is possible for First Nations peoples to provide culturally appropriate services pursuant to the Euro-western-based child and family service legislation and to maintain standards and practices within the context of insufficient resources. "The mask of today's colonialism is painted with subtle colours and is colored in the veil of empowerment and a just society" (Brown, Haddock and Kovach 2001: 146, as cited in Reid 2005: 26–28).

Many First Nations communities view the DEA as an interim measure towards self-determination and governance. Although many First Nations agencies believe they are able to benefit their children, families and communities through their work, they continue to advocate for the recognition and incorporation of their own systems of caring for children. Overall, the limited power of the delegated level of authority offered to First Nations peoples indicates that a colonial relationship with the Canadian government rooted in a relationship of power, control and racism is still strong and ongoing (Reid 2005: 26–28).

First Nations agencies and social workers face the challenge of operating under delegated authority from the very CFS system that has caused so much damage to First Nations societies, placing the First Nations social workers in the stressful position of potentially becoming a perpetrator of colonial policies and practices against their own people (Reid 2005: 26–28). "Social work needs to be redefined so that it fits with a First Nations way of working with children and families within our communities and cultural contexts" (Reid 2005: 34). This challenge for community social workers is coupled with the many processes Indigenous people are dealing with that have resulted from colonization and the ongoing ways that it manifests in their lives, such as land claims, self government initiatives, the residential school reconciliation processes, as well as social issues of racism, sexism, poverty, poor housing and inequitable services and resources on- and off-reserve. This context leads into my discussion of why I went into social work and how my Heiltsuk relationships with my family and community members have influenced my practice and assisted me in working towards reconciling and asserting Heiltsuk ways of helping.

Why I Became a Social Worker

I am only providing my own understanding and interpretation of the values and practices of the Heiltsuk people from living and working in my community and talking with my family and other community members. This is an ongoing conversation and process that I will continue to be vigilant in doing. This is also a process that my Heiltsuk community members are doing in both informal and formal ways in every aspect of community life. The Heiltsuk community asserts its traditional innovative knowledge and practices, while rebuilding and reclaiming our Heiltsuk history, language, values and helping (social work and community) practices.

I have been contemplating the reasons why I became a social worker. I immediately think about the children and youth whom I have worked with and continue to work with. The message that the children and youth send is that they want adult relationships that engage with them in a loving, respectful way, that show them they are the priority and that they belong, and that teach them how to see and be in the world. Our children and youth want to be active participants in their lives and communities. They want to have strong cultural identities. Much has been written about the impact of residential school and ongoing colonial policies on Indigenous people, communities and cultures in Canada. It has been the children and youth who have suffered the most in our communities. It is through the community social work and self-government initiatives that Indigenous communities seek to develop community and culturally based programs and economic sustainability to meet the needs of our children and families.

Another reason for becoming a social worker was because of the teachings that my parents provided and the example they modelled as community helpers. I grew up in a bi-cultural home, which has informed my understanding of what is possible as an Indigenous and non-Indigenous helper in an Indigenous community. It has been my experience through working in a mainstream school of social work that students generally want a tool box of ways to work with Indigenous people, but what I told them is that it is about developing an understanding of the stories of strength and oppression, building strong working relationships and recognizing Indigenous people as diverse peoples. There is no specific recipe or formula. When I started teaching social work I spoke with my parents about their work as community helpers and their perspectives on what needs to be done in Indigenous and non-Indigenous communities for meaningful change to happen that does not reflect a colonial relationship and reality. Many future social workers I taught gave me feedback that it was my personal practice stories, including the experiences of my parents that I shared, which were most profound in their learning. I have been looking at the generational influence of my ancestors and parents and my experiences growing up and working in my own cultural community to see how it has influenced my own values, beliefs and practices in my social work practice.

I grew up in the pristine Heiltsuk territory. My Heiltsuk grandmother, Wilhemina Reid (Juba) was from the Qvuqvuyaitxv: People of the Qvuguai or calm water people. My grandfather, George Reid was from the Yisdaaitxv — People of the Yisda. My Heiltsuk father was a community leader and my Swedish-Canadian mother worked in various capacities as a community helper. My parents have been my first and greatest teachers and have instilled in me a strong sense of values and vision about being a community helper.

It was my ancestors' and parents' teachings that that led me into social work practice and education. They instilled in me a *thloo oo wax de ya see* [a strong inner being and determined spirit] through their examples and lessons as helpers. Indigenous peoples have always been determined to maintain their cultural identities within their traditional territories and communal societies, which will sustain them and the generations to come. It is these relationships with my parents, their stories, experiences and lessons that I want to weave together into a strong cedar basket that I humbly pass on to whoever reads this.

Generations Deep

My life is generations deep,
braided with time, cultures, the living elements and spirits of love.
My life is generations deep,
wrapped in eagle's wings, rooted in cedar,
blanketed in being Heiltsuk and bi-cultural.

My life is generations deep,
Privileged with father who embraced his Heiltsuk cultural
identity and nurtured mine
Blessed with a mother who shared the gifts, beauty of being
bi-cultural.

My life is generations deep,
I am an earth woman, sustained by the sea and nourished by
all creation.
I carry in my blood and heart the songs, stories and sorrows
of my ancestors.
I hold my head high and lift my prayers to the Creator.

May each step of my journey ensure that you, my child
are wrapped in my blanket of family, community and culture.

Intergenerational Learning, Impact and Change

I believe that we learn from the generations who came before us and we pass on our teachings through our relationships to the next generations. I start the conversation with my own experiences as a social work and community helper. I see that who I am is directly connected with what I do as a helper; they are not distinct roles, but branches from the same tree.

I reflect on my experiences of assisting my community in the process of setting up a child and family service agency. It was this experience that gave me the most challenging and rich learning as a social work helper. I realized what got me through these experiences was my identity as a Heiltsuk woman and the power of interdependent community relationships to bring about some positive change. I continue to experience and witness the socio-economic impacts of colonization as a Heiltsuk woman and within the Indigenous communities in the poverty, poor housing, lack of community infrastructure and lack of services that are equitable with those of other Canadian citizens. It is extremely difficult to intellectualize and explain the depth of pain, anger and struggle that I feel as someone who has witnessed so much loss in my family and community. It is a combination of this inter-generational pain, the resilience of Indigenous peoples and the support in having non-Indigenous allies that fuels the work that I continue to do.

Effective Approaches, Skills and Practices for Community Helping

I learned many skills and lessons as I went through the child and family service (CFS) delegation process. I was filled with enthusiasm and idealism after graduating with my bachelor of social work degree and returned to my people to assist in setting up a culturally and community-based child and family service agency. I attempted to create a bridge between the main-stream teachings and my own Heiltsuk education; to build relationships at the community level with chief and council and with the provincial and federal representatives; to learn how to set up meetings and consultations with the community members and service providers; to do technical advising, implement report writing and conduct surveys to determine the communi-ties' service needs and priorities. The biggest challenge remains to reclaim the Heiltsuk traditional philosophies and approaches to helping and caring for the Heiltsuk children and families in a culturally and community-based-ways amid the dominant mainstream laws, standards and practices, which are legitimized and resourced.

I had many challenges in the process of figuring out how to ensure that there was a culturally centred and meaningful community process, despite dominant mainstream provincial and federal laws, policies, standards and practices. It was overwhelming and humbling to figure out how to do the work with the meagre government resources allotted to the child and family service delegation process, the lack of office space and the expectations of both the provincial and federal governments in conjunction with my primary responsibility to Heiltsuk community members.

I needed to build working relationships with the Heiltsuk community service providers, the community at large and federal and provincial government representatives. This process of building relationships with the other community service providers was necessary to figure out how we were going to work together under our individual mandates in order to create working protocols and integrated case management to benefit the community. It took time, money and lots of commitment to set up meetings individually with each community agency. The community services providers decided to have regular interdisciplinary meetings to share information about programs and services. These meetings helped build working relationships and a collaborative vision for community helping and more integrated services for community members.

Providing food at these meetings and setting clear guidelines that these meetings were not about case management was critical to the process. The Heiltsuk people always provide food when individuals, family or community members gather, and this is a practice that we continued within our all of our meeting processes as a way to honour one another.

Ensuring that there were regular meetings with chief and council was also vital to getting the political support and ensuring that council would not get involved as a political body in the day-to-day child and family service cases. It was important to determine how to be inclusive of the various community interest groups. A strong committee or board needed to be put in place with a cross-section of the population that represents Heiltsuk values and models ethical practice and living.

Elders were involved on the child and family service advisory committee and then later on the board. They provided cultural knowledge and wisdom about traditional Heiltsuk child rearing practices and language. Many Elders have a lot of knowledge to share to ensure an agency is culturally based. These Elders continue to be keepers of knowledge, values and practices and to pass down their teachings to the younger generations. Meeting with the Elders reminded me of the importance of using non-jargon language and communicating why it was important to have a child and family services agency.

Meeting with the community at large was most difficult because of the pain resulting from historical and current child and family service interventions and concerns about how this agency was going to address the issues in a meaningful way. Hence, the process of community consultation is essential and has to be ongoing. The strength of the Heiltsuk people has been their belief in taking care of one another and working collaboratively. It is vital in all stages of the process to discuss the needs, to build on Heiltsuk cultural and community strengths and to maintain a reciprocal relationship of accountability and responsibility between the agency and the community.

There were many components of setting up an agency that I had to learn, from how to negotiate a delegation enabling agreement, how to write reports, how to budget, how to determine what programs and services can be offered over time, how to practise ethically in a small community and how to deal with dual accountability to both the community and the provincial and federal governments. It was important to consciously engage in a process of reconciling the Heiltsuk ways of helping with the mainstream social work laws and practices. The challenge is to infuse the agency with traditional knowledge and practices while continuing to work within a dominant system that does have some valuable knowledge to offer.

What Were/Are the Challenges?

There were many challenges, rewards and learning curves in the process of setting up an agency and being a community helper. I had to learn to function within the dual relationships and responsibilities of being a community member and a Heiltsuk child and family service social worker while attempting to always maintain my focus on the children and families as the reason for doing this work. I had to learn to work in multiple roles: being on the child and family service delegation negotiating team, coordinating the agency start up and implementation process, providing front-line services. Given these multiple roles and the stress inherently involved in CFS work (even after-hours because of being in a remote island community), I had to maintain self-care and boundaries so I did not burn out (Reid 2005).

I had to learn how to be innovative and creative in working under the inequitable condition of being expected to carry out a huge mandate with insufficient resources and infrastructure. Even finding office space was a barrier in the beginning. We did find a house, but it required renovations and was not wheelchair accessible. There were jurisdictional gaps and disputes between the federal and provincial governments about who paid for which services; this was a breech of our Heiltsuk children's rights to receive the same services as those available off-reserve. In one meeting the federal and provincial representatives started to argue about who was to pay for certain services. I was sitting in our council house facing the window where I could see the Heiltsuk children playing. I immediately stated, "You want to know who pays? Our children pay." I invited them to take a walk through the elementary school and see the children's faces and to know whom they are accountable to in this process. I had to learn to have a clear sense of why I was doing this work and who it was for. The Heiltsuk have always had a commitment to think long term and plan for the future generations. I made a commitment not to leave myself as a Heiltsuk woman, my community and (most importantly) the children at the door in this process. As Reid states:

The children must never become numbers in this process.... The delegation situation was difficult because you are working between conflicting cultures, have very little shared power or control in the delegation process and are attempting to walk between two worlds, get your own world views and cultural childcare practices validated and incorporated into their programs. (2005: 30)

One of the most exciting and inspirational initiatives that I have been a part of was the 2005 child welfare conference on reconciliation, which the First Nations Child and Family Service Society of Canada organized.[1] It brought together both Indigenous and non-Indigenous people from the child welfare field. The ultimate challenge is to rebuild relationships and to reconcile across different child and family service systems, philosophies and practices. It is time to build relationships with one another and to change the nature of colonial relationships. We must learn from one another, our cultures, our different systems. Indigenous culture, values and beliefs need to be seen as the foundation of the work and process. I believe that there are many community and cultural strengths to build on. Irene Lindsay, an Ojibway Elder, told me that "we call our realities into being with our thoughts and actions" (May 2005).

How Should Heiltsuk Traditional Culture Inform Community Work?

Heiltsuk stories, values, beliefs and practices must inform the vision, the process and relationships, and the foundational structure of the agency and programs. Indigenous people often tell stories of the traditional practices and philosophies that ensured the holistic health of the community members and sustained Heiltsuk people prior to colonial contact. We need "to build on innovations that are based on thousands of years of successful caring for children, families and communities and the challenge is to find and think of ways to bridge it forward" (Blackstock 2003: 31)

Our traditional values, beliefs and practices have to be respected. The process has to be about reviving, rebuilding and renewing the culture and language when we are establishing our community programs and services and reinvigorating knowledge systems that are respectful and reflective of who we are. We must be vigilant in our strategies for change and always look at the short- and long-term impacts on our peoples and our cultures. It is important to take the time to name the agency; it is symbolic of why we do the work and to whom we are accountable. I remember when the name Kaxla was given: it refers to a philosophy of uplifting the child through supporting the family and community in culturally appropriate and accountable ways.

The process has to involve addressing the power and financial inequalities between Indigenous and non-Indigenous relations and systems. In my experience, the discussion always reverted back to how to take the mainstream legislation and limited funding and make it fit with the Heiltsuk vision and philosophy for a local child and family service agency that would ideally provide both prevention and intervention services. The Heiltsuk would talk passionately from the heart about what was needed for the children and families from their own philosophical and cultural place to mitigate the ongoing colonial impacts through culturally based preventative and intervention services.

Blackstock states: "The holistic worldview held that in order for a child, family or environment to achieve an optimal level of functioning, the physical, emotional, spiritual and cognitive must be in balance" (2001: 333). When issues arose within families regarding the care or wellbeing of children, the communities would deal with the issues within a community context that was rooted in relationships and systems of accountability. This does not imply that First Nations societies did not have social issues within their communities, but rather that there were community and cultural knowledge, processes and systems that would ensure the safety and wellbeing of the children (Reid 2005: 25).

The Heiltsuk word for children, *sasum*, refers to off-spring. There is an understanding that children are the most important members within Heiltsuk society because they will carry on the values and traditions. Children need to be loved and cared for and instilled with a strong Heiltsuk identity to prepare them to be contributing members within the community. Children are taught about values and expectations through relationships, hearing Heiltsuk stories and participation in traditional food gathering, potlatching and other practices. Children are viewed as precious gifts from the Creator and not as possessions. The parents, extended family, community members, clans, crests and other cultural structures and systems all had a role in ensuring that the children were provided with the cultural knowledge and teachings. These teaching were how the Heiltsuk peoples sustained themselves.

Significant in traditional ways were the interdependent and inter-related beliefs and practices in terms of how family was defined and who had a role in caring for Heiltsuk children. There was a belief in and practice of *wax-toos*, which recognizes the inter-relationships between immediate family, extended family and the family friends and community members. The extended family is the primary culturally and community-based resource. "The community strength is that of the extended family and adoptions which ensure that everyone is supported" (Heiltsuk Tribal Council 1994: 19). Family was not just seen as the nuclear structure and includes extended family, and each family member and community member had a role and responsibility in caring for children. It was believed that children learned how to become productive and participating members within the Heiltsuk Nation through watching their families and communities members in their daily lives. Children learned caring, sharing and responsibility within their interactions and developed strong Heiltsuk identities through their relationships with their families and community members. An Elder in a Heiltsuk study stated: "A lot of us went to residential school and do not know how to pass parenting info along" (Heiltsuk Tribal Council 1994: 19). Part of the role for Heiltsuk child and family services is to assist and support individuals, families and the Heiltsuk community to help them to re-learn and embrace their roles in caring for children. In this way, my father's teachings and experiences as a community leader and helper informed my work as a social worker.

Teachings and Lessons from My Father

My father, Cecil Reid, Gee ah thla, was born in 1930 and is a Heiltsuk man who experienced residential school and life as a registered Indian in Canada. He worked as a secondary school English and history teacher, and retired from that job before I was born. He continued to live his life as a salmon fisherman, chief councillor and Heiltsuk activist within the Bella Bella community, his traditional territory. My father has been a leader within my community and worked his whole life to find ways to redress the injustices that Indigenous people face and to ensure socio-economic sustainability for the Heiltsuk people. He said that what has kept him fighting for justice has been the resilience of the generations before him, who have given him the strength to move forward. He taught me that colonization has been a crime towards the humanity of the Heiltsuk and other Indigenous peoples around the world. My father said that the most important strategy on the part of the Canadian government was to confine our people to approximately one percent of our lands and deny us access to the resources that have sustained our people for thousands of years. The Canadian government's laws, policies and practices went after every aspect of Indian people's lives and relationships to the land, their families, communities and cultures. Part of that strategy was to create dependency on the dominant mainstream systems and cause the collapse of the Heiltsuk economic base, which resulted in poverty and social and health imbalances of our people. Ultimately, this collapse has led to the deterioration of our cultural structures. My father has always said that our people can no longer be dependent on the larger society for our livelihood and that we need to assert our Indigenous title within Heiltsuk territory and find ways to become self-sustaining within our lands. He believes that to revive our culture is to revive our economic and socio-political structures, which can sustain us as a people.

My family taught me the importance of understanding Heiltsuk history, culture, language and values and to resist colonial laws, policies and practices so that I can maintain a strong Heiltsuk identity. The Heiltsuk word for identity is *xthaway*, the source of identity and strength that is tied to the land and rooted in all the relationships and social structures. My father instilled in me a strong *qvilas*, the way we are and the laws of our ancestors. This includes the tribal laws, spirituality, customs, morals, beliefs and structures within our society. He said that our people have always lived with the belief that we are our brothers' and sisters' keepers and that we are a communal people.

The Heiltsuk peoples have always had clear accountabilities and responsibilities for the wellbeing of all of the people, and this was reflected within our own structures and relationships, which ensured that all of our resources would be sustained. For instance, our Heiltsuk people created a confederacy to ensure that intertribal warfare would not continue among the Heiltsuk tribes and that our sustainable way of living would be maintained.

My father showed me that my strength comes from having grown up within my traditional territory. My father brought my brothers and me out onto the land and sea within our territory during our *bawxla*, seasonal food gathering. He explained to us the history of the land and shared with us the *nuyim*, the Heiltsuk oral stories, which make up the history of the Heiltsuk people. The *nuyim* come from a time when our older brothers and sisters, who lived in a sacred place, could converse with all the living beings; *nuyim* is the history and social fabric that binds us together as Heiltsuk people. Out of the *nuyim* flows our holistic worldview, which is based on the philosophy of interdependence, interconnectedness, respect and balance with all life forms within our environment upon which our social structures and relationships are based.

I grew up learning some of the Heiltsuk language through the elementary school language program and through Elders who still spoke it. My father always said that maintaining and reviving the language is critical to the survival of our people because language encompasses and expresses the cultural values, beliefs and worldviews about who we are. I also had the privilege of participating in our communal and other coastal potlatches. When I was a youth I received my Heiltsuk family name, Juba, which instilled in me great pride as a ritual of passage that included clear responsibilities to be a contributing member within my society.

My father says that all of these teachings led to *kntz tho gwee masi*, we are strong. This phrase recognizes that the person's whole being is balanced and strong. He would say that colonization has created huge imbalances for our people on all levels and that it has led to *gvuxthalacx oowaxdiux*, meaning the person's whole being is out of balance. He says that the strength and power of Indigenous peoples has been evident in our resistance to being completely absorbed into the Canadian body politic and society.

My father modelled for me the importance of having a vision of why I am here as a Heiltsuk woman advocating for self-determination and self-governance for our people. He hopes that the Heiltsuk people will never sign a treaty as they exist today because it will formalize our poverty and legitimize the theft of our lands and resources. He says that the government is asking the Heiltsuk to agree to severely limiting their constitutional rights and that our people need to strategize both locally and on a much broader level as to how they can approach this issue of justice, freedom and self-determination. The struggle towards self-determination and freedom is about securing enough of our traditional territory to sustain our people within a cultural, economic and communal way of living and allow us to reclaim our own humanity within Canadian society. The Heiltsuk people's struggle is moving towards *gwees stim see mus sus wxhoo*, the way it should be.

My father always told me to be a critical thinker and to challenge the dominant worldviews and systems and to never forget who I am or where I come from. He said that a strong Heiltsuk identity would always be my strength. He spoke about the importance of relationships and being responsible and accountable within those relationships, and the need to find a balance between the Heiltsuk ways and the mainstream ways-of-knowing, being and coexisting. In the following section, my father shares his perspective, derived from working as chief and councillor for approximately twenty-three years.

Talking with My Father

Michelle Reid: What approaches, skills and practices are effective for a community helper to assist the community?

Cecil Reid: I found that you have to provide leadership. A community won't benefit if you don't. You have to look at what a village is lacking, you have to define the problems and needs and see where there are possible solutions. We had to develop a five-year plan of all the things that needed doing. That was the basis for most of the things that I did over a ten-to-fifteen year period. The basic community infrastructure wasn't here, such basic things as a store, council hall, municipal services, school. These are a major tasks, especially since everything was run by the federal and provincial government. Many of them were non-existent because they were out of region. Most of the government projects are short term and/or inequitable. We had to look at developing a basic sustainable economy.

Michelle: What skills are necessary for setting up Heiltsuk services?

Cecil: The most important skill one brings to a resolution of community problems is first to have a good grasp of the community's history so that its problems can be defined. A full identification of problems needs to be completed before possible solutions can be developed. In the work required to develop possible solutions, competent consultants and specialists can be greatly beneficial, along with ongoing community consultation. In developing proposed solutions to community problems and needs, it is a good practice to carry on consultations with the community members. These should be ongoing.

As a leader you have to plan and find consultants who can assist and flesh out ideas. Take it to Council and the people. It is important to educate and consult with the people. Once you get their approval you have a long process of jumping through hoops and getting through bureaucracies. Underlying all of this you need a leader with a vision that can be clearly articulated. In any community that is successful you will find a handful of people who think in the same way that is going to benefit the people.

The main driving force behind my actions came from my aunt Gem, who I respected because she was a proud Heiltsuk individual. She told me about my history and I wanted to honour her memory. I was aware and angry at the dispossession of the Heiltsuk people. My education came from her. She had been hurt so badly by White society that I wanted to contribute towards the kind of Heiltsuk society that she would approve of. You were proud as a Heiltsuk. Reclaim the land and access to resources. That was the impetus for most of my actions. The approval from the whole people does not always come and you have to be willing to make some difficult decision to benefit the community in general.

One of the tragedies of the residential school is that it took the place of what should have been the development of an individual child in his family, community and culture. Some of the key values were to not to lie, hurt others, especially children, not to steal, *gadsvua* — to be hard working and not to become people who talk about others.

Michelle: What were/are the challenges?

Cecil: It is difficult to witness and experience the disintegration of our social fabric. It has continued with the impacts of colonization and impoverishment of Indigenous people. One challenge is to try to make a success of all of the visions and initiatives within the community to break the dependence that has been imposed by the government. The greatest challenge facing me thirty-five years ago was the almost complete control of Heiltsuk life by the federal government through the Department of Indian Affairs (DIA). Their agent came out once a month from Bella Coola and met with our elected council. We had no powers. All services theoretically were provided by the Department of Indian Affairs, including welfare, education, new housing and largely non-existent social programs. The last thirty years has seen the attempt by the Heiltsuk to establish political and social control over our own community. Most of the program transfers were under-funded by DIA, with little funding for absolutely necessary training programs. Most program management is not up to the required levels and has been an ongoing serious problem of providing badly needed programs and services.

The other serious challenge arose from the realization that political independence cannot exist unless there is economic independence. Our history since then has been one of growing unemployment without access to our natural resources. Our community has seen poverty increase among our people with devastating social consequences. Council has built a fish processing plant, negotiated spawn-on-kelp licenses and exclusive rights to harvest manila clams, but these fall far short of the employment needed by the Heiltsuk.

The other ongoing challenge has been the need for the Heiltsuk to develop required service infrastructure, including a large general store, a hotel and fuel, home services and other basic services to run the community (water, electricity, health, social services, education, etc.). These all required enormous financial expenditures and the development of new management for all these new enterprises. All had many problems in being set up. All in all, the Heiltsuk are always seeking the goal of self sufficiency and Heiltsuk jurisdictional management of necessary services.

There is always hope, but it is easy to lose the optimism because of the depth of issues and the unresolved issues that exist within Canada for Aboriginal people. The older people appreciated what I did in the community and it was important to have their support and guidance. Relationships were important. The beautiful thing is that all of them were accountable and were willing to be responsible and respectful in the process of community change. It is easy for a society to become irresponsible with imposed poverty and dependence.

Michelle: How do the Heiltsuk traditional cultural stories, values, beliefs, laws and practices inform the community work?

Cecil: Traditional Heiltsuk beliefs have generally been the driving force in the decision-making by Heiltsuk leaders. For instance, during the course of land claims negotiations with the federal and provincial governments, after four years it became clear that federal and provincial proposed settlement offers would only lead to a further impoverishment of the Heiltsuk in terms of their land ownership and access to natural resources. There was also a proposal to seriously cap Heiltsuk rights to their lands and resources. The Heiltsuk leadership took these issues to the membership, recommending that the Heiltsuk suspend negotiations. This course of action was accepted by the Heiltsuk people. It is understood that without a just land claims settlement the Heiltsuk people will be legally impoverished, along with all of the future generations. The Heiltsuk people would only be offered about one percent of their traditional territory and receive very little financial compensation per capita. This amount would not sustain the current or future generations. Heiltsuk traditions do not always reach our young. This is a sad reflection of the cumulative results of one hundred and fifty years of European occupation of our lands and of the residential school system imposed for so long on the Heiltsuk. It is more important for all Heiltsuk to be educated in their values and traditions so that these once again permeate Heiltsuk society.

The Community School must be a part of the Heiltsuk education for our youth, along with parents. There is a 1.7 unit program of Heiltsuk history and hundreds of hours of recorded Heiltsuk oral history which must be translated and implemented in our educational system for our young people to feel proud of who they are.

The Kaxla Child and Family Service agency is about uplifting our Heiltsuk children and families. It must protect all of our children to prevent them from just being taken away. Foster parents do not fulfill the role of giving Aboriginal children an appreciation of themselves. Our children grow up knowing they should be somewhere else. We need strong culturally and community-based programs. Given the number of our children who are removed from our community, we must work towards a culturally and community-based program.

Teachings and Lessons from My Mother

My mother, Alida Reid, is a non-Indigenous woman who has lived in the Heiltsuk Nation and community of Bella Bella since 1970. She assisted in nurturing my Heiltsuk identity and has become a Heiltsuk community member and an ally in the Heiltsuk Nation's self-determination initiatives. My mother experienced both privileges as a Caucasian woman and the challenges of being a minority in the community of Bella Bella. I witnessed her experiences as a non-Heiltsuk woman, community member and inter-disciplinary helper.

My mother worked in the high school as a support worker and in health, as a community prevention coordinator and the Elders' program coordinator. She oversaw the community health nurses, mental health workers, youth workers, etc. She acted in the capacity of board member, volunteer and paid helper. I grew up with so much shame of being born bi-cultural, only to find out that the greatest teachings and lessons would come from my parents' cultural differences and their individual and shared ability to live across cultures. My mother always demonstrated an openness to learn and participate in the Heiltsuk culture and community life. When I was a child she brought my brothers and me to all of the community potlatches and gatherings, where she would often stay until the early hours of the morning. She always appeared to be respectful and accountable in building relationships across her own cultural differences. She modelled the importance of learning by observing and participating in a humble way. She volunteered on committees, especially recreational ones such as basketball, and assisted in ways that the community saw as meaningful. She took the time to engage in reciprocal relationships. Her assistance in the seasonal food gathering and preparations, such as seaweed and berry picking and fish preparations such as canning, drying and smoking, helped to keep the traditions alive in my family. She always demonstrated a spirit of generosity and caring, sharing fish, other food and resources with family and community members. She is famous for her blueberry muffins in a couple of Indigenous communities, where she bakes for fundraisers.

Despite our "normal" family challenges, my mom served as a role model and lived in a way congruent with the basic Heiltsuk values and beliefs. She encouraged my brothers and me to embrace and respect our cultures, as well as others. She encouraged me to volunteer at the Elders' gatherings and we often travelled to different communities. She demonstrates the importance of being fully present with the Elders, listening to the stories and being respectful. I have many memories of travelling with her on annual Elders' conference gatherings, where I gained a lot of knowledge and teachings.

My mom has always supported me with my cultural and academic education. She taught me that no matter where I go, I represent my Heiltsuk people as an advocate and proud member. It really was not until I began to write this chapter and reflect on the experiences and teachings from my parents that I acknowledged my mother for her contributions to my identity as a Heiltsuk woman and for the work that she contributed as a helper and ally with the Heiltsuk people. She showed me that Indigenous and non-Indigenous people can live and work together, and this gives me great hope for this generation and the generations to come. She taught me that her learning came from building a relationship with the Heiltsuk people and not to make assumptions about other Indigenous people or other cultures.

Talking with My Mother

Michelle Reid: What approaches, skills and practices work as a community helper to assist the community?

Alida Reid: The approaches, values, skills and practices are first to be a good listener. Speak your truth, but sometimes soften the blow. Always let people know through your actions that you care and love them, youth, Elders and everyone. Don't be judgmental and check out your assumptions by asking people questions.

Michelle: What were/are the challenges?

Alida: It is a challenge to learn not to rush in and just do things when you see a perceived need. I still struggle with that, and of course that has created an expectation that I will do things. [My mom talked about how it is important to accept others for who they are and to be accepted for who she is. She said that humour is important, to learn to laugh at herself, and laugh with others.]

Michelle: How do the Heiltsuk traditional cultural stories, values, beliefs, laws and practices inform the community work?

Alida: Stories are not told as much now as they were when your dad was growing up and sometimes that is sad. I know that lots of stories your dad was told did good in terms of socializing the children through stories. The only places they do this today is in the language classes. It is probably something we should get the Elders doing — along with the values. I think that with a lot of what is happening with the influence of television, we (most nations) have a tough time competing with what is advertised. If we have strong enough family connections and do some of the ceremonies like the Okanagan people with naming ceremonies, where they present their children and that they ask people to correct their children if they ever see them doing something wrong. Not everyone practises this, but it sure enforces the idea that "it takes a whole community to raise a child." We are trying hard to get the practice back for "Baby's Uplifting Ceremony" in Bella Bella. We are trying to do this through the Health Centre.

I believe that values are so important, and probably part of my frustration is that it is not adhered to in the community as much as it is in some individual homes.

I don't want to be seen as being a "Wanna be Indian." I want to have people accept me for who I am as well. The amazing thing is that so many young people do not think of me as being a White woman. A boy's mom told me a couple of years ago that she had to tell her son that I was White. He had no idea. That is the glory of the children growing up with me here, have just accepted me for who I am and not by the colour of my skin, hair or my eyes.

Communication is huge in doing this work — learning to understand through body language what they are really saying and thinking. It is important to understand why they communicate that way and how I communicate as a non-Indigenous helper with them. It is important to follow up on any assumptions that I may make about others or what they need.

It is important to understand all the hurts that have occurred through the centuries, without allowing the blame to rest on my shoulders. It is very important to listen and find out more about the people before coming or going to any new community. Find out about the people. Websites are pretty informative, but it is the relationships that will establish a good working relationship and understanding about the culture, the community and the individuals here. Listen, go to functions in the community, watch people, see how they interact. We always have to remember to not go in and "save the people." Our people are very friendly and giving, but you don't take advantage of their generosity — we need to give back and work with people.

One of the lessons I learned really early on with my work with the First Nations Skidegate.[2] People will talk about their own but don't you get caught up in it: you will soon learn that they can do it but not you. It is also really important for people to get to know people away from the workplace. Teachers always see such a different side of kids when they are on a field trip, out camping or generally away from the classroom. There are many strengths, and those should be built on.

Michelle: What are the challenges of being a non-Indigenous helper?

Alida: The challenges of being a non-Aboriginal, well, it is so long ago that I came into the community, and I didn't come in as a worker, so I am not sure. I think the biggest challenge would be to come as well prepared in knowing your job and about the people, and be prepared to do a good job at what you do; not to show off what you know but to be humble and set good work ethic patterns. Listen. I can't emphasize that enough; we need to learn from the people. We don't always have to do what they do — and do not get caught up in the community gossip!

Understanding what, as a people, they have gone through and realizing that it has affected the following generations is really important. Adults and children have all been affected and carry the burden of what went on before, but we all need to be cognizant of that. I am also the first person to say that people need to get a healing journey and I know that is easier said than done, but the sooner we do this as a people the sooner we will start being a healthier community. Meantime, we as outsiders still need to support and nourish them.

Kaxlaya Gvilas

I discussed my reasons for going into social work and my experiences as a social work helper. I have endeavoured to weave together the stories and lessons from my parents as community helpers. I recognize that every community and Indigenous culture is different, but the message is the same. The work we do for our children and families is about maintaining ourselves as cultural, self-sufficient and self-determining peoples within Canadian society. The most meaningful work and change happens because of respectful and collaborative relationships that exist in Indigenous communities and between Indigenous and non-Indigenous people. My mother showed me that it is possible to be a powerful ally and work with Indigenous people. Along with other Indigenous people, I will continue to carry forth the resilience of our ancestors and cultures and persevere in advocating for justice for our people. I will continue to invite non-Indigenous people to be allies and to work with us in bringing about meaningful change and the goal of co-existence.

As a Heiltsuk woman I will continue embrace my responsibility as *kaxlaya gvilas*, the ones who upholds the laws of our ancestors for our current generations and generations to come. I will continue to participate in a reconciliation process within social work as a profession and within child welfare to ensure that Canadian Indigenous peoples' inherent citizen rights, cultural perspectives and social work approaches are affirmed. I humbly and respectfully pass this cedar basket of personal stories and experiences to you — the reader, social worker, community helper and ally — to become engaged in a process of connecting your mind and heart in the ongoing practice of making critical, courageous and compassionate connections to the issues and lives of Indigenous people. It is a commitment of building respectful and reciprocal working relationships with Indigenous people and cultural systems. It starts with asking how you can help. The work of a helper is challenging but rewarding. It is always sacred work.

Notes

1.   The Touchstones of Hope document "draws from the rich conversations of the participants at the reconciliation event to describe why reconciliation in child welfare is needed, what reconciliation can mean in the context of child welfare, and to identify key values (touchstones) to guide reconciliation in Aboriginal child welfare." Retrieved from <http://www.fncfcs.com/docs/Touchstones_of_Hope.pdf>.

2.   Skidegate are a Haida First Nations People who are Haida Gwaii and live along the Skidegate Inlet at the end of Graham Island along British Columbia's Northern Coast. Retrieved from <http://www.skidegate.ca/Pages/VisitingSkg.html>.

Chapter 11

Gyawaglaab (Helping one Another)
Approaches to Best Practices through Teachings of Oolichan Fishing

Jacquie Green (Hemaas, Moosmagilth, Ungwa, knewq Kundoque of the Helkinew clan, knewq Haisla, Kemano and Kitselas) — Creator, Ancestors, my English name is Jacquie Green and I belong to the Killer Whale clan and am a member of the Haisla, Kemano and Kitselas peoples.

I acknowledge the story-tellers of my community and family. Over and over again, they have shared stories of our place and of our home. These stories were shared at various times and in various spaces: around the dinner table, in our feast hall, on the boat and in a car. As I have ventured through undergraduate and graduate studies, these stories have re-emerged as a strong and passionate force in my life. As I continue to journey as a social work professor and doctoral student, I find these stories are critically linked to the forms of knowledge and practices that I bring to the classroom and how I demonstrate what best practice is within Indigenous communities. I embrace the strength, passion, method and life-force of these stories in all aspects of my life. As such, this chapter is written in the ways in which I teach and practise. For me, teaching is about storying and about demonstrating with others the importance of understanding our histories, our identities and our traditional homelands through various accounts of our social, political, spiritual and economic lives. By understanding these aspects of our lives, we have a better understanding of how to interact with one another. For me, story-telling is best practice.

Identity story
Spirit Bear

Kundoque is my traditional name, which originates from Kitselas territory and means "journeying over the mountain with my belongings on my back." Kitselas people are known as "those who live by the river," and are famous for living beside the Kermode bear.

Kermode bear is known as "spirit bear" because they are black bears that are white. It is said when spirit bear meets you, you must pay attention to its actions because through its actions, the spirit bear carries a message for you.

The old people say that the only time you meet with spirit bear is when the Creator has a message for you. You never know when this meeting will take place. You could be by the river, you could be in the mountains or you could be around your home. I had the honour of meeting "spirit bear" by my home. I was home with my cousin looking out our window and saw the bear lurking around our house. We watched from the window until he trotted deep into the woods. I believe the message from this encounter is to remember my roots within Kitselas territory. I was shown through spirit bear my identity is not only Haisla, but also Kitselas. Kundoque originates from Kitselas, which is part of a vast Tsimpshian peoples. I must journey back through stories to learn and understand my place and my identity.

The information I have learned about my identity and the meaning of my name informs many aspects of a rich history in the northwest coast of British Columbia, particularly the history of the Haisla peoples. In the classroom and in my profession, I always introduce myself starting with my traditional name and where it comes from. I also share that although I am very proud of my traditional name and place, my learning of our history is lifelong and that I continue to share our history with my children while continuing to learn from my parents and many other family members about who I am and where I come from. For Indigenous people, sharing our identity, the history of our place and sometimes who our families are, gives us a sense of knowing each other. Often people introduce themselves as just coming to know who their families and places are. Acknowledging our identities to each other brings a relief and a form of comfort, knowing we all share an Indigenous identity. Yet we are so diverse. Moreover, when acknowledging our knowledge of self and place or our coming to know who we are, we illustrate the importance of knowing our history and thereby our complex identities.

Creation Story

Huncleesela was the first man to journey to the Haisla territory. Huncleesela and some of his family left Oweekeno territory, which is south of Haisla territory, because he accidentally killed his wife. It is told that the law of that time meant banishment if death happened. As a result, Huncleesela and his entire family would be punished for the death, even though it was an accident. Huncleesela escaped by journeying up toward the northwest coast of Oweekeno and continued until he reached Kluqwajeequas, just outside Haisla territory. It was told in many different villages that the reason he journeyed north was because there was a monster in this area. Because of the monster there were no people there, and he thought Kluqwajeequas would be a good place to hide. Huncleesela camped outside the territory and every once in a while the monster would open his mouth really big and make a loud noise. As he listened to the loud noise, Huncleesela made sure he watched every movement the monster made. Eventually, as Huncleesela became comfortable in his exploration of the monster, he felt brave enough to get closer. When he got as close as he could, he realized the big mouth was not a monster at all, but flocks of seagulls swooping down to grab oolichan from the river. This story tells of the discovery of Haisla territory and the relationship to oolichan, which is core to our existence, which is core to who I am as Haisla.

For Haisla people, understanding oolichan fishers and fishing is vital to understanding our community, our people and our identities. I have listened to many stories of the traditional connections between oolichan harvesting and how Haisla peoples came to be. Perhaps in my reminiscence and dreams, along with stories being shared with me, I recognize the commitment to understand our ways. Identity has to be reinforced by returning to traditional stories and understanding our traditional places. In our practice, acknowledging our willingness to learn and incorporate traditional teachings into our profession ensures the call to Indigenous praxis and to the meanings of Indigenous professionalism.

Because traditional place names can be vague, what are the ways in which you come to understand and learn the various tellings of creation stories and place names? For many Indigenous people, identity can be a complex issue. For those Indigenous people who understand and continue to learn their stories, it is essential that these stories be shared with others, shared within your profession and shared with young people. By sharing creation stories, people begin to see the richness of Indigenous history and begin to see a nation of pride!

Indigenous communities worldwide have creation stories, ceremonial stories and many stories of our families. To exhibit Indigenous knowledge in our practice, we must continue to be reflective of who we are. Our Elders offered their knowledge by sharing with us the many stories of our histories and lives, and their stories contained the teachings of how to live. For Haisla people, the central stories for our community are the telling and teachings about oolichan fishing. The practice of oolichan fishing was crucial to community and family living. The people needed to understand the seasons and weather to understand timing for the oolichan catch, just like Huncleesela had to understand the story behind the "monster" and timing of when he would confront the monster. Understanding how the seasonal rhythms for oolichan fishing inform how Haisla families are constructed is critical because of our reliance on oolichan fish and oolichan grease.

I have been told that we as Haisla people are known for oolichan and oolichan grease. Our surrounding territories often refer to our community as producers of the best oolichan grease. People from these territories often travel to our community to trade for oolichan grease. So not only do traditional teachings come through the process of oolichan fishing, there are interconnections between our various communities for oolichan grease. Therefore, in order to maintain our family traditions and our relationships with other communities and families, it is essential that we understand how to prepare and process oolichan and oolichan grease. And it is important that we as children and grandchildren learn and understand our stories, such as the teachings from Huncleesela's story.

Huncleesela ventured throughout the land to become acquainted with the monster. He was curious and adventurous. In his exploration he learned about this great fish, the oolichan, and he continued to learn more about oolichan in order for him and his family to live life in the great northwest. As professionals, the dominant systems inform us that we have become experts. However, to truly reflect Indigenous programs and practices, our practice must include an understanding of our storying about self and place. Students, clients and other people must come to understand traditional teachings by having an opportunity to freely ask questions and to openly discuss aspects of our practice that are uncomfortable or unfamiliar to them. I asked my parents to tell me the Huncleesela story over and over again. In addition, there were many times during family dinners that my parents would ask my uncles and aunts to share the story of Huncleesela with me. And so, throughout dinner, they shared the story with me again, regardless of whether I wanted to hear it or not. Our Elders, parents and other family members provide teachings through story-telling around our dinner table. They tell us that as we take in our food for sustenance we take in the teachings at the same time. Many times in the classroom, we bring food and share with each other our own traditional teachings. Or some students have an opportunity to ask questions about culture and ceremony — all of these teachings happen while we are eating together in class.

As I reflect back on how I learned about Huncleesela, I recognize the patience of my story-tellers. I recognize the creativity in how and when they shared stories with me. The commitment to teaching by our story-tellers was ever present; they provided countless opportunities for me to ask questions that were difficult or awkward for them about the Huncleesela story such as the accidental death. Sometimes the story-tellers didn't answer and sometimes they did answer about the death. There were also times when we joked about how our ancestors are "fugitives." My story-tellers ensured that Haisla teachings were taught to me in a good way and in a way where I could understand my history and my identity as a Haisla woman.

As Indigenous professionals we must also provide opportunities for people to "begin" knowing their identities and their places. At times, we get consumed with our professional demands and we don't take time to listen and observe some of the discomfort that surrounds us. Many times there are people who are Indigenous who do not know stories of their people or places. We must provide opportunities to learn about identity and place "together."

In our demonstration of Indigenous practice we must provide opportunities to grow and learn. Having said this, demonstrating learning must also include respect, honour and pride. Respect becomes very convoluted in mainstream institutions and organizations. In the classroom, for example, I teach in circle and bring in a "talking stone." Even though I explain the story behind my talking stone and my teachings about sitting in circle, many times my credentials as a "professor" are not respected. While I do acknowledge the respect I receive as an Indigenous woman, the expectations for academic course requirements are sometimes not adhered to. Let me explain further.

Through my experiences as an Indigenous professor, a life long learner of culture and tradition and a woman who predominantly lives away from home, I see the necessity of acknowledging and recognizing Indigenous knowledge as equal to other course requirements for our academic degrees. As well, I believe that students, clients and other people, and governments organizations must see the value of Indigenous knowledge as requirements for our professionalism. Occasionally, students think that because I am flexible, I have an open door policy; for example, that they do not need to hand in their assignments on time or hand them in at all!

My point in sharing these experiences is that, for me, respect is about addressing these incidents in a way so that I do not disrespect myself. As well, how do I apply institutional policies in a way that all students understand, and at the same time, ensure that I am protected? Lastly, because I get frustrated and at times furious with the lack of respect, how do I maintain my integrity despite my emotions? For me, I remember the teachings of patience during oolichan fishing. For example, Huncleesela waited for days, perhaps weeks before he faced the monster. Another example is the uncertainty of the oolichan run: our community never knows when the oolichan run will happen. Our families prepare their boats, the fishing gear, food and their camping grounds while waiting for the oolichan. Lately the oolichan have not been running every year, and all the preparations will have to be repeated in the following year. Even though the oolichan did not run, our people were at least prepared for the harvest.

In my teaching, I must continue to be prepared for any sort of incident that could occur and put my "academic teaching agenda" on hold in order to work through various dynamics that present themselves in my work. I must also remember how I carry myself with challenges, frustration and fear. Importantly I remember that how I act and speak is a reflection of my family, my grannies, my grandpas and my community. So it is just not I that faces the consequences of my actions, but also my family and community.

Oolichan Fishing Story

Oolichan fishing is one of the most important aspects of Haisla life. In our language oolichan is *za' X w en*.[1] The old people tell us our *za' X w en* is a mystery fish because they are known to spawn only once a year. They spawn in the winter months, usually just before spring weather or at the end of "north wind season." Some say you could smell the oolichan season and feel a certain chill in the air, which we refer to as "oolichan weather." Another reference to oolichan are candle fish, because at one time the old people would fish the oolichan, fully dry them and burn them for light. The main uses of oolichan are to harvest and process for *kqlateeh*,[2] preserve and use for trading with other communities for *aghingt*[3] and *xklucas*.[4]

Kqlateeh for Haisla people, and to those who seek it, is known as a delicacy. Not only is *kqlateeh* food, but also it has excellent medicinal use. The old people have used *kqlateeh* for severe cases of pneumonia, bronchitis and other such illnesses. The taste of *kqlateeh* on fish and other food sources is delicious. However, if you have it straight without accompanied by fish there is a different taste. Having it "straight" is like drinking vegetable oil by itself, only with a fishy aroma to it. Or, you can liken *kqlateeh* to olive oil or salad dressing. As you swallow *kqlateeh* it glides very slowly down your throat to your stomach. Perhaps it is the slow journey through your body that cures any illness that is there. If babies were sickly, the old women would simmer water with a bit of *kqlateeh* on the stove and the aroma would help breathing and clear the airway. Some of the old people also said that if they did not want a certain kind of visitor (like a White person), they would simmer *kqlateeh* prior to the visit. If you were not raised around oolichan the aroma is often not appealing. Visitors are then likely to leave very quickly.

Although I grew up in my territory surrounded by my family and other Haisla people, this didn't necessarily mean that I knew my history, place and identity. Well, at least I thought I did not know our history. I did however know that oolichan and *kqlateeh* were important to our existence.

As I have journeyed through academia and lived away from home I recognize the intricacies and expertise embedded within the process of oolichan fishing. Throughout academia I recognize that indeed our history is the practice of oolichan fishing today. What is challenging today is how to strengthen traditional teachings about the current process of oolichan fishing. Reflecting on our family history, our place and where our traditional names come from, I see that there is so much resiliency and strength in how our people have sustained their/our livelihood just by maintaining traditional practices. We all must remember the traditional practices that are unique to each of our diverse communities. For our people, and for my learning, I continue to be amazed at how all the uses of oolichan oil held many practices for families to sustain health, education and governance of families and communities.

Preparation Story

In the old days our people would camp and deep water fish close to oolichan time. They would set up their camps in the forest on one of the many islands in the ocean to fish for halibut, dig for clams and set crab traps. While cleaning their catch, if they found oolichan in the stomach, they knew it was time to prepare their oolichan camps. Another sign that it was oolichan time was when sea lions, seals, ducks, eagles and seagulls were dipping in the water and eating the oolichan, similar to Huncleesela's monster story.

Understanding the seasons, the weather and the animals requires fishers to be competent in preparation for oolichan fishing. Preparing for the oolichan harvest also requires that families, community members and leaders communicate efficiently so that they do not miss the oolichan run and that they are all prepared when the oolichan arrive. In the old days, each person had a role in preparation for the harvest.

It was up to the fishers to mentor young people in how to look for signs of an oolichan run among animals. Young people, or rather new learners, were mentored on how to build the required tools for fishing and for processing oolichan grease. Of course, during the preparation, children would be playing and running around the camps. The sounds of laughter, singing and splashing water gave adults the adrenaline to keep on working. Fishers needed to eat, to rest and to keep themselves clean, and so during the preparation time there was childcare, cooks and cleaners among many teachers of oolichan processing. Everyone's role at the oolichan camp was and is deemed of equal importance and value. The preparation was done collectively, each according to their age and abilities.

Once the preparation for oolichan fishing was completed, our people waited for the hereditary chief to go out and fish and return with his first catch. This first catch was celebrated, and during feasting, the people shared their plans for the new season. They shared old stories from other years and reminisced about Huncleesela's' journey, our monster story and our oolichan story.

In our work as Indigenous professionals, it is necessary that we are prepared to work with clients, students and other groups of people in a good way. Our professions require us to be honest and to seek help when we need it. Many times it is difficult to prepare a course and to teach a course knowing that students require us to know everything about social work. To prepare social work students to work with people we must be genuine in what we share in class about the course, about ourselves and about what we don't know. It is important to model leadership, just as the fishers did to new learners at the oolichan camps. I must be willing to work with students in their preparation for social work practice by perhaps having a class in the community, bringing Elders/healers (of all races, gender, ability and class) into class or perhaps sharing food in class just as we did around our dinner table.

As many of us know, the burnout rate for social workers is extremely high. When working with our own people, Indigenous people, we tend to work over and beyond our duty, because the reality is that we need to. It is imperative to know when to take time for self and for family. Just like the preparation for oolichan fishing, if someone is not fulfilling their role, then the family and maybe community loses out on oolichan for the season.

At the oolichan camps, when some knew a person was tired or hurt, they stepped in to take over for the tired person or delegated someone to assume their duties. Everyone at the camps was aware of each person's physical ability. It was crucial for people to understand and recognize each other's wellbeing during processing and preparation time. Tasks required at oolichan camps are the priority because families and the community rely on the sustenance of oolichan and oolichan grease throughout the year. Preparation of self, equipment and supplies is essential for quality work at the camps and for producing a food which is the delicacy of our nation.

Now, if we are not well prepared in our profession, then we will not be able to work efficiently with families and children. It is imperative that we as professionals take time to support one another, make time for our families and nurture our own wellbeing. We must demonstrate how we can work collectively with all people, work through our challenges, face our fears and celebrate our successes! As professionals we all must work collectively to provide fun positive visions and dreams for our children, all children.

Oolichan Grease Story

When it was time for communities to fish, their first catch after the celebration feast was used to make *kqlateeh* and was placed in oolichan bins. Haislas always used female oolichan to make *kqlateeh* because they contained more fat than males, and usually the first run of oolichan were female. The second run of oolichan were mainly used for preserving (smoking and salting).

The first catch of oolichan from the first run is then placed in bins to ferment. Before fermenting, the children would dig through all the oolichan with their hands, a cold process, and pick out large oolichan (males) for preserving by smoking and salting.[5] Once *kqlateeh* was fermented, the bins are ready to be heated to a boiling point. The Elders have shared that they would test the fermented oolichan by hanging an oolichan over a stick: if the oolichan fell apart easily, then it was fermented enough. If the "test" was passed, then the oolichan would be boiled at a steady pace for a day.

During the filling of bins, the men and women would discuss whether there was enough grease. The amount of grease processed was important because families prepared grease not only for themselves but for other family members. Furthermore, families who processed grease often traded it with families from other communities for seaweed and herring eggs or other foods that were not processed in Haisla territory. There were times when families could not make it to oolichan camps the following year, due to death or illness of family member. Families would want to know they had enough grease to last them until the next oolichan season. The women, who were the experts in skimming the grease, knew just how much grease would be produced according to how many oolichan were placed in the bins, and would therefore show the men that indeed there was enough water and grease to skim.

Throughout the preparation and first catch process, there are many areas of sharing expertise that are demonstrated through modelling, feasting and teaching. Communication among one another taught our people about what type of wood, plants and places are required to harvest oolichan. The men, with their knowledge of the land and water, knew what signs to watch for, and would in turn share these teachings with the young men who were fishing with them. Timing is of great importance as well as understanding the functions of the environment and animals. Timing included patience. Communicating in a respectful, teachable manner for all people was critical to ensuring *kqlateeh* would be processed in the best way possible. Timing included learning how to prepare equipment and tools to work with the oolichan. The entire process of oolichan fishing includes teachings of respect, honour, our relationship with the land and the importance of family and community. It required that the whole community work together to complete this daunting task that was/is so integral to the wellbeing of our people and community.

As a parent, aunt and grandmother, it has been challenging at times to let my daughters walk by themselves for the first time. It was at times difficult to watch them evolve into adulthood and face life and world challenges and richness. I suppose it has been the spirit of my ancestors who have given me strength to let them experience their own journey as young women and parents. In the classroom and in my social work practice I have also learned that families and students will make their own decisions. Each student's practice is unique and informed by their own family history and teachings. If I want to teach respect and honour, then I must engage with students and clients with respect and honour. They will make mistakes and so will I. The trick here is to recognize what a "teachable moment" is. We must be able to look at mistakes and failures as opportunities to do change and do things differently.

For those who know me, I must share a famous quote by one of my favourite inspirational athletes, Michael Jordan: "Everyday I fail, and that is how I succeed." Often in our profession, we look at failures and mistakes and react with punishments or reprimands. To break the cycles of dysfunction — not only in our families but also in our practices, our professions, classrooms and communities — change is possible if we shift how we look at issues and problems. In the oolichan camps, learners were shown how to work together with the fishers. The fishers worked collectively and communicated respectfully at all instances. Effective communication and leadership are reasons why we continue to learn and understand philosophies of oolichan fishing today.

Gyawaglaab Story

There were many different families at the oolichan camps. The different families, who were at their camps, helped each other with different tasks. Our people say *gyawaglaab*, which means "helping one another." For Haislas, oolichan fishing generates this collectivity and during the time of oolichan fishing, our entire community comes together as a collective. Traditionally, there were roles for all family members. When the oolichan barrels are *agaheestamas*[6] fishers would either take a rest or help other family fishers who hadn't filled their bins yet.

Throughout my experiences as a worker, a student and now a professional, I recognize how Indigenous people have always worked with pride and dignity with one another. I have learned through colleagues, friends and family that really there is no word for social work in our various languages. However, there are words that identify actions relevant to working with one another. For Haisla, *gyawaglaab* encapsulates how we can work effectively with one another as social workers. Within our role as leaders, understanding our identity and our traditional place and history informs what praxis could look like. For some of our people who are beginning to learn their identity as Indigenous people, this knowledge is critical. Many of our young people and older people are reconnecting to their Indigenous identities. There is a demand for our complex identities to come together as professionals. We must take time to listen and hear each other's stories. We must take time to ask courageous questions. Importantly, we must work together to implement Indigenous knowledge in our workplaces, our communities and within our families.

An Oolichan Vision

I remember as a child, I was involved in harvesting oolichan and making oolichan grease. I was about seven years of age. We were still able to fish right in the mouth of Kluqwajeequas. Our family camp was set up on the beach and there were other families around us. At the camp, people worked hard at packing and fishing oolichan, keeping the fires going, preparing the oolichan bins. There were other people who were maintaining food supplies by cooking and feeding everyone. I too had my own oolichan bucket and the job of packing oolichan. This experience and stories that were shared with me are now a distant memory. But these teachings have remained at the core of my heart and commitment to re-learn our ways. The translation of my name, Kundoque, has resurfaced for me to make the journey of re-hearing, re-telling and re-connecting to teachings of my traditional identity, place and history. The meaning of my name "journeying over the mountain with belongings on my back" is the analogy I use to carry forth the teachings of oolichan fishing, language and place to our future. Through my story, through my children's story, we will be able to keep our historical place a part of who we are as Haisla, as Kitselas, as Kemano, and our relationship to oolichan fishing.

In our workplace it is essential that we as Indigenous people continue to present our traditional teachings with pride and honour. It is essential that we model our knowledge so that young people and new learners can carry forth traditional teachings to their children, to their students and/or to their clients. I have learned through hearing stories of oolichan fishing about how to communicate effectively, how to work collectively and how to hear stories and how to re-tell stories about our Haisla ways. I will continue to demonstrate leadership in my work that reflects the wonderful teachings of my grandparents and my parents. I will continue to acknowledge my territory and my identity wherever I journey. I will acknowledge ancestors of other places and lands. Importantly, I must acknowledge and thank the Creator for the wonderful place we are living on and the abundance of resources provided to us. *Aixgwellas*!

References — *Nuuyum*
[passing on traditional teachings from our ancestors]

In academic papers we are required to cite and reference sources that have informed our writing. What is complex for academia and for me in this process of writing is that my sources are from my family, my community and my culture, and have been shared with me throughout my life.

Wa (thank you) to my family, my extended family, those I work with, those who are my friends and, importantly, my parents, my children, grandchildren and my partner for your teachings to me.

My life, my family members, my community members have all faced challenges, heartaches and tensions throughout our years. I believe the teachings of my parents have enabled my family to work through issues. I have also brought forth these teachings to inform how I work through issues/challenges in my workplace. How I deal with challenges, successes and preparation professionally are all informed by family functionality. In terms of linking my traditional teachings to "best practice," my academic teaching is a reflection of how I was raised and taught by my parents, other family members and community.

Noosa means re-telling stories, or telling stories. When we want our story-teller to share more stories, we say *noosta*. For myself, I heard various teachings and stories many times. It is now my turn to remember these stories and continue to re-tell these stories to my children, other children.

Notes

1. Pronounced as jax-quin.
2. Oolichan grease. Kwaguilth and Tshmishian say *kqleena*.
3. Herring eggs, which are one of the main sources of food of Kitsasoo, Heiltsuk and Hartley Bay.
4. Seaweed.
5. Smoking oolichan was done in smoke houses at the camps. Salting is done by placing oolichan in buckets with course salt. Both types of preserving did not require refrigeration and could be stored outdoors during other seasons.
6. Filled and sealed with oolichan.

Chapter 12

Conclusion

Michael Hart (Kaskitémahikan),
with Raven Sinclair (Ótiskewápíwskew)

This book is an anti-colonial project. It is a step in the decolonization process of the Indigenous peoples in the northern territories of Turtle Island because the Indigenous authors are asserting their traditional knowledges vis-à-vis their mainstream social work understandings, thereby creating and claiming a new territory that aligns more fully with their respective epistemologies and ontologies. Although we focus on how we work as Indigenous social workers, where our thoughts and social work practices are first and foremost based in our cultures and worldviews, we do forget that the effort to analyze and deflate the encompassing nature of colonialism and its effects on us needs to continue. This rings especially true since Amer-European worldviews continue to dominate higher education, and Amer-European thought continues to be the educational platform that is automatically considered relevant, valid and universally applicable (Morgan 2003; Sinclair 2004). In turn, Indigenous thoughts, realities and practices are marginalized through neglect or through colonial-influenced writings about Indigenous cultural knowledges, languages and colonial histories. To work in this type of learning and helping environments we, Indigenous people, often have little choice but to participate in endeavours that either devalue, belittle or simply do not acknowledge our cultural identities. As a result, we find ourselves learning and perpetuating predominantly western knowledges of helping in western *and* Indigenous environments (Morgan 2003), to the ongoing detriment to ourselves, our communities and our nations.

As Rains (1999) explains, these actions compound the social ramifications in that the knowledge we receive or transmit in our social work education practices, or don't receive or don't transmit, is, in part, what sensitizes or desensitizes all people to the current political climate and the nature of the struggles being waged by Indigenous peoples. The implications are of great concern when we note how many social workers are moving into the profession in Canada each year. The marginalization of our traditions and cultures, to the point where they are seen as obstacles to progress, demonstrates that the colonial exploitation continues. From another perspective, also shared by Rains (1999), I am deeply concerned that when we fail to include understandings of Indigenous knowledge in the curriculum, when we fail to include Indigenous ways of helping, when we fall prey to historical amnesia or when we buy into the contemporary intellectual authority, we are acquiescing to non-Indigenous jurisdiction over our lives as Indigenous people and thus, we are complicit in our own oppression. Both Fanon (1963) and Coulthard (2008) explain that this process has occurred and is occurring among Indigenous peoples. As Gail states in her chapter on Indigenous cen-tred social work, Indigenous social workers are not immune to developing a "false consciousness" through "internalized oppression" that creates cognitive and practice dissonance. De La Torre addresses internalized colonization: "We must be critical enough about our past, present, and future to recognize when we have abandoned Indigenous knowledge [and practices] for colonial reasoning" (2004: 186). In other words, we need to decolonize ourselves as social workers trained in colonial institutions literally built on the Indigenous lands and our ancestors.[1] Freire (1993) also addresses this very point when he notes that professional women and men, and this includes Indigenous social workers, are individuals who have been miseducated and socialized by a culture of domination. He also notes that these professionals are necessary to the (re)organization of the new society and ought to be reclaimed by the revolution despite their misdirection.

Decolonization requires increased Indigenous social work scholarship and practice that is based upon moral dialogue with, and the participation of, Indigenous communities. Here Ermine et al.'s (2004) concept of an ethi-cal space is a valuable framework. Ermine interprets Poole's (1972) concept of an ethical space as the space that exists when individuals from different cultures, worldviews and life experiences meet, consciously set aside their tacit infrastructures (Bohm 2003) and engage in an atmosphere of equality, respect and understanding. Such a framework would appear to epitomize social work ethics and values. Further, an ethical space approach to dialogue and interaction would intrinsically support the rights of Indigenous peoples to produce and control knowledges about ourselves, our communities, our societies and our ways of helping (Dei 2000).

Our responsibilities, as Indigenous academics, are to become creators of the discourse on Indigenous peoples and matters. Taiaiake Alfred (1999) explains this further:

> There is nothing wrong with valuing traditional knowledge. A real Indian intellectual is proud of our traditions and is willing to take a risk in defending our principles.... The traditions are powerful, real, and relevant. As intellectuals we have a responsibility to gener-ate and sustain a social and political discourse that is respectful of

the wisdom embedded within our traditions; we must find answers from within those traditions, and present them in ways that preserve the integrity of our language and communicative styles. Most importantly, as writers and thinkers, we should be answerable to our nations and communities. (1999: 143–44)

Obviously, we believe Indigenous knowledges should become a significant part of social work. This point does not just mean including curriculum that addresses Indigenous peoples and our knowledges. It also means synthesizing Indigenous knowledge into the daily workings of social work institutions and institutions effected by social work. As Sinclair (2004) explains, this synthesis would include adopting as a central goal of Indigenous social work the decolonization of Indigenous people. This goal can be enacted by recognizing and critiquing how social work is contextualized within the Canadian colonial realities and enacting healing methods based on Indigenous worldviews, epistemologies and theories of practice. A key aspect to the decolonization process is the personal responsibility of Indigenous social workers to engage in our own healing journeys based on our own knowledges (Hart 2002; Sinclair 2004). Cyndy asked the important question in her chapter: How many of us Indigenous social workers have not been impacted by colonization? By relying on our own understandings and practices, Indigenous social workers act as role models who are challenging stereotypes, addressing issues of oppression and internalized colonization, reclaiming and contextualizing Indigenous history, critically acquiring Amer-European theoretical and practice knowledge, engaging in the reconstruction of Indigenous epistemologies and pedagogical forms, and synthesizing these tasks into a form that meets the understandings of the Elders and the needs and desires of Indigenous communities and people (see also Sinclair 2004). These are a few of the many daunting tasks facing Indigenous social workers focused on Indigenist practice.

This book is a step in this communal journey. It is not the first step. There have been generations of individuals, social workers and not, who have been working on these anti-colonial tasks. But, this book is a significant step in that it is the first of its kind focusing our present understandings of social work in an Indigenist and/or Indigenous-centred way. It is clear that much work remains, including further discussion of what Indigenist or Indigenous-centred social work means and what it looks like. This raises the question: How will we as Indigenous helpers, participating in an Amer-European concept called "social work," engage in "the longest running resistance movement in Canadian history"? (Simpson 2008: 13). We do know that all social workers, Indigenous and non-Indigenous, must engage in a manner that recognizes culture as central in social work and that "mainstream or 'Western' social work is 'Indigenous' to 'Western' societies only and its relevance in other cultures and contexts must be seriously questioned and, if it is transferred, this must be done cautiously" (Gray and Coates 2008: 273). We also know that any future work will include analyses of common, and not so common, social work histories, theories and practices from an Indigenous perspective, such as Raven's critique of the child welfare scoop of past several decades and the blaming of the victims for supposedly "losing their identity," and Catherine and Dana's articulation of Métis identity and how social work can meet the needs of Métis clients. It will also include following our cultural understandings and practices in meeting the needs of our people, as exemplified by Rona's holistic focus on the wellbeing of her son who has autism, Cyndy's explanation of how she works from Indigenous worldviews in the therapeutic relationship and Kathy's experiences as an Indigenous social worker utilizing her own knowledge bundle and teachings from her people. For certain, we are committed to uphold our peoples' values, laws and beliefs, as explained by Michelle, and to incorporate the teachings from our ancestors and our lands into our analyses, as Jacquie has done.

Closing Words

I was recently re-reading Patricia Monture-Angus's (1995) comments about being a bridge between her people, Indigenous people, or more specifically the Kanien'kehaka of the Haudenosaunee Confederacy, and non-Indigenous people. I was thinking about that metaphor as it applied to me and what came to mind was the Kanien'kehaka Kaswentha. Taiaiake Alfred explains:

> The Kanien'kehaka Kaswentha (Two-Row Wampum) principle embodies this notion of power in the context of relations between nations. Instead of subjugating one to the other, the Kanien'kehaka who opened their territory to Dutch traders in the early seventeenth century negotiated an original and lasting peace based upon co-existence of power in a context of respect for the autonomy and distinctive nature of each partner. The metaphor for this relation-ship — two vessels, each possessing its own integrity, travelling the river of time together — was conveyed visually on a background of white beads (representing peace). In this respectful (co-equal) friendship and alliance, any interference with the other partner's autonomy, freedom, or powers was expressly forbidden. So long as these principles were respected, the relationship would be peaceful, harmonious, and just. (1999: 52)

In thinking of these vessels, I actually pictured two canoes — that must be the Cree in me. This picture brought out a memory of a particular canoe trip I was on with some friends. We had two canoes between the four of us. We usually paddled with the flow of the river, but on occasion we stopped paddling to admire the beautiful scenery along the Grassie River in the north-central area of Turtle Island. Some of the times when we stopped paddling, one friend from the other canoe would hold out her paddle and my friend in our canoe would grab it. At the same time, I would offer my paddle to my friend in the other canoe and he would grab it. In this way we had the two canoes side by side, joined together by hanging onto each other's paddles while the water carried us gently forward. As I thought about those times when we were joined together, I realized that our joining was voluntary. What kept us together was our desire to be together because it met the needs of the people in both canoes. At any time the two people in one canoe could let go of both paddles, or one person in each canoe could let go of the paddles. What I also realized was that a paddle could be dropped by both sides and left alone.

Unlike the bridge metaphor, where the bridge is fixed and stands re-gardless of the dynamics occurring on either side, and avoids the water or "the peace" identified in the Kanien'kehaka, the canoes and paddles fit our experiences as social workers. In spite of my awareness of the dynamics of colonialism, reification, hegemony and marginalization, I maintain my hope, perhaps naïvely, that both parties with which I am connected, the canoe of Indigenous peoples and the canoe of the social work profession and the people that comprise it, will strengthen our connections to one another so that we will maintain some mutual sense of peace, harmony and justice. I realize that my ability to connect these two worlds is dependent upon my own willingness to engage and on their desire to work with me, with us, to form such a bond. Both parties still have to reach out to one another with a paddle, which takes will. I also realize that, like the paddle, one or both could drop me at any time. So, unlike the bridge in the first story, I see myself in quite a tenuous position. This risk is heightened when one side, the Amer-European academic side, seems overwhelming. As Dei says, "To speak about Indigenous knowledges and the decolonization of the Western/ Euro-American academy is to take personal and collective risk" (2008: 112). Collectively, we are willing to embrace the necessary risks.

I also realize that as a paddle I am initially based in one canoe or the other. I know where I am based and what role I am to play for Indigenous peoples. In reality, I would have minimal difficulties being dropped by aca-demia or the mainstream social work profession, but if I am dropped by my nation for not fulfilling my commitment to our people, I am truly without a base. After all, the social work profession does not significantly influence all aspects of who I have been, who I am and who I will be, but my Creeness certainly does. So, it is with our Elders' words of "never forget where you come from" that we paddle forward as Indigenous social workers asserting our collective and individual platforms of Indigenous knowledge as the premise from which we engage in the pedagogy and practice of social work. We welcome allies and collaborators along for the ride.

Notes

1. I purposely state here "on" our ancestors because our ancestors' physical bodies became part of the land after their passing. As such, the buildings on Turtle Island are literally resting on generations of our ancestors.

References

Aboriginal Supported Child Development. 2008. *Aboriginal Supported Child Development Home Page.* <scdp.bc.ca/ASCD%20pages/mysite/index.htm>.

Absolon, K. 1993. "Healing as Practice: Teachings from the Medicine Wheel." Unpublished paper prepared for the Wunska Network.

_____. 2006. Unpublished poem. Waterloo, Ontario.

_____. 2007. Unpublished poem. Waterloo, Ontario.

_____. 2008. "Kaandosswin, This is How We Come to Know? Indigenous Graduate Research in the Academy: Worldviews and Methodologies." Unpublished doctoral thesis, University of Toronto, Toronto, ON.

Absolon, K., and E. Herbert. 1997. "Community Action as a Practice of Freedom: A First Nations Perspective." In B. Wharf and M. Clague (eds.), *Community Organizing Canadian Experiences.* Toronto, ON: Oxford University Press.

Absolon, K., J. Mitchell and A. Armitage. 1996. *The Development of the Child and Family Service Act: An Aboriginal Perspective.* Victoria, BC: University of Victoria, Child and Family Research Program, School of Social Work.

Absolon, K., and C. Willett. 2005. "Putting Ourselves Forward: Location in Aboriginal Research Methodology." In L. Brown and S. Strega (eds.), *Research as Resistance: Critical, Indigenous and Anti-oppressive Research Approaches.* Toronto, ON: Canadian Scholars Press.

Adams, H. 1975. *Prison of Grass.* Toronto, ON: General Publishing.

_____. 1999. *Tortured People: The Politics of Colonization.* Revised edition. Penticton, BC: Theytus Books.

Adams, M. 2002. *Our Son a Stranger: Adoption Breakdown and its Effects on Parents.* Montreal, QC: McGill-Queen's University Press.

Adoption Worker, Adoption Registry, Saskatchewan Department of Community Resources and Employment. Personal communication, July 13, 2007.

Alfred, T. 1999. *Peace, Power, Righteousness: An Indigenous Manifesto.* Toronto, ON: Oxford University Press.

_____. 2005. *Wasase: Indigenous Pathways of Action and Freedom.* Peterborough, ON: Broadview Press.

Alfred, T., and J. Corntassel. 2005. "Being Indigenous: Resurgences Against Contemporary Colonialism. Government and Opposition." *An International Journal of Comparative Politics* 40, 4: 597–614.

Anderson, K. 2000. *Recognition of Being: Reconstructing Native Womanhood.* Toronto, ON: Second Story Press.

Anderson, K., and B. Lawrence (eds.). 2004. *Strong Women Stories: Native Vision and Community Survival.* Toronto, ON: Sumach Press.

Angell, G.B. 2000. "Cultural Resilience in North American Indian First Nations: The

Story of Little Turtle." *Critical Social Work* 1, 1. <criticalsocialwork.com>.

Antone, R.A., D.L. Miller and B.A. Myers. 1986. *The Power Within People*. Deseronto, ON: Peace Tree Technologies.

Armitage, A. 1993. "Towards First Nations Control of Child Welfare in Canada." In B. Wharf (ed.), *Rethinking Child Welfare in Canada*. Toronto, ON: McClelland and Stewart.

_____. 1995. *Comparing the Policy of Aboriginal Assimilation: Australia, Canada, and New Zealand*. Vancouver, BC: UBC Press.

Armstrong, J. 2000. "Ekolu — A Holistic Education: Teachings from the Longhouse: We Cannot Afford to Lose One Native Child." In Maenette K.P. Nee-Benham and Joanne E. Cooper (eds.), *Indigenous Educational Models for Contemporary Practice: In our Mother's Voice*. Mahwah, NJ: Lawrence Erlbaum Associates.

Arnott, J. 1994. "Mutts' Memoir." In C. Camper (ed.), *Miscegenation Blues: Voices of Mixed-Race Women*. Toronto, ON: Sister Vision.

Arrillaga, P. 2001. "America's Lost Birds Fly Home: Adopted Indians Find Way Back to Their Tribes." <public.iastate.edu/~lhodges/2001Jun.htm>.

Arsenault, A. 2006. "The Life Cycle Experiences and Influences of Adoption Through Aboriginal Adult's Stories." Unpublished master's thesis, University of British Columbia, Vancouver, BC.

Ashcroft, B., G. Griffiths and H. Tiffin. 1995. *The Post-Colonial Studies Reader: The Key Concepts*. New York, NY: Routledge.

Ashcroft, B., G. Griffiths and H. Tiffin. 2001. *Post-Colonial Studies: Key Concepts*. New York, NY: Routledge.

Autism Canada Foundation. 2008. "What Is Autism." <autism-society.org/site/PageServer?pagename=about_home>.

Autism Society Canada. 2007. "What Is Autism Spectrum Disorder?" <autismsocietycanada.ca/pdf_word/info_ASC%27swhatisautisminfosheet_27_June_07_e.pdf>.

_____. 2007. "About Autism." <http://www.autism-society.org>.

Awasis Agency of Northern Manitoba. 1997. *First Nations Family Justice: Mee-noo-stah-tan Mi-ne-si-win*. Victoria, BC: Morriss Printing.

Baden, A. 2002. "The Psychological Adjustment of Transracial Adoptees: An Application of the Cultural-Racial Identity Model." *Journal of Social Distress and the Homeless* 112 (April): 167–91.

Bagley, C. 1991. "Adoption of Native Children in Canada: A Policy Analysis and a Research Report." In H. Altstein and R.J. Simon (eds.), *Intercountry Adoption: A Multinational Perspective*. New York, NY: Praeger Publishers.

_____. 1993. "Transracial Adoption in Britain: A Follow-up Study, with Policy Considerations." *Child Welfare* 72, 3 (May–June): 285–99.

Bagley, C., and L. Young. 1984. The Long-Term Adjustment of a Sample of Inter-Country Adopted Children. *International Social Work* 23, 16–22.

Bagley, C., L. Young and A. Scully. 1993. *International and Transracial Adoptions: A Mental Health Perspective*. Newcastle upon Tyne: Althenaeum Press.

Baikie, G., and L. Bella. 2003. *Nui Manikashuan: A Needs Assessment for Innu Social Work Education*. Memorial University of Newfoundland.

_____. 2005. "Critical Professional Self-Awareness: Using Critical Reflection to Decolonize and Create Aboriginal-Centered Social Work Theory and Practice

— An Emerging Work." Unpublished paper (May). St. John's, Newfoundland: Memorial University.

_____. 2008. "Theorizing Indigenous-Social-Work Praxis in the Borderlands Where Indigenous and Euro-western Practice Contexts Converge." Unpublished dissertation proposal, Memorial University of Newfoundland.

Ball, J. 2004. "As If Indigenous Knowledge and Communities Mattered: Transformative Education in First Nations Communities in Canada." *The American Indian Quarterly* 28, 3/4 (Summer/Fall): 454–79.

Baskin, C. 1997. "Mino-Yaa-Daa: An Urban Community Based Approach." *Native Social Work Journal* 1, 1: 55–67.

_____. 2002a. "Holistic Healing and Accountability: Indigenous Restorative Justice." *Child Care in Practice* 8: 133–36.

_____. 2002b. "Circles of Resistance: Spirituality in Social Work Practice, Education and Transformative Change." *Currents: New Scholarship in the Human Services* 1, 1. <fsw.ucalgary.ca/currents/articles/baskin_v1_n1.htm>.

_____. 2005. "Centering Aboriginal World Views in Social Work Education." *Australian Journal of Indigenous Education* 34: 96–106.

_____. 2006. "Aboriginal World Views as Challenges and Possibilities in Social Work Education." *Critical Social Work* 7, 2. <criticalsocialwork.com>.

_____. 2007. "Circles of Resistance: Spirituality and Transformative Change in Social Work Education and Practice." In John Coates, J.R. Graham, B. Swartzentruber and B. Ouellette (eds.), *Spirituality and Social Work: Selected Social Work Readings.* Toronto, ON: Canadian Scholars' Press.

Bateson, G., D.D Jackson, J. Haley and J. Weakland. 1956. "Toward a Theory of Schizophrenia." *Behavioural Science* 1: 251–64.

Battiste, M. 1998. "Enabling the Autumn Seed: Toward a Decolonized Approach to Aboriginal Knowledge, Language, and Education." *Canadian Journal of Native Education* 221: 16–27.

_____. 2000. "Maintaining Aboriginal Identity, Language, and Culture in Modern Society." In M. Battiste (ed.), *Reclaiming Indigenous Voice and Vision.* Vancouver, BC: UBC Press.

Battiste, M., and J. Barman. 1995. *First Nations Education in Canada.* Vancouver, BC: UBC Press.

Battiste, M., and J. Youngblood Henderson. 2000. *Protecting Indigenous Knowledge and Heritage: A Global Challenge.* Saskatoon, SK: Purich Publishing.

Bausch, R., and R. Serpe. 1997. "Negative Outcomes of Interethnic Adoption of Mexican American Children." *Social Work* 4, 2 (March): 136–43.

Bellefeuille, G., and F. Ricks. 2003. "A Pathway to Restoration: From Child Protection to Community Wellness." *Native Social Work Journal* 5: 23–43.

Bennett, B., and J. Zubrzycki. 2003. "Hearing the Stories of Australian Aboriginal and Torres Strait Islander Social Workers: Challenging and Educating the System." *Australian Social Work* 561 (March): 61–70.

Bennett, M., C. Blackstock and R. De la Ronde. 2005. "A Literature Review and Annotated Bibliography on Aspects of Aboriginal Child Welfare in Canada." Second edition. Ottawa. ON: First Nations Child and Family Caring Society. <fncfcs.com/docs/AboriginalCWLitReview_2ndEd.pdf>.

Bensen, R. (ed.). 2001. *Children of the Dragonfly: Native American Voices on Child Custody and Education*. Tucson, AZ: The University of Arizona Press.

Benton-Banai. E. 1988. *The Mishomis Book*. Hayward, WI: Indian Country Communications Inc.

_____. 2001. *Midewiwin Ceremonies*. Mole Lake, WI.

Berlin, S.B. 1990. "Dichotomous and Complex Thinking." *Social Service Review* 46–59 (March).

Bernard, Viola W. 1969. "Report on the First International Conference on Transracial Adoption." Archives and Special Collections, Augustus C. Long Library, Columbia University. <uoregon.edu/~adoption/archive/CACRFICTA. htm>.

Bhabha, H. 1988. "Cultural Diversity and Cultural Differences." In B. Ashcroft, G. Griffiths and H. Tiffin (eds.), *The Post-Colonial Studies Reader*. New York, NY: Routledge.

_____. 1998. "Cultures in Between." In D. Bennet (ed.), *Multicultural States: Rethinking Difference and Identity*. London, ON: Routledge.

Bishop, R. 1998. "Freeing Ourselves from Neo-Colonial Dominations in Research: A Maori Approach to Creating Knowledge." *Qualitative Studies in Education* 11, 2: 199–219.

Blackstock, C. 2000. "The Occasional Evil of Angels." *First Peoples Child and Family Review* 4, 1: 28–37. <http://www.fncfcs.com/pubs/vol4num1/Blackstock_pp28. pdf>

_____. 2001. "First Nations Child and Family Services: Restoring Peace and Harmony in First Nations Communities." In B. Mckenzie and K. Kufeldt (eds.), *Connecting Research, Policy and Practice*. Waterloo, ON: Wilfred Laurier University Press.

_____. 2006. *Reconciliation in Child Welfare: Touchstones of Hope for Indigenous Children, Youth and Families*. Ottawa, ON: First Nations Child and Family Caring Society of Canada and the National Indian Child Welfare Association.

_____. 2009. "The Occasional Evil of Angels: Learning from the Experiences of Aboriginal Peoples and Social Work." *First Peoples Child and Family Review: A Journal on Innovation and Best Practices in Aboriginal Child Welfare, Administration, Research, Policy and Practice* 4, 1: 28–37.

Blaeser, K. 1996. *Gerald Vizenor: Writing in the Oral Tradition*. Norman, OK: University of Oklahoma Press.

Blaut, J.M. 1993. *The Colonizer's Model of the World: Geographical Diffusionism and Eurocentric History*. New York, NY: Guilford Press.

Blumer, H. 1969. *Symbolic Interactionism: Perspective and Method*. Englewood Cliffs, NJ: Prentice Hall.

Boehmer, E. 1995. *Colonial and Postcolonial Literature: Migrant Metaphors*. New York, NY: Oxford University Press.

Bohm, D. 2003. *The Essential David Bohm*. New York, NY: Routledge.

Booth, R. 2009. "Louis Riel: Patriot or Rebel." <www.ebrandon.ca>.

Bopp, J., M. Bopp, L. Brown and P. Lane Jr. 1985. *The Sacred Tree*. Lethbridge, AB: Four Worlds Development.

Borg, D., K. Brownlee and R. Delaney. 1995. "Postmodern Social Work Practice with Aboriginal People." *Northern Social Work Practice. Northern and Regional Studies* 4: 116–135.

Bourgeault, R. 1983. "The Indian, the Métis and the Fur Trade: Class, Sexism and

Racism in Transition from 'Communism" to Capitalism.'" *Studies in Political Economy* 12: 45–79.

Boyko, J. 1995. *The Last Steps to Freedom: The Evolution of Canadian Racism.* Winnipeg, MB: Watson and Dwyer.

Brass, S.I. 2000. "Put on the Kettle: Study of Theoretical Premises of Muskego and Asini Cree Counseling Methods." Unpublished master's thesis, University of Saskatchewan, Saskatoon, SK.

Brendtro, L., M. Brokenleg, and S.V. Bockern. 1992. "The Circle of Courage." In *Reclaiming Youth at Risk: Our Hope for the Future.* Bloomington, IN: National Educational Service.

Brightman, R.A. 1989. *Acaoohkiwina and Acimowina: traditional narratives of the Rock Cree Indians.* Hull, QC: Canadian Museum of Civilization.

Briskman, L. 2003. "Indigenous Australians: Towards Postcolonial Social Work." In J. Allen, B. Pease and L. Briskman (eds.), *Critical Social Work: An Introduction to Theories and Practices.* Crows Nest, NSW: Allen & Unwin.

Bronte, E. 1996. *Wuthering Heights.* New York, NY: Penguin Classics Editions.

Brown, L., L. Haddock, and M. Kovach. 2001. "Watching Over Our Families: Lalum'utul Smun'eem Child and Family Services." In B. Wharf (ed.), *Community Work Approaches to Child Welfare.* Peterborough, ON: Broadview.

Brown, L., and S. Strega (eds.). 2005. *Research as Resistance: Critical, Indigenous and Anti-oppressive Research Approaches.* Toronto, ON: Canadian Scholars' Press.

Bruner, J. 1987. "Life as Narrative." *Social Research* 54, 1: 11–32.

_____. 1990. *Acts of Meaning.* Cambridge, MA: Harvard University Press.

Bruyere, G. 1998. "Living in Another Man's House: Supporting Aboriginal Learners in Social Work Education." *Canadian Social Work Review* 15, 2: 169–76.

_____. 1999. "The Decolonization Wheel: An Aboriginal Perspective on Social Work Practice with Aboriginal Peoples." In R. Delaney, K. Brownlee and M. Sellick (eds.), *Social Work with Rural and Northern Communities: Northern and Regional Studies Series*, Volume 8. Thunder Bay, ON: Centre for Northern Studies, Lakehead University.

_____. 2003. "The Lessons in our Blood: Reflections on Protecting Aboriginal Children." In D. Champagne and I. Abu-Saad (eds.), *The Future of Indigenous peoples: Strategies for Survival and Development.* Los Angeles, CA: UCLA American Indian Studies Center.

_____. 2007. "Making Circles: Renewing First Nations Ways of Helping." In J. Coates, R. Delaney, K. Brownlee and M. Sellick (eds.), *Spirituality and Social Work Practice: Selected Canadian Readings.* Toronto, ON: Canadian Scholars' Press.

Burgess, H.F. 2000. "Processes of Decolonization." In M. Battiste (ed.), *Reclaiming Indigenous Voice and Vision.* Vancouver, BC: UBC Press.

Burnett, K. 2005. "Aboriginal and White Women in the Publications of John Maclean, Egerton Ryerson Young, and John McDougall." In S. Carter (eds.), *Unsettled Pasts: Reconceiving the West Through Women's History.* Calgary, AB: University of Calgary Press.

Burstow, B. 1992. *Radical Feminist Therapy.* Newbury Park, CA: Sage Publications.

Cajete, G. 1994. *Look to the Mountain: An Ecology of Indigenous Education.* First edition. Durango, CO: Kivaki Press.

_____. 2000. *Native Science: Natural Laws of Interdependence.* San Francisco, CA: Clear

Light Publishers.

Calliou, S. 2001. "Decolonizing the Mind: A Non-empirical Reflection of Some First Nations Scholarship." In K.P. Binds and S. Calliou (eds.), *Aboriginal Education in Canada: A Study in Decolonization*. Mississauga, ON: Canadians Educators' Press.

Campbell, M. 1973. *Halfbreed*. Toronto, ON: McLelland and Stewart.

Canadian Association of Schools of Social Work. 1991. "Social Work Education at the Crossroads: The Challenge of Diversity. Report of the Task Force on Multicultural and Multiracial Issues in Social Work Education." Ottawa, ON: Canadian Association of Schools of Social Work.

Canadian Association of Social Workers. 1994. "The Social Work Profession and the Aboriginal Peoples." *The Social Worker* 62, 4 (Winter): 158.

_____. 2005. *Code of Ethics*. Ottawa, ON: Canadian Association of Social Workers.

Canadian Collaborative Mental Health Initiative. 2006. "Pathways to Healing: A Mental Health Guide for First Nations People." Mississauga, ON: Canadian Collaborative Mental Health Initiative. <ccmhi.ca>.

Cardinal, H. 1969. *The Unjust Society*. Edmonton, AB: M.G. Hurtig.

Carniol, B. 2005. *Case Critical: Social Services and Social Justice in Canada*. Fifth edition. Toronto, ON: Between the Lines.

Carrière, J. 2005. "Connectedness and Health for First Nation Adoptees." Unpublished doctoral dissertation, University of Alberta. Proquest Digital Dissertations, 1014322421, AAT NR08619.

_____. 2007. "Promising Practices for Maintaining Identities in First Nation Adoption." *The First Peoples Child and Family Review* 3, 1: 46–64.

Castellano, M.B., H. Stalwick and F. Wien. 1986. "Native Social Work Education in Canada: Issues and Adaptation." *Canadian Social Work Review* 3: 166–84.

Cavender W.A. 1996. "Grandmother to Granddaughter: Generations of Oral History in a Dakota Family." *American Indian Quarterly* 20, 1: 7–14.

Cheah, C.S.L., and L.J. Nelson. 2004. "The Role of Acculturation in the Emerging Adulthood of Aboriginal College Student." *International Journal of Behavioral Development* 28, 6: 495–507.

Chestang, L. 1972. "The Dilemma of Biracial Adoption." *Social Work* 17: 100–105.

Chrisjohn, R., and S. Young. 1997. *The Circle Game: Shadows and Substance in the Indian Residential School Experience in Canada*. Penticton, BC: Theytus Books.

Chung, Y.M. 2003. "A Grounded Theory Study on Culture And Social Workers: Towards Dialectical Model of Cross-Cultural Social Work." Unpublished doctoral dissertation. University of Toronto.

Churchill, W. 1992. *Fantasies of the Master Race: Literature, Cinema and the Colonization of American Indians*. Monroe, ME: Common Courage Press.

_____. 2003. "I am Indigenist: Notes on the Ideology of the Fourth World." In *Acts of Rebellion: The Ward Churchill Reader*. New York, NY: Routledge.

Clark, M. 1995. "Changes in Euro-American Values Needed for Sustainability." *Journal of Social Issues* 514: 63–82.

Coates, L., N. Todd and A. Wade. 2003. "Violence and Resistance." Paper presented at the Coming to Terms: Summer Intensive on Anti-Violence, Duncan, BC.

Coates, L., and A. Wade. 2004. "Telling It Like It Isn't: Obscuring Perpetrator Responsibility for Violence." *Discourse and Society* 15: 499–526.

Coleman, H., Y. Unrau and B. Manyfingers. 2001. "Revamping Family Preservation Services for Native Families." *Journal of Ethnic and Cultural Diversity in Social Work* 10, 1: 49–68.

Colorado, P. 1988. "Bridging Native and Western Science." *Convergence* XXI, 2/3: 49–67.

Cottell, S. 2004. "My People Will Sleep for One Hundred Years: Story of a Métis Self." Unpublished master's thesis, University of Victoria, Victoria BC.

Coulthard, Glen. 2008. "Beyond Recognition: Indigenous Self-determination as Prefigurative Practice." In L. Simpson (ed.), *Lighting the Eighth Fire: The Liberation, Resurgence, and Protection of Indigenous Nations*. Winnipeg, MB: Arbeiter Ring.

Cournane, J. 2007. "Are Rural American Indian Adolescents Becoming a Race of Angels?" *First Peoples Child and Family Review* 31: 127–32.

Crofoot G.T.L. 2002. "Using Reasons for Living to Connect to American Indian Healing Traditions." *Journal of Sociology and Social Welfare* XXXIX, 1: 55–75.

Crosby, A. 2004. *Ecological Imperialism: The Biological Expansion of Europe, 900–1900.* Cambridge: Cambridge University Press.

Cross, T. 2000. "Drawing on Cultural Tradition in Indian Child Welfare Practice." *Social Casework: The Journal of Contemporary Social Work* 67, 5: 283–89.

Davis, Bill. 2001. *Breaking Autism's Barriers: A Father's Story.* Philadelphia, PA: Jessica Kingsley Publishers.

de Certeau, M. 1984. *The Practice of Everyday Life.* Berkeley, CA: University of California Press.

De La Torre, J. 2004. "In the Trenches: A Critical Look at the Isolation of American Indian Political Practices in the Nonempirical Social Science of Political Science." In D.A. Mihesuah and A.C. Wilson (eds.), *Indigenizing the Academy: Transforming Scholarship and Empowering Communities*. Lincoln, NB: University of Nebraska Press.

Dei, G.J.S. 2000. "Rethinking the Role of Indigenous Knowledges in the Academy." *International Journal of Inclusive Education* 4, 2: 111–32.

Deloria, P.J. 1998. *Playing Indian.* New Haven: Yale University Press.

Denham, A.R. 2008. "Rethinking Historical Trauma: Narratives of Resilience." *Transcultural Psychiatry* 45, 3: 391–414.

Densmore, F. 1979. *Chippewa Customs.* Whitefish, MT: Kessinger Publications.

Department of Justice Canada. 1982. "Constitution Act." Ottawa, ON: Government Publications. <laws.justice.gc.ca/en/const/annex_en.html>.

Donalek, J. 2001. "First Incest Disclosure." *Issues in Mental Health Nursing* 22: 573–91.

Dorais, L.J. 1993. "Language, Culture and Identity: Some Inuit Examples." *The Canadian Journal of Native Studies* 15, 22: 293–308.

Dumbrill, G., and J. Green. 2008. "Indigenous Knowledge in the Social Work Academy." *Social Work Education* 27, 5: 489–503.

Dumont, M. 1996. "The Red and White." In C. Camper (ed.), *Miscegenation Blues: Voices of Mixed Race Women*. Toronto, ON: Sister Vision.

Dunn, Martin. n.d. <www.othermetis.net>.

Duran, B., and E. Duran. 1995. *Native American Postcolonial Psychology.* Albany, NY:

State University of New York Press.

Duran, B., E. Duran and M. Yellow Horse Brave Heart. 1998. "Native Americans and the Trauma of History." In M. Battiste and J. Barman (eds.), *First Nations Education in Canada: The Circle Unfolds.* Vancouver, BC: UBC Press.

Durst, D. 2000. "It's Not What, But How? Social Service Issues Affecting Aboriginal Peoples: A Review of Projects." Regina, SK: University of Regina, Social Policy Research Unit, Faculty of Social Work and Human Resources Development Canada.

Durst, D., J. Mcdonald and C. Rich. 1995. "Aboriginal Governance of Child Welfare Services: Hobson's Choice?" In J. Hudson and B. Galaway (eds.), *Child Welfare in Canada: Research and Policy Implications.* Toronto, ON: Thompson Educational Publishers.

Dybicz, P. 2004. "An Inquiry into Practice Wisdom." *Families in Society: The Journal of Contemporary Social Services* 852: 197–203.

Eco, U. 1983. *The Name of the Rose.* New York, NY: Harcourt.

Edelson, S.M. 2006. "Why is Autism on the Rise?" In K. Simmons (ed.), *The Official Autism 101 Manual: Everything You Need to Know About Autism From Experts Who Know and Care.* Autism Today.

Elliott, J., and A. Fleras. 1992. *Unequal Relations: An Introduction to Race and Ethnic Dynamics in Canada.* Scarborough, ON: Prentice-Hall.

Ellison, E., and F. Ellison. 1996. "Culturally Informed Social Work Practice with American Indian Clients: Guidelines for Non-Indian Social Workers." *Social Work* 41, 2: 147–51.

Ermine, W. 1995. "Aboriginal epistemology." In M. Battiste and J. Barman (eds.), *First Nations Education in Canada: The Circle Unfolds.* Vancouver: UBC Press.

Ermine, W., R. Sinclair and B. Jeffery. 2004. "The Ethics of Research with Indigenous Peoples." Saskatoon, SK: Indigenous Peoples' Health Research Centre. <iphrc.ca>.

Fanon, F. 1963. *The Wretched of the Earth.* New York, NY: Grove Press.

_____. 1995. "National Culture." In B. Ashcroft, G. Griffiths and H. Tiffin (eds.), *The Post-colonial Studies Reader.* New York, NY: Routledge.

Fanshel, D. 1972. *Far from the Reservation: Transracial Adoption of American Indian Children.* Metuchen, NJ: Scarecrow Press.

Farquharson, A. 1999. "Commentary on Chapter 19: Finding the Mix: Lay and Professional Helping." In R. Delaney, K. Brownlee and M. Sellick (eds.), *Social Work with Rural and Northern Communities.* Thunder Bay, ON: Lakehead University.

Feigelman, W., and A. Silverman. 1984. "The Long-Term Effects of Transracial Adoption." *Social Service Review* 48: 588–602.

Fiddler, S. 2000. "Strategic Human Resources Analysis of the Aboriginal Social Work Sector." In M. Stephenson, G. Rondeau, J. Michaud and S Fiddler, *Critical Demand: Social Work in Canada: Findings of the Sector Study.* Ottawa, ON: CASSW.

Fogg-Davis, H. 2002. *The Ethics of Transracial Adoption.* Ithaca, NY: Cornell University Press.

Foley, D. 2003. "Indigenous Epistemology and Indigenous Standpoint Theory." *Social Alternatives* 22, 1: 44–52.

Fook, J. 2002. *Social Work: Critical Theory and Practice.* London: Sage Publications.

Fook, J., and F. Gardner. 2007. *Practising Critical Reflection: A Resource Handbook.* Berkshire, UK: Open University Press.

Ford, T.L., and C.B. Dillard. 1996. "Becoming Multicultural: A Recursive Process of Self — and Social Construction." *Theory Into Practice* (Autumn) 232–38.

Four Worlds Development Project. 1984. *The Sacred Tree.* Lethbridge, AB: Four Worlds Press.

Fournier, S., and E. Crey. 1997. *Stolen from our Embrace: The Abduction of First Nations Children and the Restoration of Aboriginal Communities.* Vancouver, BC: Douglas and McIntyre.

Freire, P. 1993. *Pedagogy of the Oppressed.* Revised edition. New York, NY: Continuum.

_____. 1995. *Pedagogy of the Oppressed.* New York, NY: Continuum.

_____. 1996. *Pedagogy of the Oppressed.* Twentieth anniversary edition. New York, NY: Continuum.

Frideres, J. 1976. "Racism in Canada: Alive and Well." *The Western Canadian Journal of Anthropology* 14: 124–45.

_____. 1988. "Native People." In B. Singh Bolaria and P. Li. (eds.), *Racial Oppression in Canada.* Toronto, ON: Garamond Press.

Frideres, J.S., and R.R. Gadacz. 2001. *Aboriginal People in Canada: Contemporary Conflicts.* Sixth edition. Toronto, ON: Prentice Hall.

Friesen, John W. 1991. "Native Cultures in a Culture Clash." In J.W. Friesen (ed.), *The Cultural Maze: Complex Questions on Native Destiny in Western Canada.* Calgary, AB: Detselig Enterprises.

Gair, S., J. Thomson, D. Miles and N. Harris. 2002. "It's Very 'White' Isn't It! Challenging Mono-Culturalism in Social Work and Welfare Education." Unpublished manuscript, James Cook University, Townsville, Australia.

Gandhi, L. 1998. *Postcolonial Theory: A Critical Introduction.* New York, NY: Columbia University Press.

Garroutte, E.M. 2003. *Real Indians: Identity and the Survival of Native America.* Berkeley, CA: University of California Press.

Gilchrist, L. 1995. "Aboriginal Street Youth in Vancouver, Winnipeg and Montreal." Doctoral dissertation, University of British Columbia, Proquest Digital Dissertations 742854381. AAT NN05963.

Giroux, H.A. 2005. *Border Crossings: Cultural Workers and the Politics of Education.* Second edition. New York, NY: Routledge.

Goffman, E. 1963. *Stigma: Notes on the Management of Spoiled Identity.* Englewood Cliffs, NJ: Prentice Hall.

Goulet, J.P. 1998. *Ways of Knowing: Experience, Knowledge, and Power Among the Dene Tha.* Lincoln, NB: University of Nebraska Press.

Goyette, L. 2003. "The "X" Files: By Signing Applications for Land Grants, Were the Prairie Métis Drawn into One of the Largest Property Swindles in Canadian History?" *Canadian Geographic* (March/April).

Grande, S. 2004. *Red Pedagogy: Native American Social and Political Thought.* New York, NY: Rowman and Littlefield.

Graveline, F.J. 1998. *Circle Works: Transforming Eurocentric Consciousness.* Halifax, NS: Fernwood Publishing.

_____. 2000. "Circle as a Methodology: Enacting an Aboriginal Paradigm." *Qualitative*

References

Studies in Education 134: 361–70.

_____. 2004. *Healing Wounded Hearts*. Halifax, NS: Fernwood Publishing.

Gray, M., and J. Coates. 2008. "Conclusion." In M. Gray, J. Coates and M. Yellow Bird (eds.), *Indigenous Social Work Around the World: Towards Culturally Relevant Education and Practice*. Burlington, VT: Ashgate Publishing.

Gray, M., and J. Fook. 2004. "The Quest for a Universal Social Work: Social Work Issues and Implications." *Social Work Education* 23, 5 (October): 625–44.

Gross, L.W. 2002. "Bimaadiziwin, or the 'Good Life,' as a Unifying Concept of Anishinabe Religion." *American Indian Culture and Research Journal* 211: 15–32.

_____. 2003. "Cultural Sovereignty and Native American Hermeneutics in the Interpretation of the Sacred Stories of the Anishinaabe." *Wicazo Sa Review* 18, 3: 127–34.

Grow, L., and D. Shapiro. 1974. *Black Children White Parents: A Study of Transracial Adoption*. Research Centre, Child Welfare League of America, Inc.

Guzmán, T.L.D. 2005. "'Diacuí Killed Iracema': Indigenism, Antionalism and the Struggle for Brazilianness." *Bulletin of Latin American Research* 24, 1: 92–122.

Hains, S. 2001. "An Emerging Voice: A Study Using Traditional Aboriginal Research Methods to Better Understand Why Native Students Drop Out of School." Unpublished doctoral dissertation, Saybrook Graduate School and Research Centre, San Francisco, CA.

Hamilton, A.C., and C.M. Sinclair. 1991. "Child Welfare: Chapter 14." *Report of the Aboriginal Justice Inquiry of Manitoba*. Winnipeg, MB.

Hamilton, L.M. 2000. *Facing Autism: Giving Parents Reason for Hope and Guidance for Help*. Colorado Springs, CO: Waterbrook Press.

Harris, L.D., and J. Wasilewski. 2004. "Indigeneity, an Alternative Worldview: Four R's Relationship, Responsibility, Reciprocity, Redistribution vs. Two P's Power and Profit. Sharing the Journey Towards Conscious Evolution." *Systems Research and Behavioral Science* 21: 489–503.

Harris, W. 1973. *Tradition, the Writer and Society*. London, ON: New Beacon.

Hart, M.A. 1997. "An Ethnographic Study of Sharing Circles as a Culturally Appropriate Practice Approach with Aboriginal People." Unpublished master's of social work, University of Manitoba, Winnipeg, MB.

_____. 1999. "Seeking Minopimatasiwin: An Aboriginal Approach to Social Work Practice." *Native Social Work Journal* 21: 91–112.

_____. 2001. "An Aboriginal Approach to Social Work Practice." In T. Heinonen and L. Spearman (eds.), *Social Work Practice: Problem Solving and Beyond*. Toronto, ON: Irwin Publishing.

_____. 2002. *Seeking Mino-pimatisiwin: An Aboriginal Approach to Helping*. Halifax, NS: Fernwood Publishing.

_____. 2003. "Am I a Modern Day Missionary? Reflections of a Cree Social Worker." *Native Social Work Journal/Nishnaabe Kinoomaadwin Naadmaadwin* 5: 299–309.

_____. 2006. "An Aboriginal Approach to Social Work Practice." In T. Heinonen and L. Spearman (eds.), *Social Work Practice: Problem Solving and Beyond*. Second edition. Toronto, ON: Irwin Press.

_____. 2007. "Cree Ways of Helping: An Indigenist Research Project." Unpublished doctoral thesis, University of Manitoba, Winnipeg, MB.

_____. 2008. "Critical Reflections on an Aboriginal Approach to Helping." In M.

Gray, J. Coates and M. Yellow Bird (eds.). *Indigenous Social Work around the World*. Burlington, VT: Ashgate Publishing.

Hart, M.A., and Y. Pompana. 2003. "Establishing the Aboriginal Social Work Associations: Sharing the Manitoba Experience." *Native Social Work Journal* 5: 243–60.

Harvey, G., and C.D. Thompson Jr. 2005. "Introduction." In G. Harvey and C.D. Thompson Jr. (eds.), *Indigenous Diasporas and Dislocations*. Aldershot, UK: Ashgate Publishing.

Heiltsuk Tribal Council. 1994. "The Native Brotherhood of British Columbia, The Cooperative University-Provincial Psychiatric Liaison." Department of Psychiatry, University of BC. Heitlsuk Wellness: Shared Vision (March).

Henderson, J.Y. 2000a. "Ayukpachi: Empowering Aborigional Thought." In M. Battiste (ed.), *Reclaiming Indigenous Voice and Vision*. Vancouver, BC: UBC Press.

_____. 2000b. "Challenges of Respecting Indigenous World Views in Eurocentric Education." In R. Neil (ed.), *Voice of the Drum: Indigenous Education and Culture*. Brandon, MB: Kingfisher Publications.

_____. 2000c. "Postcolonial Ghost Dancing: Diagnosing European Colonialism." In M. Battiste (ed.), *Reclaiming Indigenous Voice and Vision*. Vancouver, BC: UBC Press

Henry, F., and C. Tator. 1995. *The Colour of Democracy*. Toronto, ON: Harcourt Brace and Company.

Hermes, M. 1998. "Research Method as a Situated Response: Towards a First Nations' Methodology." *Qualitative Studies in Education* 11, 1: 155–68.

Heshusius, L. 1994. "Freeing Ourselves from Objectivity: Managing Subjectivity or Turning toward a Participatory Mode of Consciousness?" *Educational Researcher* 233 (April): 15–22.

Hick, S. 2002. *Social Work in Canada: An Introduction*. Toronto ON: Thompson Educational Publishing.

_____. 2006. *Social Work in Canada: An Introduction*. Second edition. Toronto, ON: Thompson Educational Publishing Inc.

Higman, C.L. 2000. *Noble, Wretched, and Redeemable: Protestant Missionaries to Indians in Canada and the United States, 1820–1900*. Calgary, AB: University of Calgary Press.

Hollingsworth, L.D. 1999. "Symbolic Interactionism, African American families and the Transracial Adoption Controversy." *Social Work* 445: 443–54.

Holmes, L. 2000. "Heart Knowledge, Blood Memory, and the Voice of the Land: Implications for Research Among Haqaiian Elders." In G.J.S. Dei, B.L. Hall and D.S. Rosenberg (eds.), *Indigenous Knowledges in Global Contexts: Multiple Readings of Our World*. Toronto, ON: University of Toronto Press.

Holtan, B., and B. Tremitiere. 1996. "Looking Back: How Have They Fared: An Outcome Study of Three Populations of Adoptees." Report to the NACAC Conference, August 1996. New York: Tressler Lutheran Services.

hooks, b. 1990. *Yearning: Race, Gender, and Cultural Politics*. Boston, MA: South End Press.

_____. 1992. *Black Looks: Race and Representation*. Toronto, ON: Between The Lines.

_____. 1993. *Sisters of the Yam: Black Women and Self-recovery*. Toronto, ON: Between The Lines.

_____. 1994. *Outlaw Culture: Resisting Representations.* New York, NY: Routledge.

Howard, G. 1991. "A Narrative Approach to Thinking, Cross-Cultural Psychology and Psychotherapy." *American Psychologist* 46, 3: 187–97.

Howse, Y., and H. Stalwick. 1990a. "Social Work and the First Nations Movement: Our Children, Our Culture." In B. Wharf (ed.), *Social Work and Social Change in Canada.* Toronto, ON: McClelland and Stewart.

_____. 1990b. "The First Nation movement." In B. Wharf (ed.), *Social Work and social Change in Canada.* Toronto, ON: McClelland and Stewart.

Hughes, D., and E. Kallen. 1974. *The Anatomy of Racism: Canadian dimensions.* Montreal, QC: Harvest House.

Hughes, Langston. 1959. "Dreams." From *Selected Poems of Langston Hughes.* New York, NY: Vintage Books.

Hughes, Lotte. 2003. *The No-Nonsense Guide to Indigenous Peoples.* Toronto, ON: New Internationalist Publications.

Hull, G. 1982. "Child Welfare Services to Native Americans." *Social Casework: The Journal of Contemporary Social Work* (June): 340–47

Hurdle, D. 2002. "Native Hawaiian Traditional Healing: Culturally Based Interventions for Social Work Practice." *Social Work* 47, 2: 183–92.

Indian Act. R.S.C., 1875, c.1-5.

International Federation of Social Workers. 2004. "International Policy Statement on Indigenous People." Unpublished document. Bern, Switzerland.

Jalbun Lodge. <miditrax.com/redroad.htm>.

Jamies Guerrero, M.A. 2003. "'Patriarchal Colonialism' and Indigenism: Implications for Native Feminist Spirituality and Native Womanism." *Hypatia* 18, 2: 58–69.

Johnston, B. 1990. *Ojibway Heritage.* Toronto, ON: McClelland and Stewart.

Johnson, Patrick. 1983. *Native Children and the Child Welfare System.* Toronto, ON: James Lorimer in association with the Canadian Council on Social Development.

Judgment. 2004. SKQB 503, Dec. 10, 2004, <http://www.lawsociety.sk.ca/judgments/2004/QB2004/2004skqb503.pdf>.

Kakakaway and Associates. <kakakaway.com>.

Kelly, L. 1988. *Surviving Sexual Violence.* Minneapolis, MN: University of Minnesota Press.

Kim, D. 1978. "Issues in Transracial and Transcultural Adoption." *Social Casework* 598 (October): 477–86.

Kimmelman, Justice E.C. 1985. "No Quiet Place: Review Committee on Indian and Métis Adoption and Placements." Manitoba Community Services.

King, C. 1997. "Here Come the Anthros." In I. Biolsi and L.J. Zimmerman (eds.), *Indians and Anthropologists: Vine Deloria Jr. and the Critique of Anthropology.* Phoenix, AZ: University of Arizona Press.

King, T. 2003. *The Truth About Stories: A Native Narrative.* Toronto, ON: House of Anansi.

Kirmayer, L.J., G.M. Brass and C.L. Tait. 2000. "The Mental Health of Aboriginal Peoples: Transformations of Identity and Community." *Psychiatry* 45, 7: 607–16.

Kline, M. 1992. "Child Welfare Law, 'Best Interests of Child' Ideology, and First Nations." *Osgoode Hall Law Journal* 30, 2: 375–425.

Koegel, L., and C. Lazebnik. 2004 *Overcoming Autism: Finding the Answers, Strategies, and*

Hopes that Can Transform a Child's Life. New York, NY: Penguin Group.

Kondrat, M.E. 1999. "Who is the "Self" in Self-Aware: Professional Self-Awareness from a Critical Theory Perspective." *Social Service Review* 734: 451–77.

_____. 2002. "Actor-centered Social Work: Re-visioning "Person-in-environment" Through a Critical Theory Lens." *Social Work* 474 (October): 435–48.

Kovach, M.E. 2005. "Emerging from the Margins: Indigenous Methodologies." In L.A. Brown and S. Strega (eds.), *Research as Resistance: Critical, Indigenous and Anti-Oppressive Approaches*. Toronto, ON: Canadian Scholars' Press.

_____. 2006. "Searching for Arrowheads: An Inquiry into Approaches to Indigenous Research using a Tribal Methodology with a Nêhiýaw Kiskêýihtamowin Worldview." Uunpublished doctoral dissertation, University of Victoria, Victoria, BC.

Kranowitz, C. 1998. *The Out-Of-Sync Child*. New York, NY: Berkley Publishing.

Krech, Paul. R. 2002. "Envisioning a Healthy Future: A Re-Becoming of Native American Men." *Journal of Sociology and Social Welfare* 29, 1: 77–91.

Kreitzer, L. 2006. "Social Work Values and Ethics Issues of Universality." *Currents: New Scholarship in the Human Services* 5, 1.

Kroetch, R. 1995. "Unhiding the Hidden." In B. Ashcroft, G. Griffiths and H. Tiffin (eds.), *The Post Colonial Studies Reader*. New York, NY: Routledge.

Kulusic, T. 2005. "The Ultimate Betrayal: Claiming and Re-Claiming Cultural Identity." *Atlantis* 29, 2: 1–8.

Kuokkanen, R. 2007. *Reshaping the University: Responsibility, Indigenous Epistemes, and the Logic of the Gift*. Vancouver, BC: UBC Press.

Ladner, J. 1977. *Mixed Families: Adopting Across Racial Boundaries*. London: Doubleday.

LaPrairie, C. 1987. "Native Women and Crime: A Theoretical Model." *The Canadian Journal of Native Studies* 7, 1: 121–37.

LaRocque, E. 1991. "Racism Runs Through Canadian Society." In O. McKague (ed.), *Racism in Canada*. Saskatoon, SK: Fifth Street Publishers.

Lee, K.J., and Associates. 1992. *Liberating Our Children, Liberating Our Nations*. Report of Aboriginal Committee — Community Panel, Family and Children's Service, Legislation Review in British Columbia. Victoria, BC.

Lee, Y. 2001. "A Study of the Transformative Learning Process Among Prominent Taiwan Puyuma Aborigines." *Australian Journal of Adult Learning* 41, 2 (July): 186–207.

Levitt, K., and B. Wharf (eds.). 1985. *The Challenge of Child Welfare*. Vancouver, BC: UBC Press.

Lindholm, B., and J. Tavliatos. 1980. "Psychological Adjustment of Adopted and Non-Adopted Children." *Psychological Reports* 46: 307–10.

Little Bear, L. 2000. "Jagged Worldviews Colliding." In M. Battiste (ed.), *Reclaiming Indigenous Voice and Vision*. Vancouver, BC: UBC Press.

Locust, C. 2000. "Split Feathers: Adult American Indians Who Were Placed in Non-Indian Families as Children." Ontario Association of Children's Aid Societies. <oacas.org/resources/oacasjournals/2000October/Feathers.pdf>.

Long Claws, L. 1994. "Social Work and the Medicine Wheel Framework." In Beulah Compton and Burt Galaway (eds.), *Social Work Processes*. Fifth edition. Pacific Grove, CA: Brooks/Cole Publishing.

References

Loomba, A. 1998. *Colonialism/postcolonialism.* New York, NY: Routledge.

Losey, M.B. 2007 *Children of Now — Crystalline Children, Indigo Children, Star Kids, Angels on Earth, and the Phenomenon of Transitional Children.* Franklin Lakes, NJ: Career Press.

Lynn, R. 2001. "Learning from a 'Murri Way'." *British Journal of Social Work* 31: 903–16.

MacDonald, K. 2000. "First Nation Summit Action Committee for First Nations Children and Families Discussion Paper." Vancouver, BC: First Nations Summit.

_____. 2002. *Missing Voices: Aboriginal Mothers Who Have Been at Risk of or Who Had Their Children Removed From Their Care Phase 2 Report.* Vancouver, BC: NAC-BC Region and Legal Service Society — Native Programs Dept.

MacDonald, N., J. Gloade and F. Wien. 2005. "Respecting Aboriginal Families." In M. Ungar (ed.), *Handbook for Working with Children and Youth: Pathways to Resilience across Cultures and Contexts.* Thousand Oaks, CA: Sage Publications.

MacDonald, N., and J. MacDonald. 2007. "Reflections of a Mi'kmaq Social Worker on a Quarter of a Century Work in First Nations Child Welfare." *First Peoples Child and Family Review* 3, 1: 34–45.

Mackie, R. 1997. *Trading Beyond the Mountains.* Vancouver, BC: UBC Press.

Mafile'o, T. 2004. "Exploring Tongan Social Work." *Qualitative Social Work* 33: 239–57.

Mandelbaum, D.G. 1979. *The Plains Cree: An Ethnographic, Historical, and Comparative Study.* Canadian Plains Studies 9. Regina, SK: University of Regina.

Manual, G., and M. Posluns. 1974. *The Fourth World: An Indian Reality.* New York, NY: Free Press.

Mastronardi, L. 1990. "The Inuit Community Workers' Experience of Youth Protection Work." In L. Davies and E. Shragge (eds.), *Bureaucracy and Community: Essays on the Politics of Social Work Practice.* Black Rose Books.

Mawhiney, A.M. 1995. "The First Nations in Canada." In J.J. Turner and F.J. Turner (eds.), *Canadian Social Welfare.* Third edition. Scarborough, ON: Allyn and Bacon.

McCormick, R. 1995. "The Facilitation of Healing for the First Nations People of British Columbia." *Canadian Journal of Native Education* 21: 251–322.

_____. 2005. "The Healing Path: What can Counselors Learn from Aboriginal People about How to Heal?" In R. Moodley and W. West (eds.), *Integrating Traditional Healing Practices into Counseling and Psychotherapy.* Thousand Oaks, CA: Sage Publications.

McDonald, R.J., P. Ladd, et al. 2000. *First Nations Child and Family Services Joint National Policy Review.* Final report prepared for the Assembly of First Nations with First Nations Child and Family Service Agency Representatives in partnership with the Department of Indian Affairs and Northern Development. Ottawa: Assembly of First Nations and Department of Indian Affairs and Northern Development (June).

McGaa, E.E.M. 1995. *Native Wisdom: Perceptions of the Natural Way.* Minneapolis, MN: Four Directions Publishing.

McGregor, D. 2004. "Coming Full Circle: Indigenous Knowledge, Environment, and Our Future." *American Indian Quarterly* 28, 3/4: 385–410.

McKenzie, B., and P. Hudson. 1985. "Native Children, Child Welfare, and the Colonization of Native People." In K. Levitt and B. Wharf (eds.), *Challenge of Child Welfare*. Vancouver, BC: UBC Press.

McKenzie, B., and V. Morrisette. 2003. "Social Work Practice with Canadians of Aboriginal Background: Guidelines for Respectful Social Work." In A. Al-Krenawi and J.R. Graham (eds.), *Multicultural Social Work in Canada: Working with Diverse Ethno-Racial Communities*. Don Mills, ON: Oxford University Press.

McKenzie, B., E. Seidl and N. Bone. 1995. "Child and Family Service Standards in First Nations: An Action Research Project." *Child Welfare* LXXIV, 3: 633–53.

McLeod, J. 2000. *Beginning Postcolonialism*. New York, NY: Palgrave.

McRoy, R., L.A. Zurcher, M. Lauderdale and R. Anderson. 1982. "Self-Esteem and Racial Identity in Transracial and Inracial Adoptees." *Social Work* 27, 6: 522-26.

McRoy, R., L.A. Zurcher, M. Lauderdale and R. Anderson. 1984. "The Identity of Transracial Adoptees." *Social Casework: The Journal of Contemporary Social Work* 65: 34–39.

Mead, G. 1934. *Mind, Self and Society*. Chicago, IL: University of Chicago Press.

_____. 1977. *On Social Psychology: Selected Papers*. Chicago, IL: University of Chicago Press.

Meadows, K. 1990. *The Medicine Way: A Shamanic Path to Self Mastery*. Rockport, MA: Element Books.

Melichercik, J. 1987. "Child Welfare Policy." In S. Yelaja (ed.), *Canadian Social Policy*. Waterloo, ON: Wilfred Laurier University Press.

Memmi, A. 1965. *The Colonizer and the Colonized*. Boston, MA: Beacon Press.

_____. 1991. *The Colonizer and the Colonized*. Boston, MA: Beacon Press.

Menard, A. 2001. "The Halfbreed Blues." *Prairie Fire* 2, 3: 32–33.

Midgley, J. 1981. *Professional Imperialism: Social Work in the Third World*. London, ON: Heinemann.

Mihesuah, D.A. 1996. *American Indians: Stereotypes and Realities*. Atlanta, GA: Clarity Press.

_____. 1998. *Natives and Academics: Researching and Writing about American Indians*. Lincoln, NB: University of Nebraska Press.

_____. 2003. *Indigenous American Women: Decolonization, Empowerment, Activism*. Lincoln, NB: University of Nebraska Press.

Mihesuah, D.A., and A.C. Wilson (eds.). 2004. *Indigenizing the Academy: Transforming Scholarship and Transforming Communities*. Lincoln, NB: University of Nebraska Press.

Miller, J.R. 1996. *Shingwauk's Vision: A History of Native Residential Schools*. Toronto, ON: University of Toronto Press.

Milloy, J. 1999. *A National Crime: The Canadian Government and the Residential School System, 1879 to 1986*. Winnipeg, MB: University of Manitoba Press.

Monture-Angus. P.A. 1995. *Thunder in My Soul: A Mohawk Woman Speaks*. Halifax, NS: Fernwood Publishing.

_____. 1999. *Journeying Forward: Dreaming First Nations Independence*. Halifax, NS: Fernwood Publishing.

Moore, K., V.F. Cordova, K. Peters, T. Jojola, A. Lacy and L. Hogan (eds.). 2007. *How it Is: The Native American Philosophy of V. F. Cordova*. Tucson, AZ: University of Arizona Press.

Morgan, D.L. 2003. "Appropriation, Appreciation, Accommodation: Indigenous Wisdoms and Knowledges in Higher Education." *International Review of Education* 49, 1–2: 35–49.

Morrisseau, C. 1998. *Into the Daylight: A Wholestic Approach to Healing*. Toronto, ON: University of Toronto Press.

Morrissette, V., B. McKenzie and L. Morrissette. 1993. "Towards an Aboriginal Model of Social Work Practice: Cultural Knowledge and Traditional Practices." *Canadian Social Work Review* 101 (Winter): 91–108.

Mullaly, B. 2002. *Challenging Oppression: A Critical Social Work Approach*. Don Mills, ON: Oxford University Press.

Mussell, W.J. 2006. *Warrior-Caregivers: Understanding the Challenges and Healing of First Nations Men*. Ottawa, ON: Aboriginal Healing Foundation.

Nabigon, H. 2006. *The Hollow Tree: Fighting Addiction with Traditional Native Healing*. Montreal and Kingston: McGill-Queen's University Press.

Nabigon, H., R. Hagey, S. Webster and R. Mackay. 1999. "The Learning Circle as a Research Method: The Trickster and Windigo in Research." *Native Social Work Journal* 21: 113–37.

Napoli, M., and E. Gonzalez-Santin. 2001. "Intensive Home-Based and Wellness Services to Native American Families Living on Reservations: A Model." *Families in Society* 82, 3: 315–26.

National Archives of Canada. "Policy Matters regarding Care of Children in Private or Foster Homes: 1958–1960." Record Group 10, Volume 6937. National Archives of Canada.

National Indian Brotherhood. 1972. "Indian Control of Indian Education: Policy paper presented to the Minister of Indian Affairs and Northern Development by the National Indian Brotherhood." Ottawa.

National Institute of Mental Health. 2004, "Autism Spectrum Disorders." NIH Publication No. 04-5511. <bridges4kids.org/articles/1-05/NIH4-04.htm>.

Neu, D., and R. Therrian. 2003. *Accounting for Genocide. Canada's Bureaucratic Assault on Aboriginal Peoples*. Black Point, NS: Fernwood/Zed Books.

Niezen, R. 2003. *The Origins of Indigenism: Human Rights and the Politics of Identity*. Berkeley, CA: University of California Press.

Nimmagadda, J., and C.D. Cowger. 1999. "Cross-cultural Practice: Social Worker Ingenuity in the Indigenization of Practice Knowledge." *International Social Work* 42, 3: 261–76.

Noël, L. 1994. *Intolerance: A General Survey*. A. Bennett (trans.). Kingston, ON: McGill-Queen's University Press.

Nuttgens, S. 2004. "Life Stories of Aboriginal Adults Raised in NonAboriginal Families." Doctoral dissertation, University of Alberta. ProQuest Digital Dissertations 813777181. AAT NQ96311.

O'Brien Caughy, M., P.J. O'Campo and C. Muntaner. 2004. "Experiences of Racism among African American Parents and the Mental Health of their Pre-School Children." *American Journal of Public Health* 94, 121 (December): 2118–24.

Oetting, E.R., and F. Beauvais. 1991. "Orthogonal Cultural Identification Theory: The Cultural Identification of Minority Adolescents," *The International Journal of the Addictions* 25, 5A–6A: 655–85.

O'Gorman, K., and R. Delaney. 1996. "Natural Helpers in the Northern Context: Women who Made a Difference in Northwestern Ontario." In R. Delaney, K. Brownlee and M.K. Zapf (eds.), *Issues in Northern Social Work Practice*. Thunder Bay, ON: Lakehead University.

O'Keefe, B., and I. MacDonald. 2001. *Merchant Prince: Alexandra Duncan Macrae*. Victoria, BC: Heritage House.

O'Shaughnessy, T. 1994. *Adoption, Social Work and Social Theory: Making the Connections*. Brookfield, VT: Avebury Publishing.

Ohio Developmental Disabilities Council. 2007. "Autism: Reaching for a Brighter Future — Service Guidelines for Individuals with Autism Spectrum Disorder/ Pervasive Development Disorder." <ddc.ohio.gov/pub/ASDGuide.htm>.

Okimaw Ohci Healing Lodge. <csc.scc.gc.ca/text/prgrm/fsw/fsw30/fsw30eol_e. shtml>.

Osmond, J. 2006. "A Quest for Form: The Tacit Dimension of Social Work Practice." *European Journal of Social Work* 92 (June): 159–81.

Otway, Linda. "Otway Consulting." <uregina.ca>.

Palmer, S., and W. Cooke. 1996. "Understanding and Countering Racism with First Nations Children in Out-of-Home Care." *Child Welfare* 756 (November/ December): 709–25.

Pe Sakastew Centre. <psepc-sppcc.gc.ca/publications/Corrections/ccra/aborigi- nal_offender_e.asp>.

Philp, M. 2002. "The Land of Lost Children." *Globe and Mail* December 21.

Pinderhughes, E. 1989. *Understanding Race, Ethnicity, and Power: The Key to Efficacy in Clinical Practice*. Toronto, ON: Maxwell Macmillan.

Poe, Edgar Allen. 1984. "Eleonora." In P.F. Quinn (ed.), *Poetry and Tales by Edgar Allen Poe*. New York, NY: Library of America.

Polkinghorne, D. 1988. *Narrative Knowing and the Human Sciences*. Albany, NY: State University of New York Press.

Poole, R. 1972. *Towards Deep Subjectivity*. New York, NY: Harper and Row.

Poonwassie, A., and A. Charter. 2005. "Aboriginal Worldview of Healing: Inclusion, Blending, and Bridging." In R. Moodley and W. West (eds.), *Integrating Traditional Healing Practices into Counselling and Psychotherapy*. Thousand Oaks, CA: Sage Publications.

Pratt, M.L. 2004. The Anti-Colonial Past. *Modern Language Quarterly* 65, 3: 443–56.

Puff, R. 1993. "In the Best Interests of the Child?" Unpublished paper. SW 468: History of Social Services (December). Saskatoon.

Ragab, I. 1990. "How Social Work can Take Root in Developing Countries." *Social Development Issues* 123: 38–51.

Rains, F.V. 1999. "Indigenous Knowledge, Historical Amnesia and Intellectual Authority: Deconstructing Hegemony and the Social and Political Implications of the Curricular 'Other.'" In L.M. Semali and J.L. Kincheloe (eds.), *What Is Indigenous Knowledge: Voices from the Academy*. New York, NY: Falmer Press.

RCAP (Royal Commission on Aboriginal Peoples). 1996. <ainc-inac.gc.ca/ch/rcap/ sg/ci2_e.pdf>.

Red Horse, J., R. Lewis, M. Feit and J. Decker. 1978. "Family Behavior of Urban American Indians." *Social Casework* 67–72.

Red Horse, J., C. Martinez, P. Day, D. Day, J. Poupart, and D. Scharnberg. 2000.

Family Preservation: Concepts in American Indian Communities. Portland, OR: National Indian Child Welfare Association.

Reid, M. 2005. "First Nation Women: Workers Speak, Write, and Research Back." *First Peoples Child and Family Review* 2, 1: 21–40.

Reissman, C. 1993. "Women in South India." *Gender and Society* 14, 1: 111–35.

Resnick, R. 1984. "Latin American Children in Intercountry Adoption." In P. Bean (ed.), *Adoption: Essays in Social Policy, Law, and Sociology.* New York: Tavistock Publications.

Rheault, D. 1999. *Anishinaabe Mino-bimaadiziwin: The Way of a Good Life.* Peterborough, ON: Debwewin Press.

Rice, B. 2005. *Seeing the World with Aboriginal Eyes: A Four Dimensional Perspective on Human and Non-human Values, Cultures, and Relationships on Turtle Island.* Winnipeg, MB: Aboriginal Issues Press.

Richardson, C. 2005. "Cultural Stories and Métis Self-Creation." *Relational Child and Youth Care* 18, 1: 55–63.

Richardson, C., and B. Nelson. 2001. "Embodying the Oppressor and Oppressed: My Perspective as a Métis woman." *The International Journal of Narrative Therapy and Community Work* 1: 84–85.

_____. 2004. "Becoming Métis: The Relationship Between the Sense of Métis Self and Cultural Stories." Unpublished doctoral dissertation, University of Victoria, Victoria, BC.

_____. 2007. "A Change of Residence: Government Schools and Foster Homes as Sites of Forced Aboriginal Assimilation: A Paper to Provoke Thought and Systemic Change." *First Peoples Child and Family Review* 3, 2: 75–83.

Robbins, S., P. Chatterjee and E. Canda. 1998. *Contemporary Human Behaviour Theory: A Critical Perspective for Social Work.* London, ON: Allyn and Bacon.

Roberts, R. 1990. *Lessons from the Past: Issues for Social Work Theory.* New York, NY: Tavistock/Routledge.

Roberts, T.L., and L. Anderson Smith. 2002. "The Illusion of Inclusion: An Analysis of Approaches to Diversity Within Predominantly White Schools of Social Work." *Journal of Teaching in Social Work* 223, 4: 189–210.

Robertson, P., M. Jorgensen and C. Garrow. 2004. "Indigenizing Evaluation Research: How Lakota Methodologies are Helping 'Raise the Tipi' in the Oglala Sioux Nation." *American Indian Quarterly* 28, 4/5: 499–526.

Rosaldo, R. 1989. *Culture and Truth: The Remaking of Social Analysis.* Boston, MA: Beacon Press.

Rue, M., and L. Rue. 1984. "Reflections on Bicultural Adoption." In P. Bean (ed.), *Adoption: Essays in Social Policy, Law, and Sociology.* New York, NY: Tavistock Publications.

Rutherdale, M. 2002. *Women and the White Man's God: Gender and Race in the Canadian Mission Field.* Vancouver, BC: UBC Press.

Ryant, J. 1984. "Some Issues in the Adoption of Native Children." In P. Sachdev (ed.), *Adoption: Current Issues and Trends.* Toronto, ON: Butterworths.

Sacks, O. 1995. "Foreword." In Temple Grandin, *Thinking in Pictures and other Reports From My Life With Autism.* New York, NY: Vintage Books.

Said, E. 1993. *Culture and Imperialism.* New York, NY: Alfred A. Knopf.

Sakamoto, I., and R.O. Pitner. 2005. "Use of Critical Consciousness in Anti-oppressive Social Work Practice: Disentangling Power Dynamics at Personal and Structural Levels." *British Journal of Social Work* 35: 435–52.

Saskatchewan Indian. 1977. "Indian Children Taken Illegally." 7, 1: 11.

Sawchuk, J. 2001. "Negotiating an Identity: Métis Political Organizations, the Canadian Government, and Competing." *American Indian Quarterly* 25, 1.

Schick, C., and V. St. Denis. 2001. "Race Matters: A Challenge for anti-Racist Pedagogy in Teacher Education." Paper presented at the Canadian Society for the Study of Education, Twenty-ninth Annual Conference, Quebec City, QC (May).

Schon, D. 1987. *Educating the Reflective Practitioner.* San Francisco, CA: Jossey-Bass

Schratz, M., and R. Walker. 1998. "Towards an Ethnography of Learning: Reflection on Action as an Experience of Experience." *Studies in Culture, Organizations, and Societies* 4: 197–209.

Schriver, J. 2001. *Human Behaviour and the Social Environment: Shifting Paradigms in Essential Knowledge for Social Work Practice.* Third edition. London, ON: Allyn and Bacon.

Scofield, G. 1999. *Thunder Through my Veins: Memoirs of a Métis Childhood.* Winnipeg, MB: Pemmican Press.

Scott, J. 1990. *Domination and the Arts of Resistance: Hidden Transcripts.* New Haven, CT: Yale University.

Seniantha, A. 1991. "Assumption Reserve." In D. Meili (ed.), *Those Who Know: Profiles of Alberta's Native Elders.* Edmonton, AB: NeWest Press.

Shebib, B. 2007. *Choices: Interviewing and Counseling Skills for Canadians.* Third edition. Toronto, ON: Pearson Education Canada.

Sheppard, M., S. Newstead, A. DiCaccavo and K. Ryan. 2000. "Reflexivity and the Development of Process Knowledge in Social Work: A Classification and Empirical Study." *British Journal of Social Work* 30: 465–88.

Shewell, H. 2004. *'Enough to Keep Them Alive': Indian Welfare in Canada, 1873–1965.* Toronto, ON: University of Toronto Press.

Shilling, R. 2002. "Journey of Our Spirits: Challenges for Adult Indigenous Learners." In E.V. O'Sullivan, A. Morrell and M.A. O'Connor (eds.), *Expanding the Boundaries of Transformative Learning: Essays on Theory and Practice.* Toronto, ON: Palgrave Publishers.

Shireman, J., and P. Johnson. 1986. "A Longitudinal Study of Black Adoptions: Single Parents, Transracial and Traditional." *Social Work* 31, 3: 172–76.

Shriver, J. 2004. *Human Behavior and the Social Environment: Shifting Paradigms in Essential Knowledge for Social Work Practice.* Fourth edition. Toronto, ON: Allyn and Bacon.

Siegel, B. 1998. *The World of the Autistic Child: Understanding and Treating Autistic Spectrum Disorders.* Toronto, ON: Oxford University Press.

Silverman, A., and W. Feigelman. 1981. "The Adjustment of Black Children Adopted by White Families." *Social Casework* 62: 529–36.

_____. 1990. "Adjustment in Interracial Adoptees: An Overview." In D. Brodzinsky and M.D. Schechter (eds.), *The Psychology of Adoption.* New York: Oxford University Press.

Simmons, K. (ed.). 2006. *The Official Autism 101 Manual.* Sherwood Park, AB: Autism Today.

References

Simon, R. 1998. "Adoption and the Race Factor: How Important Is It?" *Sociological Inquiry* 682 (May): 274–79.

Simon, R., and H. Alstein. 1977. *Transracial Adoption*. New York: John Wiley and Sons.

_____. 1981. *Transracial Adoption: A Follow-Up*. MA: Lexington Books.

_____. 1992. *Adoption, Race, and Identity: From infancy through Adolescence*. New York: Praeger Publishers.

Simpson, L. 2008. "Oshkimaadiziig, the New Peoples." In L. Simpson (ed.), *Lighting the Eighth Fire: The Liberation, Resurgence, and Protection of Indigenous Nations*. Winnipeg, MB: Arbeiter Ring.

Simpson, L.R. 2001. "Aboriginal Peoples and Knowledge: Decolonizing our Processes." *Canadian Journal of Native Studies* XXII: 137–48.

_____. 2004. "Anticolonial Strategies for the Recovery and Maintenance of Indigenous Knowledge." *American Indian Quarterly* 28, 3/4: 373–84.

Sinclair, Judge M., D. Phillips and N. Bala. 1991. "Aboriginal Child Welfare in Canada." In J. Bala, J. Hornick and R. Vogl (eds.), *Canadian Child Welfare Law: Children: Families and the State*. Toronto, ON: Thompson Educational Publishing.

Sinclair, R. 2004. "Aboriginal Social Work Education in Canada: Decolonizing Pedagogy for the Seventh Generation." *First Peoples Child and Family Review* 11: 49–61.

_____. 2007a. "Identity Lost and Found: Lessons from the Sixties Scoop." *First Peoples Child and Family Review* 31: 65–82.

_____. 2007b. "All my Relations: Native Transracial Adoption: A Critical Case Study of Cultural Identity." Unpublished doctoral dissertation, University of Calgary (September).

Sindelar, R. 2004. "Negotiating Indian Identity: Native Americans and Transracial Adoption." Unpublished master's thesis, Loyola University, Chicago.

Sixkiller Clarke, A. 1994. "OERI Native American Youth at Risk Study." Bozeman, MT: Montana State University.

Slemon, S. 1995. "The Scramble for Post-Colonialism." In B. Ashcroft, G. Griffiths and H. Tiffin (eds.), *The Post-Colonial Studies Reader*. New York, NY: Routledge.

Smith, A. 2005. *Conquest: Sexual Violence and American Indian Genocide*. Cambridge, MA: South End Press.

Smith, G.H. 2000. "Protecting and Respecting Indigenous Knowledge." In M. Battiste (ed.), *Reclaiming Indigenous Voice and Vision*. Vancouver, BC: UBC Press.

Smith, L.T. 1999. *Decolonizing Methodologies: Research and Indigenous peoples*. New York, NY: Zed Books.

Somekh, B. 2006. "Constructing Intercultural Knowledge and Understanding Through Collaborative Action Research." *Teachers and Teaching: Theory and Practise* 12, 1: 87–106.

Sorosky, A., A. Baron and R. Pannor. 1975. "Identity Conflicts in Adoptees." *American Journal of Orthopsychiatry* 45, 1: 18–27.

St. Denis, V. 2007. "Aboriginal Education and Anti-Racist Education: Building Alliances Across Cultural and Racial Identity." *Canadian Journal of Education* 30, 4: 1068–92.

Stalwick, H. 1986. "Demonstration of Strategies for Change: A Review of Indian and Native Social Work Education in Canada: What Was Said?" Study guide one. *The Taking Control Project*, Social Administration Research Unit, University of Regina.

Stannard, D. 1992. *American Holocaust: The Conquest of the New World*. New York, NY: Oxford University Press.

Steinhauer, P. 2001. "Situating Myself in Research." *Canadian Journal of Native Education* 25, 2: 183–87.

Sterling Consulting and Nzen'man Child and Family Development Centre Society. 2007. "Aboriginal Supported Child Development Needs Assessment Rep ort for the Thompson-Nicola-Lillooet Zone." Unpublished report.

Stevenson, W. 2000. "Decolonizing Tribal Histories." Unpublished dissertation, University of California, Berkeley, CA.

Stewart-Harawira, M. 2005. *The New Imperial Order: Indigenous Response to Globalization*. New York, NY: Zed Books.

Stolen Generations. 2003. *Book of Voices: Voices of Aboriginal Adoptees and Foster Children*. Winnipeg, Manitoba: Stolen Generations.

Strickland, C.J., E. Walsh and M. Cooper. 2006. "Healing Fractured Families: Parents' and Elders' Perspective on the Impacts of Colonization and Youth Suicide Prevention in a Pacific Northwest American Indian Tribe." *Journal of Transcultural Nursing* 17: 5–12.

Struthers, R. 2001. "Conducting Sacred Research: An Indigenous Experience." *Wicazo Sa Revie* 16, 1: 125–33.

Swidrovich, C. 2004. "Positive Experiences of First Nations Children in Non-Aboriginal Foster or Adoptive Care: Deconstructing the 'Sixties Scoop.'" Unpublished master's thesis, University of Saskatchewan, Saskatoon, SK.

Taoua, P. 2003. "The Anti-Colonial Archive: France and Africa's Unfinished Business." *Substance* 103, 32, 3: 146–64.

Taylor, E.W. 1997. "Building Upon the Theoretical Debate: A Critical Review of the Empirical Studies of Mezirow's Transformative Learning Theory." *Adult Education Quarterly* 48, 1 (Fall): 34–59.

Ten Fingers, K. 2005. "Urban Dakota and Dene Peoples: Quality of Life Indicators Project." Winnipeg, MB: Research and Policy Development Unit Assembly of Manitoba Chiefs. <cnpr.ca/Publications/CNPR%20-%20532109.pdf>.

Thomas, R., and J. Green. 2007. "A Way of Life: Indigenous Perspective on Anti-Oppressive Practice." *The First Peoples Child and Family Review* 3, 1: 91–104.

Thompson, K. 1999. "The History of the Adoption Myth: Adoption Policies in Saskatchewan." Unpublished master's thesis, University of Regina.

Timpson, J. 1995. "Four Decades of Literature on Native Canadian Child Welfare: Changing Themes." *Child Welfare* 74, 3: 525–46.

Timpson, J., S. McKay, S. Kakegamic, D. Roundhead, C. Cohen and G. Matewapit. 1988. "Depression in a Native Canadian in Northwestern Ontario: Sadness, Grief or Spiritual Illness?" *Canada's Mental Health* 5, 8.

Titley, B. 1986. *A Narrow Vision: Duncan Campbell Scott and the Administration of Indian Affairs in Canada*. Vancouver, BC: UBC Press.

Todd, N., and A. Wade. 2003. "Coming to Terms with Violence and Resistance: From a Language of Effects to a Language of Responses." In T. Strong and D. Pare (eds.), *Furthering Talk: Advances in the Discursive Therapies*. New York, NY:

Kluwer Academic Plenum.

Tough, F. 2002. *Putting the Métis Back on the Map: An Historical Geography of the Métis Nation 1870–1901.* Edmonton, AB: University of Alberta Press.

Treaty of Waitangi. New Zealand History On-line. Retrieved July 3, 2009 from http://www.nzhistory.net.nz/category/tid/133

Triseliotis, J. 1989. "Some Moral and Practical Issues in Adoption Work." *Adoption and Fostering* 132: 21–27.

Trudeau, L. 1999. *Spirit Knows.* Victoria, BC: Trafford Publishing.

Umar, A. 1993. "The Protest Tradition in Nigerian Adult Education: An Analysis of NEPU's Emancipatory Learning Project 1950–1966." *Convergence* 26, 4: 19–33.

United Nations. 1948. *Convention on the Prevention and Punishment of the Crime of Genocide.* Adopted by Resolution 260 III A of the United Nations General Assembly on 9 December 1948. <hrweb.org/legal/genocide.html#Article%202.5>.

Universal Energy Training and Learning Centre. <universalreiki.ca/>.

Van Kirk, S. 1983. *Many Tender Ties.* Norman, OK: University of Oklahoma Press.

Vedan, R. 2005. "CASSW and the Aboriginal Social Work Educators Network." <aboriginalsocialwork.ca>.

Wade, A. 1997. "Small Acts of Living: Everyday Resistance to Violence and Other Forms of Oppression." *Contemporary Family Therapy* 19: 23–40.

_____. 2000. "Resistance to Interpersonal Violence: Implications for the Practice of Therapy." Unpublished doctoral dissertation, University of Victoria, Victoria, BC.

Waller, M.A., and S. Patterson. 2002. "Natural Helping and Resilience in a Diné Navajo Community." *Families in Society* 83, 1: 73–84.

Walters, K.L., and J.M. Simoni. 2002. "Reconceptualizing Native Women's Health: An 'Indigenist' Stress-Coping Model." *American Journal of Public Health* 92, 4: 520–24.

Walton, R.G., and M.M. Abo El Nasr. 1988. "Indigenization and Authentization in Terms of Social Work in Egypt." *International Social Work* 312: 135–44.

Waseskun Network. <waseskun.net>.

Watzlawick, P., J. Beavin Bavelas and D. Jackson. 1967. *Pragmatics of Human Communication: A Study of Interactional Patterns, Pathologies and Paradoxes.* London, ON: W.W. Norton.

Weaver, H. 1997. "Training Culturally Competent Social Workers: What Students Should Know About Native People." *Journal of Teaching in Social Work* 15, 1/2: 97–111.

_____. 1998. "Indigenous People in a Multicultural Society: Issues for Human Services." *Social Work* 43, 3: 203–11.

_____. 1999. "Indigenous People and the Social Work profession: Defining Culturally Competent Services." *Social Work* 44, 3: 217–25.

_____. 2000. "Activism and American Indian Issues: Opportunities and Roles for Social Workers." *Journal of Progressive Human Services* 11, 1: 3–22.

_____. 2001a. "Culture and Professional Education: The Experiences of Native American Social Workers." *Journal of Social Work Education* 363 (Fall): 415–28.

_____. 2001b. "Indigenous Identity." *American Indian Quarterly* 25, 2.

_____. 2004. "The Elements of Cultural Competence: Applications with Native American Clients." *Journal of Ethnic and Cultural Diversity in Social Work* 13: 19–35.

Weaver, H.N., and B.J. White. 1997. "The Native American Family Circle: Roots of Resiliency." *Journal of Family Social Work* 2, 1: 67–79.

Weaver, H.N., and M. Yellow Horse Brave Heart. 1999. "Examining Two Facets of American Indian Identity: Exposure to Other Cultures and the Influence of Historical Trauma." *Journal of Human Behaviour and the Social Environment* 2, 1–2: 19–33.

Weber-Pillwax, C. 2001. "Orality in Northern Cree Indigenous Worlds." *Canadian Journal of Native Education* 25, 2: 149–65.

Wesley-Esquimaux, C.C., and M. Smolewski. 2004. *Historical Trauma and Aboriginal Healing: The Aboriginal Healing Foundation Research Series.* Ottawa, ON: The Aboriginal Healing Foundation.

Wharf, B. (ed.). 1990. *Social Work and Social Change in Canada.* Toronto, ON: McClelland and Stewart.

_____. 1993. *Rethinking Child Welfare in Canada.* Toronto, ON: McClelland and Stewart.

White, M. 1997. *Reflections of Therapists' Lives.* Adelaide, SA: Dulwich Centre Publications.

_____. 2000. *Reflections on Narrative Practice: Essays and Interviews.* Adelaide, SA: Dulwich Centre Publications.

Whitepath Consulting. <whitepathconsulting.ca>.

Williams, E.E., and F. Ellison. 1996. "Culturally Informed Social Work Practise with American Indian Clients: Guidelines for Non-Indian Social Workers." *Social Work* 41, 2: 147–51.

Willis, J.W. 2007. *Foundations of Qualitative Research: Interpretive and Critical Approaches.* Thousand Oaks: Sage Publications.

Wilson, A. 2004. "Decolonization and the Recovery of Indigenous Knowledge." In D. Mihesulah and A. Wilson (eds.), *Indigenizing the Academy: Transforming Scholarship and Empowering Communities.* Lincoln, NB: University of Nebraska Press.

Wilson, S. 2001. "What Is Indigenous Research Methodology?" *Canadian Journal of Native Education* 25, 1: 175–79.

_____. 2003. "Progressing Towards an Indigenous Research Paradigm in Canada and Australia." *Canadian Journal of Native Education* 27, 2: 161–80.

Wilson, W.A. 2004. "Indigenous Knowledge Recovery is Indigenous Empowerment." *American Indian Quarterly* 28, 3/4: 359–72.

Windsor, J.E., and J.A. McVey. 2005. "Annihilation of Both Place and Sense of Place: The Experience of the Cheslatta T'En Canadian First Nation Within the Context of Large-Scale Environmental Projects." *The Geographic Journal* 171, 2: 146–65.

Wood, P.J., and M. Schwass. 1993. "Cultural Safety: A Framework for Changing Attitudes." *Nursing Praxis* 81 (March): 4–15.

Wotherspoon, T., and V. Satezwich. 1993. "Chapter 7." *First Nations: Race, Class, and Gender Relations.* Scarborough, ON: Nelson Canada.

Wright, R. 2004. *A Short History of Progress.* Toronto, ON: Anansi.

Yellow Bird, M., and A.W. Wilson (eds.). 2006. *For Indigenous Eyes Only: A Decolonization Handbook.* Santa Fe, NM: School of American Research Press.

Yellow Horse Brave Heart, M., and L.M. DeBruyn. 1998. "The American Indian Holocaust: Healing Historical Unresolved Grief." *American Indian and Alaska Native*

Mental Health Research Journal of the National Center 8, 2: 60–82.

York, G. 1992. *The Dispossessed: Life and Death in Native Canada.* Toronto, ON: Little Brown Canada.

Young, M. 2003. "Anishinabemowin: A Way of Seeing the World Reclaiming My Identity." *Canadian Journal of Native Education* 271: 101–107.

Young, R.J.C. 2001. *Postcolonialism: An Historical Introduction.* Malden, MA: Blackwell Publishers.

Zapf, K. 2002. "Geography and Canadian Social Work Practice." In F.J. Turner (ed.), *Social Work Practice: A Canadian Perspective.* Don Mills, ON: Pearson Education Canada.

Zastrow, C. 1977. *Outcome of Black Children-White Parents Transracial Adoptions.* San Francisco: R&E Research Associates.